6.75

STUDIES IN HISTORY, ECONOMICS AND PUBLIC LAW

Edited by the
FACULTY OF POLITICAL SCIENCE OF COLUMBIA UNIVERSITY

NUMBER 527

THE PROGRESSIVE MOVEMENT OF 1924

BY

KENNETH CAMPBELL MAC KAY

THE PROGRESSIVE
MOVEMENT OF 1924

BY

KENNETH CAMPBELL Mac KAY

1966

OCTAGON BOOKS, INC.

New York

Reprinted 1966
by special arrangement with Columbia University Press

OCTAGON BOOKS, INC.
175 FIFTH AVENUE
NEW YORK, N. Y. 10010

LIBRARY OF CONGRESS CATALOG CARD NUMBER: 66-18046

Printed in U.S.A. by
NOBLE OFFSET PRINTERS, INC.
NEW YORK 3, N. Y.

PREFACE

This study grew out of a desire to know more about the principles and personalities of the third party movement of 1924. Perhaps other students of American political history have been as perplexed as the author by the curiously recondite and inadequate statement in many standard texts that " a Progressive ticket, headed by Senator LaFollette, obtained about five million votes in the 1924 election." To learn more about these Progressives of 1924, to discover what had brought them together, to appraise the contributions they had made, to seek the reasons for the rapid dissolution of their party machinery after Election Day, these were some of the goals of this research. It soon became apparent that a satisfactory undertaking of this sort would, at least, attempt some evaluation of the role the 1924 effort played in relation to the whole progressive movement which has been so integral a part of the American scene since the turn of the century. That was the general contribution this work could make. In addition, it could furnish a specific contribution: a detailed and comprehensive analysis of the campaign and election problems which beset the Progressives of 1924. Possibly some hardy band of reformers, preparing to enter the lists on another occasion against the entrenched representatives of our two-party system, might profit by such foreknowledge.

One method of this research has been to utilise, to the fullest, the opportunity still available to speak with the men and women of '24, to " get the feel " of the entire movement through personal interview and association. To whatever extent I have been successful in accomplishing this, the credit must go where it belongs, to those generous and kindly persons who gave unstintingly of their time and effort to make this a more intelligible record of the 1924 campaign. Their unquenchable faith in the coming of a better world provided a constant stimulus which made this task both a privilege and pleasure.

Special thanks are due Miss Fola LaFollette, whose vibrant interest in the progressive movement is alone enough to inspire those fortunate to know her; Dr. Mercer Green Johnston, whose wealth of material—so generously made available —was only excelled by his Southern hospitality; Miss Nina Hillquit, custodian of the papers of her father, the late Morris Hillquit; and Mr. Robert W. Hill, Keeper of Manuscripts, at the New York Pubiic Library. The kindness shown by a host of librarians, including Miss Evelyn N. Pehlke of the State Historical Society of Wisconsin, Miss Alma Schultz of the Cleveland Public Library, Dr. St. George L. Sioussat and Miss Florence S. Hellman of the Library of Congress, must not go unmentioned.

In conclusion, I am happy to acknowledge my indebtedness to Professor Allan Nevins, of Columbia University, without whose critical counsel and unflagging patience this study would never have been possible.

K. C. M.

Madison, N. J.

TABLE OF CONTENTS

THE PROGRESSIVE
MOVEMENT OF 1924

CHAPTER I
STRANDS OF AN UNBROKEN THREAD

In 1924, when nearly five million citizens went to the polls to vote for Robert M. LaFollette as President and for Burton K. Wheeler as Vice President, more votes were cast for the candidates of a minor-party organization than at any other election in American history.

Hindered by their hastily improvised campaign machinery, restricted by the pathetically inadequate financing of their ticket, divided by the innumerable problems which plague any political movement bold enough to defy the sacrosanct two-party system in America, tempted by the seductive allurements to keep cool with Coolidge, these progressive voters cast their ballots for a different kind of America. More than that, in spite of the ethical confusion and captivating enticements of lush prosperity, these five million persons, at the polls on November 4, 1924, registered their disapproval of Tweedledum and Tweedledee. La-Follette had been the " monstrous crow " which " frightened both the heroes so ". Without the emergence of the progressive movement, the 1924 campaign might have been as dull as that of Roosevelt and Parker in 1904. With the Progressives in the field, the 1924 campaign provided a lively challenge to the bosses of the entrenched parties, with an opportunity for real issues to be debated and decided.

Another distinctive feature of the progressive movement in 1924 is the fact that it represented the first formal alliance of organised labor in America with farmers and Socialists. The American Federation of Labor, departing momentarily from its traditional policy of non-partisan political action, endorsed the candidacies of LaFollette and Wheeler. It was the nearest American workers have ever come to a farmer-labor alliance independent of the major parties. Fighting with a strange earnestness which belied the desperate nature of their cause, these farmers, workers, and intellectuals of 1924—a

9

colorful melange of variegated beliefs and doctrines, recruited from such dissimilar sections of the nation—may have written the prologue to the history of successful farmer-labor co-operation in the United States.

Essentially, the progressive movement in 1924 was an optimistic force, inspired by a confidence and faith in man's ability to conquer his faults and loosen his shackles. Like John Stuart Mill, the 1924 Progressives could not doubt for a moment that most of the great positive evils of the world were in themselves removable and would, if only we availed ourselves of our opportunities, be finally reduced within narrow limits. Man's accomplishments in the past were a guarantee of his attainments in the future. The future beckoned, with its promise of an American—and universal—life richer in both spiritual and material values. They preferred the dreams of the future to the history of the past.

With perspicacity, the whole insurgent movement has been described as " on the whole Jeffersonian rather than Hamiltonian in character; it was liberal rather than radical; it was optimistic rather than desperate. Its roots went down deep into American experience, but it profited immensely from the teachings and practices of the more enlightened European nations. It was romantic in its philosophical implications but realistic in the sense that it recognised the economic bases of politics.   It was basic in its criticism but opportunistic in its program, accepting in practice Mr. Justice Holmes' dictum that ' legislation may begin where an evil begins '. Its accomplishments, both social and legislative, were impressive, and though many of those accomplishments were forfeited in the war and the post-war years, it may be said to have laid both the philosophic and legislative foundations for the New Deal of the 1930's." [1] The Progressives of 1924, obstinately resisting the floodtide of post-war political reaction and moral relaxation, provide the link between the days of Lloyd, Altgeld, Ross and

1 Morison, S. and Commager, H. S., *The Growth of the American Republic,* 3rd Ed., Vol. II, p. 357.

Riis, and the days of Frankfurter, Wallace, Tugwell and Hopkins. A farewell to reform there may have been, but the reformers had not departed.

Since important political movements are rarely begun for the attainment of remote and imperfectly comprehended ends, the Progressives of 1924, envisioned definite, tangible accomplishments, a program closer to reach than the stars. So it was that in this first presidential campaign in which organized labor formally participated with Socialists, farmers and intellectuals, the platform of the insurgents called for specific and immediate reforms. LaFollette's platform promised to uproot monopoly ("the great issue before the American people"), establish public ownerships of water power, achieve eventual public ownership of the railroads, deprive the Supreme Court of its right to declare laws of Congress unconstitutional, provide for the popular election of the judiciary, recognise the right of workers to organize and bargain collectively, enact an anti-injunction law and child-labor amendment to the Constitution, and provide for the following: the direct nomination and election of the President, the use of the initiative and referendum, the use of a popular referendum before a declaration of war, downward tariff revision, more governmental aid to farmers, and more direct public control of the Federal Reserve System. On such a platform did LaFollette and Wheeler make their appeal to the country. Much of it echoed the Populist pleas of the late nineteenth century. More of it anticipated the reforms of the New Deal.

The progressive movement in 1924 may have been the last of the old and the first of the new. For a moment, Populist and Socialist joined hands. For a moment Northwest farmers, veterans of many an agrarian crusade, made common cause with garment workers from New York's East Side. In a strange, esoteric blending of past and future, the voice of workers demanding collective bargaining, factory reforms, and safeguards against industrial tyranny, was raised with that of the farmers who once again were clamoring for redress and protection against the monopolies and the special interests. Across the years, out of America's past, were heard the familiar complaints of the Populists, the resurgent enthusiasm of men who had cheered Bloody Bridles Waite and had voted for James B. Weaver. Out of the past, as in 1912, came another embattled host to stand at Armageddon. At the Progressive convention which endorsed Robert M. LaFollette in 1924, they sang " Onward, Christian Soldiers " quite as sincerely, if not so lustily, as at Chicago in 1912. These were all kinds of men, these Progressives of 1924. Populists, Single-taxers, Socialists, writers from the East, farmers from the West, railroad men, Bull Moosers, Greenbackers, politicians, college students, dreamers and opportunists, they were all here. Some wanted to reassert old values; others were anxious to break with the past. Most of them hoped to see their diverse elements crystallise into a new political party, an American counterpart, possibly, of the British Labour Party. Accepting too eagerly the obvious fact of its failure, we are now too apt to overlook the significance of the nearly five million votes which were cast for LaFollette and Wheeler in 1924, incontrovertible statistical evidence that there existed, even in the palmiest days of Coolidge prosperity, a vast reservoir of liberal thought and opinion, a reservoir merely concealed and not obliterated by the political successes of the reactionaries and the economic sedatives of the 'Twenties.

With our penchant for over-simplification and hasty judgment, it has become customary to speak of the years 1900 to 1917 as the period covering the progressive movement in America. Not infrequently reference is made to the " death " of progressivism in 1912 when Roosevelt's bid for the Presidency ended in failure. Sometimes, we hear of Roosevelt " killing " the progressive movement in 1916 when he refused to lead a third party again. One purpose of this history is to demonstrate that—far from being dead—the progressive movement, supported by agrarian malcontents, militant labor forces, and far-visioned Socialists and intellectuals, remained alive and energetic throughout the 'Twenties. A long thread of continuity reaches down through the years from the Liberal Republicans, the Greenbackers, the Populists and the Bull Moosers, the Progressives of 1924 to the days of the New Deal. Sometimes attaching themselves to one of the old parties, occasionally striking out as independents in bold defiance of their elders, the dissident elements, liberals, radicals, agrarians, laborites, particularists, have made a contribution to American political history which has been too much neglected. To assume that the progressive movement disappeared with the defeat of the Bull Moosers, or at Chicago in 1916 when Roosevelt spurned the opportunity to run again, or at the outbreak of the World War, is, in effect, to believe that all the voters who had balloted in protest had suddenly passed away or been transported to a remote desert island. These protestants were neither dead nor gone. They voted for LaFollette in 1924 and waited; in 1932 the great majority of them voted for Franklin D. Roosevelt. Within the broad panoply of the New Deal there was room not only for bosses and bourbons; there was also a place for the men who had followed LaFollette in 1924. The farmers who had expressed their disapproval of Coolidge by voting for LaFollette delivered the Mid-West to Franklin D. Roosevelt. The huge Democratic majority in the Mid-West in 1932 was a heritage of William J. Bryan and LaFollette. The organised workers who had experimented with a farmer-labor alliance in 1924 saw a similar alliance build the Roosevelt victory in 1932 to landslide proportions.

Too many historians look upon the progressive movement in American politics, as a variable, fluctuating erratically from election to election, spasmodically reaching for office. We would more nearly approximate the truth by conceiving of it as a constant, moving sometimes within the framework of one of the major parties (as in 1896 and 1932) and sometimes— when what Ostrogorski has described as " moral decomposition " afflicts the old parties—moving away to form its own party structure and formulate its own policies free of the compelling force of compromise and concession.

William Allen White has said that the " insurgent movement was nothing in God's world but political implementation of the deepening moral intelligence of the American people ".[2] If we grant the validity of Mr. White's statement, the picture of American progressive thought and action becomes one not of periodic, almost accidental eruptions, but rather of a permanent course of political behaviour, a devotion to the principle of orderly and early development of social democracy.

Although the deep-seated sources of insurgency and pro-gressivism remain fairly constant, the third parties which from time to time represent their protest against the existing order are usually short-lived. The Greenbackers and the Populists were precipitated as separate, independent political organisms in response to temporary conditions and issues. A schism in the Republican party accounts for the Bull Moose movement in 1912. The manner in which the Republicans crowded out the Whigs in the 1850's is an exception to the rule that third parties live but briefly, an exception explained only by the singular sectional nature of American politics in the days immediately preceding the Civil War.

Moreover, third parties are short-lived because the major parties have become exceedingly dexterous in stealing those planks of the minor party platforms that meet with public ap-proval. In so generously providing the old-line parties with a house to loot, the third parties—unwittingly and unwillingly—make perhaps their most significant contribution to the Ameri-can party system. Thus a constant process of " permeation " endures in our political system, with the old parties adopting—or kidnapping—the likeliest looking issues of the newer parties.[3] By presenting to the electorate the need for a change,

2 W. A. White to Kenneth Hechler, quoted in K. Hechler's *Insurgency*, p. 220.

3 See Ostrogorski, M., *Democracy and Political Parties*, Vol. II (1922 Ed.), pp. 455-459.

the third party performs a genuine service. Familiar to most students of American history is the early espousal, by the Populists, of such " radical " reforms as the federal income tax, direct election of United States Senators, regulation of public utilities and immigration control.

By invariably proposing some kind of change and by their frontal assaults upon the vested holdings of the entrenched organizations, third parties instill a much needed vitality into the old parties. Third party activity is a splendid antidote for the political indolence and stagnation which so often debilitate American politics.

> Parties are constant associates though not officially boon companions. They tend to neutralize each other by copying each other's tactics and by a more reluctant acquiescence to each other's principles. The more conservative will tend to become slightly less conservative and the liberal will tend to become conservative. After a few decades the two will oppose each other more for the sake of party than principles because there will, in reality, be no great difference in principles. The party leaders who are gifted with imagination and a sense of humor will have to exercise self-restraint to avoid laughing when they face each other across the legislative chambers in their stereotype debates. This is the third party's opportunity to force a fusion of its two elder brothers, or drive one of them out of existence.[4]

Sometimes, as was the case with the Farmer-Labor bloc in the Senate during part of the 'Twenties, the insurgent forces can hope to represent the balance of power between the two old parties. But usually a third party, viewed as a political structure, is a make-shift device, a colorful mosaic of the motives and desires of its component parts, in imminent danger of falling apart into its many sections.

This is the story of a small band of political intransigeants of dissimilar social and economic backgrounds and of widely

4 Johnson, C. O., " Third Parties," *The Quarterly Journal*, University of North Dakota, 15:1, Nov. 1924, p. 41.

differing, sometimes of contradictory, political convictions, who braved the apathetic complacency of Coolidge's America to register their protest against reaction, exploitation, and corruption and to renew their faith in the promise of American life. Despite the corrosive effects of the cynical materialism which saturated the American character in the dreary decade after the World War, these men—and women—, their vision unimpaired by the roseate atmosphere of a superficial prosperity, foresaw the black days of depression, the weary disillusionment which was to come at the end of the reckless, heedless 'Twenties.

Most of us, readily accepting superficial appearances, look back on the 'Twenties as a kind of moral desert devoid of either spiritual guidance or intellectual integrity. To such persons the spectacle of several million Americans voting for Robert M. LaFollette, in the midst of this period of American history so readily stereotyped as cynical and debauched, may seem completely incongruous. What prompted these millions to vote for LaFollette? Some saw in Senator LaFollette the embodiment of cherished and traditional American values in danger of being submerged in the tide of post-war disillusionment and hardened materialism. Others perceived in the progressive movement the promise of a renovated America, the beginnings of a society, co-operative rather than acquisitive. Ranging far and wide between these two poles of political thought was the great bulk of the five million, intelligent enough to be apprehensive about the misbehaviour of the Administration, vaguely aware of the necessity for vigilance and fortitude in the face of temptations to relax and to retreat. These progressives were not convinced, as were many of the worshipers of Mammon in 1924, that telephones, washing machines, and six-cylinder automobiles were necessarily an index of political morality and economic well-being. At a time when the great majority of the American citizenry was too engrossed with the making of money and the promotion of its own economic advantages, a group of responsible farm and labor leaders, together with a scattering of "intellectuals" and "practical politicians"—odd combination!—risked their political futures as they stood, like Canute, against the rising flood of Coolidge complacency.

They called themselves "Progressives" in 1924. What did the term mean? To be accurate, we must admit, at once, that the term probably meant all things to all people. But if we analyse the 1924 movement with reference to earlier progressive movements, protest and reform forces, a bond of common interest and purpose—reaching back to the policies of such early insurgent organizations as the Greenbackers of 1876, the Union Labor party of 1888, and the Populists of the 'Nineties and extending forward to account for many of the reforms and experiments of the New Deal—holds them all together.

Three tendencies, held in common, seem to distinguish the progressive movements in American history, according to an astute observer of American politics.[5] The first of these is their insistence that special minority and corrupt influences in government be removed. The second tendency is found in the desire to change the structure of government to make it more difficult for control to rest in the hands of the few, easier for it to rest in the hands of the many. The conviction that the restricted functions of government must be increased and extended to relieve social and economic distress is the third tendency by which a progressive movement can be discerned. "These three tendencies with varying emphasis are seen ... in the platform and program of every political party; they are manifested in the political changes and reforms that are advocated and made in the nation, the states and the cities; and, because of their universality and definiteness, they may be said to constitute the real progressive movement."[6] When, as in 1912 and 1924, some members of the old parties believed that the emphasis upon these three tendencies was too light or casual, they organ-

5 Dewitt, B., *The Progressive Movement,* pp. 4-5.
6 *Ibid.,* p. 5.

ised, within a new third party, an agency for the promotion of
their progressive ideals.

But progressivism meant more than certain political convictions. There was in the faith of the progressive, whether he
be the progressive of 1900 or of 1924, an acute awareness of an
economic problem which, upon analysis, underlay any political
tendencies observed on the surface. The whole problem was
never so succinctly stated as when Herbert Croly noticed
the changes which were taking place in American life:[7]

> The American democracy has confidently believed in the
> fatal prosperity enjoyed by the people under the American
> system. In the confidence of that belief it has promised to
> Americans a substantial satisfaction of their economic needs;
> and it has made that promise an essential part of the American
> national idea. The promise has been measurably fulfilled hith-
> erto, because the prodigious natural resources of a new con-
> tinent were thrown open to anybody with the energy to ap-
> propriate them. But those natural resources are now in large
> measure passed into the possession of individuals, and Ameri-
> can statesmen can no longer count upon them to satisfy the
> popular hunger for economic independence. An ever larger
> proportion of the total population of the country is taking to
> industrial occupations, and an industrial system brings with
> it much more definite social and economic classes, and a di-
> minutive of the earlier social homogeneity. The contemporary
> wage-earner is no longer satisfied with the economic results
> of being merely an American citizen. His union is usually of
> more obvious use to him than the state, and he is tending to
> make his allegiance to his union paramount to his allegiance
> to the state. This is only one of many illustrations that the
> traditional American system has broken down. The American
> state can regain the loyal adhesion of the economically less in-
> dependent class only by positive service. What the wage-
> earner needs, and what it is to the interest of a democratic
> state he should obtain, is a constantly higher standard of liv-

7 Croly, H., *The Promise of American Life*, pp. 205-206. By permission
of the Macmillan Company, publishers.

ing. The state can help him to conquer a higher standard of living without doing any necessary harm to his employers and with a positive benefit to general economic and social efficiency. If it is to earn the loyalty of the wage-earners, it must recognize the legitimacy of his demand, and make the satisfaction of it an essential part of its public policy.

Appealing to Progressives was this warm-hearted resolve that a better, a much better, America would emerge from industrial turmoil and technological adjustment if only the government recognised its responsibility to provide the little man with a higher standard of living through making a morally and socially desirable distribution of wealth the " dominant and constructive national purpose ".[8] Whether or not they had read *The Promise of American Life,* most Progressives, during the first quarter of this century, were striving for the kind of ideal to which Croly had given expression.[9]

The years of political and social agitation preceding the World War, years characterised by public indignation of corruption in high places and monopoly in the market place, by the rapid growth of the Socialist party, by thunderous demands on the floor of Congress, in the press, by muckrakers, for sumptuary controls over the malefactors of great wealth, had been years of hope and accomplishment for the progressives.

But " the technique of liberal failure ", as John Chamberlain has pointed out, intervened.[10] " The brave days disappeared. The spirit of reform, variously interpreted by a Croly, Weyl or Veblen, variously translated into action by a resourceful Tom Johnson, vigorous Bob LaFollette, or opportunistic Teddy Roosevelt, was quenched as America turned eastward to launch a great crusade to make the world safe for democracy. The

8 *Ibid.,* p. 23.

9 ". . . Herbert Croly and his *The Promise of American Life* has been too much ignored by those who have traced the development of the Progressive party "—H. Pringle in *Theodore Roosevelt,* p. 540. Pringle, of course, was thinking primarily of the development of the Bull Moose-Progressive party.

10 Chamberlain, J. A., *A Farewell to Reform,* p. 304.

progressive movement, in which Roosevelt had so abruptly displaced LaFollette as the knight errant, was formally interred at Chicago in 1916 when Roosevelt and his patron, George Perkins, decided to support the Republican ticket.[11] The small remnant of Progressives went home, bewildered and confused, to a world they never made. The progressive movement had, indeed, come upon evil days. American participation in the World War applied the *coup de grace* to pre-war progressivism. President Wilson's speech, on April 6, 1917, asking for a declaration of war against Germany closed the doors on an era once pregnant with the promise of reform. Here was the farewell to reform, a temporary farewell, to be sure, but none the less impressively abrupt.

The identity of names has led, in some quarters, to a misunderstanding regarding the organic relation of the progressive movement of 1924 to that of 1912. The preservation of the name might lead one to expect considerable similarity in the two movements. Both, of course, as progressive movements, endorsed the general principles upon which our definition of progressivism stands. The Bull Moosers of 1912 were primarily bolters from the Republican party, following their Prophet of Reform wherever he might lead them. The progressive movement of 1912 was a kind of " moral up-lift " society, more intent upon having Teddy work wonders than upon establishing any firm basis for a party of reform. Motivated by genuine humanitarian impulses, an indignant electorate rebelled in 1912 against the machinations of old-line politicians and against the manipulators of business and government. When Roosevelt crowded out LaFollette for the nomination of the Progressive party, they followed him without too many qualms of conscience about the intensity of his devotion to reform or without too many suspicions about his eleventh-hour conversion to progressivism.

11 See Ickes, H. L., "Who Killed the Progressive Party?", *Mississippi Valley Historical Review*, 46:2, Jan. 1941, pp. 306-337.

If the progressivism of 1912 had been a spontaneous explosion of American political and social idealism, the progressivism of 1924, by contrast, was a calculated, determined experiment in group resistance to the economic and social classes in control of political authority. The devotion and enthusiasm of Teddy Roosevelt's supporters swept up and over the walls of class distinction, submerging the differences which in 1924 formed the foundations of the Conference for Progressive Political Action; 1912 had been Armageddon, and the embattled legions, in the exhilarating cadence of *Onward, Christian Soldiers,* had marched ahead for the Lord and Theodore Roosevelt. 1912 had been a noisy crusade of reformers; 1924 was to be a grim attempt to establish a party of farmers and workers. To be sure, the moral enthusiasms, the zest for humanitarianism, the challenge to fulfill destiny's assignment which had stirred imaginations and buoyed Bull Moose hopes in 1912 were still in evidence in 1924. But 1924, unlike 1912, was not so much a crusade as an instinctive class movement. The progressives of 1924 were convinced of the necessity of organising, at the earliest possible date, a political party devoted to the principle of political reform and economic democracy. Their intent was not merely to create temporary schisms in the old parties; they planned to organize a permanent political structure whose foundations would endure far longer than the momentary stage appearances of popular favorites and glamourous political personalities.

CHAPTER II

RETREATING TO NORMALCY

THE story of America's return to normalcy, of the retreat from wartime enthusiasms and Wilsonian ideals has already been amply told by numerous historians. Here we are only concerned with the post-war years as they affect the growth of the discontent—both agrarian and industrial—which was to culminate in the Progressive movement of 1924.

Disillusionment might have followed close on the heels of the armistice, but depression waited until 1920. In fact, the extravagant expectations of a revived foreign trade, the continued extension of credit and speculation, and, above all, the reconversion to production of consumers' goods, now greatly in demand after the period of wartime restrictions, all these factors postponed the primary post-war depression. This unexpected and almost spectacular post-war prosperity which preceded the collapse might be dated from the Spring of 1919 to the middle of 1920. The full effects of the collapse were being felt by the beginning of 1921. As civilian supplies were replenished in 1919, and as the demobilised soldiers enhanced the civilian demand, credit continued to expand, and American banking houses stepped in to finance European reconstruction and recovery. Here at home the steady rise in prices and the optimistic speculation in Wall Street facilitated supplies of credit.

Six distinct characteristics of this 1919-1920 boom require comment.[1] First of all, there was a fantastic rise in prices. A government price index moved from 129.8 in February, 1919, to 167.2 in May of the same year.[2] Second, the volume of bank credit expanded. The bellows of inflation were moving and money became " easier and easier." There was an over-all rise

[1] See Chapter V of *Recent Social Trends*, Vol. I, " Trends in Economic Organization " by Gay, E., and Wolman, L.

[2] *Ibid.*, p. 222.

in industrial activity. Factories were humming. The demand seemed insatiable. Wages increased and hours were reduced. Profits and surpluses for the corporations were fat and generous.

The forces of labor were riding high at the end of the war. The unprecedented demand for manpower and the willingness of a friendly administration to recognize the demands of organized labor had resulted in labor's greatest period of expansion. By 1920, the membership of the American Federation of Labor was twice as great as in 1916.[3] Its total enrolled membership, for the first time in its history, was over four million. The loss during the ensuing three years was to be almost as spectacular as the expansion from 1917-1920.

Germane to this study of post-war progressivism is the fate of labor and agriculture in the trying days that began with the turning of the business cycle in 1920. Both took a terrible beating. The ranks of labor were deserted wholesale; against labor, the forces of business and reaction launched a nationwide offensive. The courts openly proclaimed their antipathy to strikes and strikers. Agriculture fared no better. The giddy days of world markets and two-dollar wheat were over and, by 1921, the farmers were left with only their mortgages and surplus crops.

Labor found itself on the defensive even before the depression began. As Wilson's crusading idealism was replaced by disillusionment and cynicism, American dislike for things European expressed itself in a violent fear of alien thoughts and practices. This exaggerated nationalism of the post-war period easily played into the hands of labor baiters and conservative politicians. The famous red-hunt ensued. Attorney-General Palmer was applauded as he rounded up alleged radicals, often with little or no justification, and shipped them off to Russia. During this shameful period, five regularly elected Socialist assemblymen were denied their seats in the New York Legislature.

3 *American Labor Year Book*, 1921, p. 119.

During the height of the 1920 frenzy over the Reds, Sacco and Vanzetti were found guilty of a crime in a case which was destined to become a *cause célèbre* for years to come.

As prices went up in 1919, labor demanded higher wages. When the request was not granted labor—confident of itself as a result of its wartime successes—decided to strike. Besides, labor no longer considered it unpatriotic to strike. In September, 1919, occurred the great steel strike, involving 300,000 workers. By importing Negro strikebreakers and stirring up racial hatreds among the strikers, the steel companies broke the strike. A coal strike by 450,000 miners was defeated by a government injunction.[4]

Labor had miscalculated the temper of the American people and the extent to which domestic conditions had changed since the war. The labor organizations played right into the hands of the labor baiters by allowing the strikes to go to excess. A five-day general strike in Seattle, in 1919, obviously led by foreign labor agitators, alienated public opinion. The police in Boston struck after being denied the right to join a union. When the Police Commissioner refused to reinstate the police after their strike had been broken, Sam Gompers intervened on their behalf. Calvin Coolidge, then Governor of Massachusetts, dramatized the whole public reaction to this wave of strikes by his famous telegram that " there is no right to strike against the public safety by anybody, anywhere, anytime ". Not only did Coolidge's statement serve to focus national attention on the extent and seriousness of the strikes; it sky-rocketted its author into second place on the Republican ticket in 1920. It is idle to debate whether the strikes of 1919 and 1920 really represented a threat to the security of the nation. The fact remains that, in 1919-1920, the conservative element shrewdly took advantage of labor's plight. With the press as its disposal and an administration and judicial system apprehensive over " bolshevism " and foreign doctrines, it was relatively easy for

4 A comprehensive yet succinct account of this period may be found in Parkes, H. B., *Recent America*, ch. XXX.

the nation's reactionaries, aided by a middle-class yearning for " normalcy, " to take the offensive against labor.

By 1921, labor was retreating. By 1922, its retreat was almost a rout. The losses in membership of the American Federation of Labor were as follows :[5]

$$1921.......... \quad 84,000$$
$$1922.......... \quad 883,000$$
$$1923..........1,052,000$$

This represented a total decrease by 1923 of 24 per cent. Obviously, the gains of labor during the war had been superficial and transitory. When the nation returned to normal, labor could not consolidate its gains. Perlman and Taft have made a significant observation on one of the peculiar shortcomings of American labor overlooked by the sanguine leaders of 1919. Referring to the sharp decline in membership from 1920-1923, these historians of American labor say :

> This 24 per cent decline was in part due to the abnormal and forced nature of the preceding expansion. The war policy of the government was by far the greatest factor for it was the government that opened the doors to unionism in industries heretofore closed—not that unionism forced the doors open by its own strength. The government, by virtue of its war-time power and prestige, gave the unions the all-important right to organise against a temporarily confounded and half rebellious employing group.[6]

To substantiate this statement, Perlman and Taft point out that the unions which prospered most during the war tended to lose most during this period of retrenchment. " On the contrary, the unions which best maintained their membership were

5 Commons, J. R., et al., *History of Labor in the United States,* Vol. IV, "History of the Labor Movement" by Perlman, S. and Taft, P., p. 523.

6 *Ibid.*

those which had received no or only incidental aid from the government during the war. The building trades, the printing trade, the miners, and the clothing group more than held their own." [7]

Organised labor's position grew progressively weaker. As the nation entered the depression in 1920-1921, the blows against labor were manifold. In substance they consisted of:

(1) unemployment
(2) wage reductions
(3) drive for " the open shop "
(4) unfavorable court decisions,
both federal and state.

The unemployment and wage reductions were, of course, concomitants of the business depression. In such a period they were to be expected. But never before had they so affected union membership. Union organization, by itself, was impotent to stop layoffs. Within a year, four million men were out of work.[8] Part of the post-war shrinkage was due, of course, to the almost complete disappearance of shipbuilding and the munitions industries, both of which had employed great pools of manpower.

With labor reeling from these economic blows, the National Association of Manufacturers, co-operating with other management organizations, launched its campaign for " the open shop." The general public was receptive. Euphemistically termed the " American Plan," the open shop conjured up a picture of free enterprise, of high wages in a plant like Ford's of smiling, self-respecting workers. The open shop campaign was well-timed. It coincided with the revulsion of feeling against European ideas and European practices. And, in the minds of many Americans, the labor movement was indigenous to the soil of Europe, a strange and barren seed in the land of

7 *Ibid.*

8 Kirkland, E. C., *A History of American Economic Life*, p. 572.

freedom and individualism. Each new act of " violence " on the part of a labor leader simply further confirmed this conviction.

In many respects the long list of judicial blows that labor had to take in the period from 1919-1923 was a measure of how completely apathetic the nation had grown to the demands of labor. The courts had been emboldened by the attitude of the American public.

In 1919 a government injunction had been employed to break a strike of coal miners. In 1922 the famous " Daugherty injunction " was used, with stinging effect, against the striking railroad shopmen.[9] Of outstanding importance in this period were the three cases involving litigation in the federal courts, in each one of which the federal judges decided against labor. These three cases were the *Duplex* case and *Truax* v. *Corrigan,* both settled by the Supreme Court in 1921, and the *Coronado* case, decided in 1922.[10] In the Duplex case, the Court decided that the immunities granted by the Clayton Act applied only to the employees directly involved. *Truax* v. *Corrigan* upheld the use of the injunction in labor disputes. In the famous *Coronado* case, the Court expressed the view that unincorporated labor unions did not escape liability as entities. This, of course, was similar to the renowned Taft-Vale decision in England, which had so effectively crippled trade union action. All in all, these decisions proved that " the courts again demonstrated that the labor provisions of the Clayton Act had not altered the common law of criminal conspiracy, repealed the damaging clauses of the Sherman Anti-Trust Act, nor seriously hampered the use of injunctions in labor disputes." [11]

Labor, indeed, had fallen upon evil days. The victories of 1917 and 1918 stood revealed as sham and misleading. The

9 See page 31.

10 *Duplex Printing Press Corporation v. Deering,* 254 U. S. 443.
 Truax v. Corrigan, 257 U. S. 312.
 United Mine Workers v. Coronado Coal Company, 259 U. S. 344.

11 Kirkland, *op. cit.,* p. 596.

company union and the open shop were making headway. The government belonged to Big Business and the foes of labor. The courts had, in effect, repealed laws for which long years of arduous effort had been sedulously devoted. Labor lost much in the early 'Twenties. When, consequently, the next period of business revival returned—by 1923—the war-time gains of labor had been, for the most part, obliterated, and the retreat had taken labor far back into another era of reaction and hardship. Labor stood on the defensive, in some states badly battered by hostile legislation intended to destroy the labor union movement. In Kansas and Colorado, compulsory arbitration bills, despised by labor, had already been made into law.[12] Wherever labor looked, in the states, at the courts, at the National Administration, even in Congress, the scene was unfriendly.

As labor fell back before the aggressive attacks of its enemies in the post-war period, only one group of organised workers was able to consolidate the gains which it had secured during the war years. The Railroad Brotherhood unions were, politically and economically, far more powerful than before the war. Because of the leading role these unions were to play in fostering independent political action in 1924, it is necessary to consider their organization in greater detail and to trace the events leading up to their promotion of a progressive movement in the early 'Twenties.

The history of these brotherhoods has been one of constant growth and ever-increasing political influence and effectiveness. They had been organised originally as beneficiary societies, a policy dictated by the refusal of insurance companies to insure men engaged in train service.[13] As fraternal societies intent

12 The Supreme Court of the United States eventually declared, in two successive decisions, the Kansas compulsory arbitration law to be unconstitutional. *Wolff Packing Co. v. Court of Industrial Relations*, 262 U. S. 522. The Colorado law, while not actually compelling arbitration, forbade strikes pending investigation of the dispute by a state board.

13 Commons, H. R., et al., *History of Labor in the United States*, Vol. II, pp. 309-310.

upon a stable program of insurance coverage, the brotherhood unions remained aloof from the more spectacular nineteenth century labor movements like the Knights of Labor. Even the conservative American Federation of Labor made no appeal to these railroad unions concentrating upon the task and peculiar problems confronting them within their own trade. The Brotherhood of Locomotive Engineers was the first to be founded, establishing a beneficiary fraternal order in 1855. Within a generation, three other brotherhoods, the Order of Railway Conductors of America, the Order of Locomotive Firemen, and the Brotherhood of Railroad Trainmen, had been formed. These four brotherhoods have usually been referred to as the " Big Four " of the railway unions, customarily taking the lead—through their numbers and experience—in raising standards and formulating policy.[14] The Brotherhood of Railroad Trainmen was, numerically, by far the largest organization of railroad employees in the country. It had approximately 350,000 members by the end of the war.[15]

When the United States went to war against Germany, the government took over the railroads. For the ensuing three years, the railroad transportation system of the United States was co-ordinated under the management of the Federal Railroad Administration, created by Congress in 1917 to grapple with the gigantic problems of transporting millions of men and tons of equipment.

Government operation served to strengthen and promote the railroad labor movement. The railroad brotherhoods came out of the war with perhaps the strongest and most deeply entrenched organization anywhere in the American labor movement. Administered by William Gibbs McAdoo, a friend of labor alive to the problems of rising prices, the Federal railroad management granted pay rises to the workers and recognised

14 Haynes, F. E., *Social Politics in the United States*, pp. 109-116.
15 *Ibid.*, p. 114.

the principle of collective bargaining.[16] Adjustment boards were established in insure just and equitable settlement of disputes between the unions and management. "The war gave the unions their first taste of real power and their first opportunity to engage in experiments with the joint control of industry." [17]

When the war ended and the government prepared to turn back the railroads to their owners, the unions rallied their forces to prevent any return to the labor conditions which had prevailed before 1917. The more sanguine threw themselves into the fight for government ownership, despite the dim prospects of success. Glenn E. Plumb, general counsel for the Brotherhood, formulated the plan which carries his name. The Plumb Plan was a proposal to effect government ownership. Through a bond issue, the government was to buy all railroad properties and then lease them through operation of a national non-profit corporation.[18] After setting aside earnings for operating expenses, interest on the bonds and retirement of the principle in fifty years, any profits were to be shared by all employees.

Enthusiastically the Brotherhood threw itself into promotion of the Plumb Plan. A Plumb Plan League was formed, with Sam Gompers as president. The weekly journal, *Labor,* was launched to publicize the scheme. Headquarters in Washington were established to " push, popularize and publicize " the movement. The discontented farmers of the Northwest—expressing their opinions through such organizations as the Non-Partisan League—joined in support. But the railroad interests had money, publicity and a lobby too. But the Esch-Cummins bill

16 The best account of this period of railroad history is in Hines, W. D., *War History of American Railroads.*

17 *Recent Social Trends,* "Labor Groups in the Social Structure," by Wolman, L. and Peck, G., Vol. II, ch. CVI, p. 836.

18 See Plumb, G. E., *Labor's Plan for Government Ownership and Democracy in the Operation of the Railroads,* (pamphlet issued by Plumb Plan League, Washington, D. C., 1919).

became law, and the railroads went back to their private owners.[19]

As a concession to the railroad workers, the Transportation Act of 1920 included a provision establishing a Railway Labor Board consisting of nine members appointed by the President. Management, labor and the public were each to have three representatives. In spite of their disappointment at losing the Plumb Plan, the railroad unions were not without solace. They now had representation, the right to sit down alongside management in the Labor Board. Collective bargaining had, in effect, been recognized—at least in the railroads—by the Transportation Act of 1920.[20] The principle of government arbitration had been established, or more correctly, retained from war-time practice.

But trouble lay ahead. By 1921 the primary post-war depression was in full swing. The railroads, more affected than most business, decided to cut wages. The Railway Labor Board allowed the reduction.[21] As a result, in 1922, seven shop crafts —of the sixteen railroad unions—went out on strike. In some sections of the country violence occurred as the railroads extensively employed strikebreakers in this so-called " Shopmen's Strike " of 1922.

Two developments within this strike deserve particular attention in assaying the temper of the railroad men. One is the " extraordinary and incongruous " stand—in view of the eighty years of striking in America—taken by the Railroad Labor Board, on July 3, 1922, that the strikers, by stopping work, had severed their connections with the carriers that had employed them. As a student of American railroad history has observed, " while strike leaders may have loosely stated that they were leaving the carriers' employ, this constituted neither excuse nor justification for the ill-advised decision of the

19 See Harris, H., *American Labor*, pp. 253-254.

20 See MacVeagh, R., *The Transportation Act of 1920*.

21 Approximately a twelve per cent reduction.

board." [22] The workers, as a result, were demoralized and embittered. The companies were encouraged to hire strike-breakers and organize company unions. When finally a settlement was arranged, the question of seniority—caused by the railroads taking thousands of new men into the " vacancies " created by the strikers—remained to plague all parties.

The second development was perhaps of greater political than economic consequence. When the unions found the plan of settlement that he had proposed inacceptable, President Harding allowed the whole issue to pass into the incredibly inept hands of Attorney-General Daugherty. On September 1, Daugherty obtained a sweeping temporary injunction against the strikers from a federal district court in northern Illinois. After the presentation of evidence, the injunction was continued. With insult heaped upon injury this way, there was little for the strikers to do but return to work. In vain did the non-striking brotherhoods attempt to secure honorable terms of settlement. The strike was definitely broken, broken by a strange but strong alliance of property and government.[23] By September, the workers had been forced back to their jobs, but indeed, it must have been a Pyrrhic victory for the managers. The railroad men had lost respect for President Harding; Daugherty had incurred their unrelenting hatred; and, more than ever before, they were convinced of the impossibility of securing justice in courts prejudiced against labor. They were ready to experiment with direct political action. The sixteen railroad brotherhood unions represented a strong, compact organization, composed of proud and skilled workers.[24] Nowhere in the country was there such a homogeneous labor group, capable of direct political action, experienced and tested in battle. There were approximately 1,500,000 members in the associated railroad brotherhoods in 1922, an interest group no politician

22 Wood, L. A., *Union-Management Co-operation on the Railroads*, p. 77.

23 Wood, L. A., *op. cit.*, pp. 77-78.

24 See Appendix No. 1.

could afford to overlook without risking grave political consequences.[25]

The political reaction which placed Warren G. Harding in
the White House and gave the Republicans control of Congress
and most of the states was a concomitant of the post-war economic forces which dealt the farm and labor movements such
heavy blows. The high idealism of the war days had been
abandoned. A kind of war neurosis had left the American
people tired of crusades and callous towards idealism. " There
might be no such word in the dictionary as normalcy, but
normalcy was what they wanted." [26]

The Republicans, unable to agree upon either General
Leonard Wood or Governor Frank Lowden, had—as so often
occurs in American politics—agreed upon a compromise candidate. And—following the pattern of American political behaviour—they selected a man whose chief virtue was his
mediocrity, the fact that while he had made few real friends,
he had made few enemies. Harding embodied most of the
foibles and shortcomings of his " average " countryman. A
small town editor, he had been graduated from the school of
Ohio politics, eventually arriving in the United States Senate
as a reward for his party regularity. His record of faithful devotion to party lines and principles was maintained, of course, in
the Senate. Standpat on most issues, he believed that what
helped business helped all. Uncertain and—through his own indolence—ill-informed on most questions, he was content to
follow the Penrose-Smoot-Lodge cabal in the upper house.
Again and again, his actions in the Senate demonstrated the
superficiality of such political convictions as he may have
possessed.[27] When—as in the case of the Prohibition and
Women's Suffrage amendments—he was forced to express an
opinion by voting yes or no, he would stall as long as possible

25 *American Labor Year Book*, 1924, p. 43.

26 Allen, F., *Only Yesterday*, p. 125.

27 See Adams, S. H., *Incredible Era*, ch. VI.

and finally take the "safe" course measured in terms of the voting public.[28] He had a penchant for evasive language; he promised so often to give a bill "earnest and careful consideration". Out of thirty-two calls on various angles of the Prohibition question, he voted Wet thirty times. But in the final showdown he was counted on the affirmative for the Prohibition Amendment; he even went further and helped override Wilson's veto of the Volstead Act.[29] Subservient to his political masters, he enjoyed Senate life immensely. There was an amplitude of good fellowship and high living there. It took some diligence on the part of Harry Daugherty and Mrs. Harding ("the Duchess") to convince him to seek the nomination. Abysmally ignorant in so many matters, Mr. Harding, at least, had a prescience of his own shortcomings as President.

The Democrats, futilely resisting the full flood of reaction against Wilsonian idealism, nominated—after a long convention battle involving William McAdoo and A. Mitchell Palmer —James A. Cox, governor of Ohio, to whom Irving Stone, in his study of defeated presidential aspirants, pays this tribute— "He is one of the clearest cases in all American history of the best man having been defeated. He was the right candidate running at the wrong time." ...[30] "If Cox had been elected in 1920 he would have saved the nation from its most wrecking scandals since the administration of Grant. If Cox had been elected there would have been no sabotage of the League of Nations; the chance of avoiding World War II might have been greatly increased."[31]

The dominant but confusing issue in the campaign was a vote of confidence in Wilson's administration and policies, "Wilsonism," as it was sometimes called. In vain did the Democrats speak of a "solemn referendum" on the League of

28 *Ibid.*, pp. 86-87.

29 *Ibid.*, p. 86.

30 Stone, I., *They Also Ran*, p. 19.

31 *Ibid.*, p. 33.

Nations. The Republicans, and their nominee for President, deliberately vague and ambiguous, effectively prevented any expression of public approval of the League. Harding's disingenuous platitudes were gauged to be equally palatable to the isolationists and the reservationists. The political apathy and intellectual torpor of the times concealed the brazen outlines of Republican hypocrisy. And the trick worked. All things to all people, Republicans—regardless of their opinions on international co-operation—went to the polls to vote not for Harding, but against Wilson. The campaign of deliberate confusion had worked. " The voice of the weasel was heard in the land."[32]

Harding's administration confirmed, needless to say, all the apprehensions felt in 1920 by those who had not been rocked to sleep by the lullaby of normalcy. Significantly, Harding's nomination, effected by a Senate cabal, assured the temporary ascendancy of an alliance of pressure groups whose representatives could be found on the floors of Congress. Strong leadership, White House guidance, executive controls over Congress, all disappeared as Harding replaced Wilson in the Presidency. " The administration of Harding covering a period of twenty-nine months did not materially alter the alignment of interests within the Republican party. The President's conception of party leadership made it possible for the regular party organization to dominate in the administrative domain of party interest, particularly in matters of routine and of patronage, at the same time that it permitted, indeed encouraged, the continued development in Congress of the programs, as well as the reputation, of various powerful and ambitious chieftains. "Thus in 1923, as in 1903, the Republican party was a coalition of leaders and of interests, only more so." [33]

This shifting of the center of political gravity from the White House to Capitol Hill as Harding succeeded Wilson was one of the most significant developments of the new Admini-

32 Adams, *op. cit.,* p. 178.

33 Robinson, E. E., *The Evolution of American Political Parties,* p. 345.

stration. Another major change was the appearance of the wealthy and shrewd Andrew Mellon upon the Washington scene and his selection as Secretary of the Treasury. If it is true that the real issue—taxation—lay hidden under the verbal torrents about the League during the 1920 campaign, then Mr. Mellon deserves far more attention than most historians have paid him. To the men who dominated the Republican party, the all-absorbing interest was who would pay for the war expenditures. Mellon represented everything they were looking for as a Secretary of the Treasury. One of the wealthiest men in the country, with huge holdings in aluminum, oil and banking, he could be depended upon to work his wonders in behalf of those interests which traditionally backed the Republican party in return for tax and tariff favors. " Senator Knox could not have suggested to Harding a happier choice for the Treasury. The Secretary's fabulous wealth was to throw about him a cloak of immunity from criticism by those elements—decisive in the nation—who worshiped wealth. If a million dollars could do no wrong, a hundred millions had a positive genius for being right. On the other hand, his obscurity, his lack of a personal history, his origin in Pittsburgh, removed the obvious label of " Wall Street " which demagogues would have delighted to pin on him. In fact, there was nothing material for the opposition sharpshooters to aim at; he glided, wraith-like, into the Treasury, a spirit unburdened by a personal record." [34] Certainly he was no roaring bull of Wall Street, despite his wealth. The Senate confirmed him without an opposing vote. Within nine months, Mellon had fulfilled his promise. The new revenue bill, made into law by President Harding's signature on November 23, 1921, repealed the excess profits act (saving stockholders $1,500,000,000 a year) and reduced the maximum surtax from 65 per cent to 50 per cent.[35] The saving for the Secretary, his

34 O'Connor, H., *Mellon's Millions*, p. 124.

35 *Ibid.*, p. 129.

family and his interests, was estimated to be close to a million dollars for the one year, 1922.[36]

Mellon's inflluence, already great, was to reach extraordinary heights when Harding died and Calvin Coolidge succeeded him. Harding and Mellon were not on intimate terms. They shared no abiding friendship. Then, too, as long as Harding lived, the Senators retained their influence at the White House. But between Coolidge and Mellon there appeared instantaneously a relationship curiously close and unreserved for two men with such antithetical backgrounds and environments. William Allen White goes so far as to say that Coolidge was " blinded " by Mellon.[37] Mellon's political fortunes zoomed. With business organizations and service clubs beating the drums, the highly-publicised " Mellon Plan " was announced in November 1923.[38] It was a far-reaching program of tax reduction, most effective in the upper brackets. It called for reduction of the surtax from 50 to 25 per cent along with moderate downward revisions all along the line. Republicans, conservatives, editorial writers and business men outdid each other in paying homage to the greatest Secretary of the Treasury since Alexander Hamilton. Senator Smoot, not to be outdone by the *Saturday Evening Post,* declared that Mellon had actually displaced Hamilton as the greatest Secretary of the Treasury.[39]

White sums up Coolidge's attitude this way : " Andrew W. Mellon was President Coolidge's bad angel. The President could cope with Daugherty or with Denby, two men of vastly different political minds—and each a wide variant from Coolidge. He and Fall could get to terms—but they would be Coolidge's terms—in short order . . . but Mellon was too much for Coolidge. For Mellon's millions spoke gospel to Coolidge. He represented in those years, by his social attitudes, by his

36 *Ibid.*

37 White, W. A., *A Puritan in Babylon,* p. 241.

38 *New York Times,* Nov. 11, 1923.

39 O'Connor, H., *op. cit.,* p. 132.

official policy, a strictly plutocratic philosophy of life. He was the guardian angel of all that the Chamber of Commerce held sacred in its white marble palace." [40]

More and more, as the 1924 campaign approached, the Republicans, following Coolidge's cue, couched their political appeal in terms of the Mellon treatment—reduction of taxes, encouragement of investment and freedom of business enterprise. Perhaps, subconsciously, as the scandals were exposed and his faith in other members of the cabinet was swept away, Coolidge moved into closer spiritual and economic agreement with his Secretary of the Treasury. Small wonder that newspapermen in Washington facetiously remarked upon the well-worn path between the Treasury Building and the East Door of the White House!

This bewildering alliance of Big Business, personified by Andrew Mellon, and government, under Harding and Coolidge, temporarily paralyzed the forces of liberalism. Still licking their wounds from the battle of 1920, there was not much to do, save the occasional lifting of a voice like LaFollette's, until the election of 1922. Paradoxically, as farm mortgages were foreclosed and labor lost its wartime gains, Coolidge, Mellon and the Administration went on their way, heedless of the cries from the Unions and from the West. Rejected by the Republicans and ignored by the Democrats, labor and agrarian leaders thought ever more seriously of a third party. Out of these thoughts was born the idea of a Conference for Progressive Political Action in 1922.

40 White, W. A., *op. cit.*, p. 396.

CHAPTER III

THE LAND OF LOST CONTENT

AMERICAN agriculture will not soon forget the First World War. Not only did it provide the farmer with his dizziest period of success and prosperity; it also bestowed upon him his worst and most persistent economic hang-over. Even before America became involved in the world struggle, the farmer was beginning to feel its effects. By January, 1917, an index of prices of farm products had already climbed to 166 (1913 = 100).[1] Europe began to call for food; millions left the fields to fight. All his traits of self-interest, humanitarianism and patriotism were stimulating the American farmer to added production by 1917. " Food," he was told, in a thousand government posters, " will win the war." Not only was he asked to produce; he was called upon, in the name of national security and interest, to increase his holdings and yield. Consequently, with the compensation derived from the highest prices he had ever known, the American farmer invested heavily in land, more land and machinery. He plowed under the buffalo grass and, confident that he was in step with economic needs, cultivated even the marginal land. Moreover, he invested in social utilities, in churches, roads and schools, unmindful of the accounting that the future would make in taxes and interest charges. In effect, much of his payment was in terms of mortgages on prospective profits. " With money easy to borrow, and the ratio of prices he received to those he paid more than 10 per cent above the 1910-1914 levels, he was as unassailed by doubts about the future as were the urban prophets of perpetual prosperity in 1928-1929." [2]

1 Based on statistics in the *Yearbook of Agriculture 1918,* U. S. Dept. of Agriculture, p. 701.

2 *Recent Social Trends,* Vol. I, ch. X, " Rural Life," by Klob, J. H. and Brunner, E., p. 488.

As in the case of labor, the post-war crash in agriculture did not come immediately. So long as America continued to feed Europe and so long as the abnormal domestic boom continued, farm prices and returns remained high. But 1920 brought an end to all that. When the crash came to agriculture, the effects were even more penetrating and lasting than in the case of labor. Farm prices went lower and stayed there longer.

The reasons for agriculture's plight after the World War are so numerous and complex that, at best, we can only outline some of the more obvious factors. It is well to note the far-reaching international character of some of these factors.[3]

1—Purchasing power was crippled in Europe. This meant almost an automatic termination of the extraordinary foreign demand which had encouraged the American farmer to break all his records for production.

2—Hungry and bankrupt nations were beginning to raise their own food. Their soldiers were demobilized; and in the devastated areas, the horse and plow had reappeared. Economic self-sufficiency was being practiced in many nations.

3—New foreign competition, stimulated by war-time needs, had been established. In particular, the British Dominions and South America had come into the world's wheat market.

4—The internal market was limited by the decrease in the rate of population growth.

5—Dietary habits had changed. Consumption habits were turning away from American agricultural staples like wheat and corn toward fruit and vegetables, many of which came from abroad.

6—Fashions also had changed. The desire of the American lady to stay slim (or become slim) had more than a casual effect upon the law of supply and demand. There was less demand for cotton and related products as clothes became scantier and legs were sheathed in silk.

3 For a more extensive account, see *Recent Social Trends,* Vol. I, Ch. X, *op. cit.*

7—The displacement of draft animals removed the demand for certain farm products.

8—The machine, whose invasion of the farm had been facilitated by the easy credit of the war years, increased the per-man efficiency of the farm faster than workers migrated to the city. Between 1919 and 1932 productivity per agricultural worker increased 25 per cent.[4]

9—The marginal and submarginal lands first cultivated during the World War increased the cost of production, thus causing a wider differential between the farmer's cost and the farmer's price than would otherwise have been the case.

In 1920 came the smash. Prices collapsed. The exchange value of the farmers' products disappeared almost from sight. Based on a 1913 = 100 computation, the index of farm product prices was 235 in May, 1920. By October, the index was down to 178. By the next May it was 112![5] Senator Capper has vividly described the farmers' plight during this dramatic deflation. "During the period of high prices in 1919, when corn was worth one dollar-and-a-half a bushel, a farmer could get five gallons of gasoline for a single bushel. A year later at the farm price that bushel of corn would buy only one gallon of gasoline; and two years later the same bushel of corn would buy about half a gallon of gasoline. In 1919 it took only six bushels of corn to buy a ton of coal; while a year later it cost forty bushels of corn and two years later, sixty bushels of corn."[6]

Farm incomes fell off more than 50 per cent during 1921. The export crop diminished 85 per cent the same year. Farm bankruptcies, which had averaged 1.5 per 10,000 farms in the period from 1905-1914, rose to 20. in 1920 and 21.51 in 1922

4 Parkes, H. B., *Recent America,* p. 407.

5 Genung, A. B., "The Purchasing Power of the Farmer's Dollar from 1913 to Date," *Annals of the American Academy of Political and Social Science,* 126:206, Jan. 1925, p. 30.

6 Capper, A., *The Agricultural Bloc,* p. 38.

and were to continue on up to an average of about 100 for the rest of the 'Twenties. The mortgage debt on owner-operated farms, which had been 1.7 billion dollars in 1910, was already four billion dollars by 1920.[7]

Even more disconcerting than the cold figures of falling production and stranded farmers are the statistics showing the gap between income and outgo, between effort and reward. The farmer's purchasing power, in terms of non-agricultural commodities, fell from 118 in May, 1919, to 68 by August, 1922.[8] The ratio of prices of farm products to tax and interest payments fell from 104 to 56 within a year.[9] The rate earned on all capital invested in agriculture, 1920-1921, was 0.6. During this same time the rate of interest paid on mortgages and other indebtedness by agriculture was 6.8.[10] During the five years before the war the average farm family earned $396. In 1918 and 1919 this amount increased to more than $1200 but declined during the collapse of 1921-1922 to $292, the lowest return of the last decade and a half.[11] The net result of the tremendous increase in farm mortgages and farm tenancy was that a large proportion of the gross income took on the nature of tribute paid the city by the country. Instead of purchasing goods with his slim profits, the farmer had to placate the city banker or entrepreneur to whom he was indebted.

Perhaps the chief difference between the agricultural and industrial depressions of the early 'Twenties is the fact that industry recovered by 1923, bringing higher wages back to the industrial worker and dividends once more to the stockholder. But the farmer's depression stayed on. By 1923, credit extended

7 *Recent Social Trends*, Vol. I, *op. cit.*, p. 499.

8 Genung, A. B., *op. cit.*, p. 24.

9 *Ibid.*, p. 25.

10 Bean, L., and Stine, O. C., " Income from Agricultural Production," *Annals of the American Academy of Political and Social Science*, 126:206, Jan. 1925, p. 30.

11 *Ibid.*, p. 31.

to Europe by American bankers was stimulating the export of finished goods. For reasons already stated, the farmer did not share in this foreign trade. Installment buying accounted for a spurt in domestic industrial activity. Industry and commerce, by 1923, were well on their way into that fantastic interim that we label today as the days of " Coolidge Prosperity ".

As industry revived, agriculture, in some instances, actually became more distressed. The industrial prosperity, from 1923 on, increased the spread between the rural and urban dollar, consequently depriving the farmer of his purchasing power. In the period 1922-1923 the farm price index averaged 135 of the pre-war level. During the same period, industrial wages averaged 221.[12]

Taxes and interest, relative to the farmer's income, mounted rapidly. Taxes, which tend to be a fixed cost, had to be paid for out of prices realized on products whose values were declining. Taxes, accentuated by an antiquated system of collection, on the American farmer had risen to 232 per cent of the pre-war level by 1922.[13] As freight rates rose and selling and servicing charges increased, the American farmer felt more desperate than ever before. His debt became more oppressive. His prospects of liquidating his obligations, even the less ambitious objective—making both ends meet—seemed more and more unlikely. In Washington was an Administration earnestly promoting the interests of Business and Wall Street, reducing taxes on millionaires and constructing tariff walls for the manufacturers but ready to look upon any proposal of the farm bloc congressmen as an attack upon either American financial institutions or the system of free enterprise.

Early in the Harding administration, it became evident to the farm lobby groups and to some of the congressmen from the agricultural sections that some definite plan of action would have to be formulated to promote the interests of the farmer.

12 *Recent Social Trends,* Vol. I, *op. cit.,* p. 500.
13 *Ibid.*

At a meeting called by Senator Kenyon, May 9, 1921, held at the Washington office of the American Farm Bureau Federation, twelve Senators decided upon a program of immediate action.[14] These Senators included W. S. Kenyon of Iowa, A. Capper of Kansas, G. W. Norris of Nebraska, F. R. Gooding of Idaho, E. F. Ladd of North Dakota, R. M. LaFollette of Wisconsin, E. D. Smith of South Carolina, J. B. Kendrick of Wyoming, D. U. Fletcher of Florida, J. E. Ransdell of Louisiana, J. T. Heflin of Alabama, and Morris Sheppard of Texas.[15] A similar organization of House members was affected. The purpose of the group, as declared by Senator Kenyon, was direct action by Congress to aid the farmer. Four committees were appointed on the following subjects: Transportation, Federal Reserve Act, Commodity Financing and Miscellaneous Agricultural Bills. The names of these committees suggest, of course, the general nature of the legislation that the Bloc was to sponsor—measures to facilitate farm credit, to control the distributors and middlemen, to promote co-operative marketing and to revive foreign trade. The McNary-Haugen Bill, designed to accomplish the latter, was perhaps its best-known and most widely discussed proposal.

American agriculture, like American labor, found itself on the defensive in the years following the World War. Like labor, agriculture had no plan of direct national political action. Both labor and agriculture had their pressure groups and lobbies. Yet neither had a definitive policy of action upon which they could join forces. Both faced a common enemy—an unholy alliance of Big Business and the conservative Administration. Faced by common danger, yielding to the same enemy, some leaders of labor and agriculture began to think in terms of direct political action. The old parties, deaf to their pleas for assistance, offered little hope or promise.

14 Capper, A., *op. cit.*, p. 9.

15 Other members of the Senate, including Charles McNary of Oregon, and Peter Norbeck of South Dakota, joined soon thereafter.

But there was one distinct difference between farm and labor preparation for political action in the 'Twenties. Labor, endorsing the Wilson war administration, had built no instrument of revolt. The farmers, never entirely forgetting their Populist tradition, had started to organize actively, through the Non-Partisan League, even before the World War.

Still involved, despite all the fleeting blandishments of wartime prosperity, in " a long and perhaps a losing struggle—the struggle to save agricultural America from the devouring jaws of industrial America ", the American farmer renewed his faith in a creed which had inspired the agrarian movements of the latter part of the preceding century.[16] This creed of the American farmer, stemming from the grass roots which had flourished where once there had been land in abundance and opportunity without end, was twofold: first, the conviction that " the people " must control the government; second, that the government must curb the selfish tendencies of the few who have gained disproportionate wealth and power. Such a political faith squared with the individualistic philosophy which the rugged, self-reliant life on the frontier had nurtured in agrarian thinking. Above all, the American farmer prized his " rights ". The demands of the Populists—for trust legislation and railroad control, for currency and credit reform, for conservation and direct democracy—had reflected the indignant temper of the farmers of America against those who—it was believed— were engaged in a well-contrived scheme to thwart freedom and steal the common man's rights. The leaders of revolt and reform identified themselves with the early patriots who had thrown off the yoke of British tyranny and had guaranteed human rights to their posterity. As Professor Curti has so well remarked: [17]

> Faith in man's dignity, in his natural rights to liberty, to equality of opportunity, and to happiness, was a heritage

16 Hicks, J., *The Populist Revolt*, p. 237.
17 Curti, M., *The Growth of American Thought*, p. 610.

of the Enlightenment. It was also a heritage of actual experience on American soil. The *philosophes* had emphasized man's power through reason to tear down dungeons and build mansions. The conquest of the American physical environment by individuals, families, and groups seemed in the minds of American men and women to be living evidence of human ability to do this very thing. The old American society of relatively equal opportunity was changing, but belief in the individual continued.

Without possessing more than a sharp awareness of the grievances which plagued them, the mortgaged homes, the paltry purchasing power of their crops, the constant distress and dread insecurity, the farmers knew that somewhere there lay a cause for all these grievances. If that cause could be removed through the instrumentality of the government, then the land of lost content could be regained. If others had, through artful political manipulation, achieved an ascendancy in the State, then farmers too would have to organise. In union they could find strength. Aroused and truculent, they were in a receptive mood for political action and organization when the Non-Partisan League came along.

Whether or not, as two historians of American labor politics have stated, the Non-Partisan League was the real starting point for the movement that culminated in Robert LaFollette's candidacy for the Presidency in 1924, the remarkable and spectacular rise and fall of the League—or " Townleyism ", as critics chose to say—must not be slighted in any historical evaluation of the attempt of farmers and laborers to organise along political lines.[18] The grass roots caught fire in 1915 and the smoke and flames of politics lay over the prairies, not under control until the early 'Twenties.

Although the Non-Partisan League was not organised until 1915, other movements had been going on for some time, movements which were indicative of the growing discontent

18 Commons, J. R., et al., *History of Labor in the United States*, Vol. IV, " History of the Labor Movement," by Perlman, S. and Taft, P., p. 525.

and resentment of farmers long suspicious of North Dakota's conservative groups and institutions. And one of the most conservative of these institutions was its state constitution, under whose terms it was impossible legally to authorize state-owned elevators and mills. The immediate predecessor of the League, the Equity Society, had been advocating this reform, the patent advantages of which had been amply demonstrated by Professor Ladd of the Agricultural College. Despite authorization by the voters at the polls, the state legislature, in 1915, refused to carry out the mandate to revise the constitution to allow for this degree of public ownership. When the representatives of the Equity Society were ignored by the legislators, someone called upon the farmers to remember the insult at the polls, " to go home and slop the hogs ". The slogan clicked. " Slop the hogs " became the objective of every farmer in North Dakota who felt that the legislature had been unduly influenced by conservative and private-interest groups.[19]

At this propitious moment, the man and the time coincided. A born salesman, a promoting genius was there ready to sell the farmers what they wanted.

The man who ignited the prairies deserves recognition as one of the most skillful organizers the country has ever seen, whose methods combined all the resourceful manipulation of a Tammany precinct leader with the fervent zeal of a frontier evangelist.

By 1915, Arthur C. Townley, although he was only thirty-five, had learned much about the farmer's problems. Born on a farm in the northern section of the state, he had seen his own parents struggle relentlessly against not only the soil but far-off creatures who came to be known as the " Interests ". As a young country schoolteacher, reading and getting acquainted with his neighbors, he discovered how close so many of these farmers were to financial disaster. And then, in 1912, when he

19 Rowell, C., " Political Cyclone in North Dakota," *World's Work*, 46:1, July 1923, p. 269.

had returned to the profession of his parents, he learned a personal lesson in the vagaries of farming. He had, in a short time, become known to his neighbors as a highly successful farmer, even, occasionally, being referred to as the " Flax King ". Townley had prospered with his flax crop and, too confident of the future, expanded to the limit of his ability.[20]

Then came the disastrous season of 1912. On top of a short crop, caused by the dry season, the price broke sharply under a market drive by speculators; and Townley found himself, like so many farmers before him, suddenly bankrupt.

" A few months before I had been a good fellow and an able farmer," says Townley, " but after the failure nobody in town wanted to speak to me or to see me. I was a fool, a dub, and a crook, and everybody had always known that I was going to blow up sooner or later. All because somebody in Chicago or Minneapolis sought to break somebody else who was buying flax." [21]

For a while Townley joined the Socialists but he found their long-range planning and theorising irksome to his active nature. The Northwest was simmering with unrest. The farmers complained of their declining purchasing power, their helplessness before the bankers and speculators, their insecurity and, in so many cases, their poverty. In Canada crop-insurance plans had been instituted and co-operative organizations had obtained great political influence. Townley, sensing the trend of the times, motivated by his own personal bitterness perhaps as much as by his dream of farmer independence, decided to organise the state for the Socialist Party. But Townley and the Socialists soon parted. To them, he was an opportunist, building a vast personal political machine. To Townley, they were

20 A detailed account of Townley's life and the formation of the Non-Partisan League appears in H. E. Gaston's *The Non-Partisan League,* ch. VI. C. E. Russell's *The Story of the Nonpartisan League* is extremely friendly to Townley and his movement.

21 Gaston, H. E., *The Non-Partisan League,* p. 50.

visionary and impractical people safe within their Ivory Tower.[22]

With a Ford car and sixteen dollars, Townley went to work organizing the farmers of the Northwest.[23] He provided a program, an application blank and a sincerity that was usually more than convincing. Within three years, by the end of 1918, two hundred thousand farmers had joined the Non-Partisan League.[24]

The program was exactly what the farmers were looking for. There were five main planks in his platform, as follows: [25]

1—State ownership of terminal elevators, flour mills, packing houses, and cold storage plants.

2—State inspection of grain and grain dockage.

3—Exemption of farm improvements from taxation.

4—State hail insurance on the acreage tax basis.

5—Rural credit banks operated at cost.

Two remarkable facts—organising farmers and winning primaries—stand out about the early days of the Non-Partisan League. Unparalleled is the singular success that Townley achieved by his emphasis upon " organization " among the farmers. " Organization " was the key word. The " Interests " had long been organised. The farmers, to protect themselves, would have to organise. This would necessitate an extensive League organization, well-financed and ably managed.

No one could ever accuse Townley of being a piker when he set out to organise his League. He decided from the start to set high dues. At first they were $2.50 a year. The figure was

22 The author is indebted to the Hon. John M. Baer, of North Dakota, first Non-Partisan Congressman, for an intimate and detailed description of Townley's personality and motives.

23 See Haynes, F. E., *Social Politics in the United States,* ch. XIII. An excellent appraisal of Townley's genius for organization.

24 *Ibid.,* p. 323.

25 Gaston, H. E., *op. cit.,* p. 60.

raised several times until, by the end of 1916, they were stan-
dardized at $16.00 for two years—the period of time from one
election to another.[26] The high prices that the farmers now
began to get because of the insatiable demand of a world at
war enabled them to pay the dues and join the organization.
The sixteen-dollar fee included something more tangible than
the inward delight of joining a new movement and the distant
promise of farmer victories at the polls. The dues included a
subscription to the *Non-Partisan Leader,* official weekly organ
of the League, founded in 1915, and a year's subscription to
Pearson's Magazine. Pearson's Magazine, in exchange for this
unexpected source of increased circulation, agreed to publish a
series of articles on the League written by Charles E. Russell,
one of Townley's closest advisers and an editor of the *Leader.*[27]

Some attention should be paid to the variety of activities
that the Non-Partisan League entered. As Nathan Fine has
well pointed out, the League was more than a political organization. Mr. Fine mentions the extensive agents of publicity,
not only the *Non-Partisan Leader,* but two dailies, one in
Fargo and one in Grand Forks. *Leaders* were established in
different states. Co-operatives and banks, owned and operated
by farmers, were started.[28]

The political strategy of the Leaguers became apparent as
the elections of 1916 approached.

Townley's experience with the Socialists had lost him what
little faith he had had in third parties. Instead of using a third
party for his purposes, Townley set out to utilize an electoral
device—the direct primary. No organization in America has
ever made such wide use of this democratic machinery. True
to its name, the Non-Partisan League, under Townley, made
no attempt either to organise a party of its own or to capture
the old parties. Its strategy was to enter its own candidates in

26 Fine, N., *Labor and Farmer Parties in the United States,* p. 368.

27 Gaston, H. E., *op. cit.,* p. 72.

28 Fine, N., *op. cit.,* p. 368.

the primaries, throw the full weight of the organization behind them and then support them regardless of the party affiliation. In the event of defeat in the primaries, the League felt no compulsion to support the victorious candidates. Having pledged no loyalty to any party, it was free to take any kind of independent action.

The first election showed how efficacious this method could be. The June, 1916, primaries resulted in sweeping victories for the Non-Partisan supporters. Out of a total Republican vote of approximately 75,000 in North Dakota, Frazier, the League candidate, secured about 40,000, a majority over his three opponents combined.[29] Every man on the state ticket endorsed by the League was nominated. The Non-Partisan League had captured the legislature. Final victory in the November elections was a foregone conclusion.

Meanwhile Townley and his men kept canvassing the state in their Fords, reaching the homes of farmers who had always been inaccessible. The Townley organizers picked out dependable, esteemed farmers as local " boosters,"whose function was to be a kind of agrarian precinct leader, reporting trends and portents to general headquarters. The *Non-Partisan Leader* poured out advice on political action and constantly reminded the farmers of their inequalities and the necessity for political cohesion. When it came time to vote, no farmer could truthfully say, above the din of League publicity and organizational activity, that he was ignorant of the issues.

Victory followed victory. In a special election, in 1917, the League sent John M. Baer, the North Dakota cartoonist who had been drawing for the *Leader,* to Congress. By 1917, national headquarters—an entire floor of an office building— had been opened in St. Paul, Minnesota. Organisers were already at work, in the first month of 1917, in Minnesota, Montana and South Dakota.[30] It was in Minnesota that the League

29 Gaston, H. E., *op. cit.,* p. 124.

30 *Ibid.,* p. 156.

began to sponsor the idea of a farmer-labor alliance. So long as the League had remained in North Dakota, it had been dealing almost exclusively with farmers. But Minnesota was different. Here there were large city populations composed of substantial union memberships. In Montana, also, there were union men, miners who resented the monopolistic domination of the great copper interests.[31]

The dramatic growth of the League carried over into the early 'Twenties despite war frenzy and the attempts to stigmatize the Non-Partisan people as pro-German.[32] But when the movement started to wane, its fall was quite as dramatic as its rise. The state government returned to conservative hands in the recall election of 1921. The meteor was disappearing into the night. The old parties had caught their second wind and were finding ways and means of combating this new kind of attack. In some states, the Old Guard moved against the League by a frontal attack on its instrument of popular expression—the direct primary. In Idaho the leaders of the old parties manipulated the abolition of the primary. In Montana a similar scheme succeeded. Where the Non-Partisan League continued to use the primary to win office, the conservatives retorted by refusing to vote for Non-Partisan endorsees.[33]

Probably a far more important reason for the rapid decline of the Non-Partisan League—by 1923, Townley had resigned, the *Leader* had ceased publication and the national organization had practically disappeared—was the financial difficulty that faced the organization as a result of both the unusual methods of financing that Townley had employed and the unparalleled economic distress in the agrarian areas after the World War boom.

31 *Ibid.,* p. 164.

32 For his alleged " pro-German activities " during the World War, Townley was forced to serve a term in prison. His followers looked upon the charge and subsequent trial as a shameless " frame-up." See *The Nonpartisan Leader,* " *Did Townley Have a Fair Trial?* ", May 16, 1921.

33 Fine, N., *op. cit.,* p. 375.

Ever since the organization of the League in 1915, Townley had been accepting post-dated checks to finance the League. Money comes in once a year for North Dakota farmers—when they sell their crops. So Townley accepted their post-dated checks when they joined and filled out their membership blanks. The system worked so long as money came in for the crops. But when the war was over and the crops were no longer needed, the post-dated checks became as worthless as the wheat that no one seemed to want.[34]

Appreciating neither the speed nor the seriousness of the decline of the Non-Partisan movement in the early 'Twenties, progressives were encouraged by the remarkable readiness of farmers to join a political organization devoted to liberal principles. If the emboldened farmers could elect congressmen and revise state constitutions, why could not some similar organization contribute to a great national victory of farm and labor groups?

34 *The Nonpartisan National Leader* (formerly *The Nonpartisan Leader*), in its last issue, July 1923, explained at length the difficulties of the League.

CHAPTER IV
THE PROGRESSIVES PREPARE

IN addition to the politically conscious railroad brotherhoods and the farmers represented by groups like the Non-Partisan League, both of which have been previously considered in this account, two other organizations played an important role in the formation and proceedings of the CPPA. One of these was the Socialist party; the other, the Committee of Forty Eight.

The Socialist party, which joined other progressive groups at the first meeting of the CPPA, had had a turbulent history. The war and internal friction had dealt roughly with the lusty party that had been able to cast nearly 900,000 votes for Debs in 1912. The party had been scarred by internal strife ever since the turn of the century and by the cleavage between the " Socialist Labor " wing and the " Social Democrats ". Daniel DeLeon and his Socialist labor party had gone one way, subscribing dogmatically and rigidly to the principles of Karl Marx, putting forward immediate demands and expecting an early collapse of capitalism.[1] Adopting the name " Socialist Party " in 1901, the less revolutionary group enjoyed continued success that culminated in the high-water mark of 900,000 votes for Eugene Debs in 1912. This was six per cent of the total vote, a record unequalled by the party in any subsequent election. The World War came on, casting aspersions upon the loyalty and patriotism of Socialists. The establishment of the soviet state in Russia and the world-wide activities of the Third International split the Socialist party at the moment of its greatest crisis. The vote fell off to 585,000 in 1916 and 900,000 in 1920, when women had the vote for the first time and the aggregate for all parties was 45 per cent above that of 1916. The membership in the Socialist party even more vividly revealed the fruits of the internecine battles occasioned by the

1 For a comparison of the Socialist Labor and Socialist Parties, see Sait, E. M., *American Parties and Elections*, p. 187 ff.

enthusiastic and well-organised protagonists of Russian Communism. Socialist membership, which had reached an all-time high of 118,045 in 1912 and still remained above 100,000 in 1919, dwindled to 26,766 in 1920, the year of the split with the group later to be known as the Workers' Party, later still as the Communist Party. By 1922 the membership had melted to 11,019.[2]

Despite these unimpressive figures, the importance of the Socialists in the CPPA must not be minimised. From an organizational point of view, it was highly desirable that the Socialists co-operate with the progressives. They had the local organizations which could provide the framework for the construction of the new party, and, moreover, unlike many of the promoters of a progressive party, whose enthusiasm exceeded their experience, they had had rich knowledge of how to conduct campaigns, in meeting the tactics of the old parties, in exchanging blow for blow in practical politics. The Socialists had their name on the ballots in almost all the states—a priceless heritage for the Progressives, as the latter were to find out in the heat of the 1924 campaign. The Socialists had appealing and tried leaders, men like Debs and Hillquit, whose influence and renown would mean much in a national campaign.

With a knowledge of Communist tactics gained by first-hand experience, the Socialists steered clear of the unstable and unpredictable Farmer-Labor convention in 1920. But the persistent talk of a united front of the liberals had its effect upon the Socialists. By 1921, they were making overtures to the other progressives. At the national convention held that year in Detroit, Mayor Hoan offered a resolution to inquire into the possibility of a Labor Party, a permanent third party.[3] The invitation of the Railroad Brotherhoods found the Socialists most receptive.[4] To the early meetings of the CPPA went—

2 *American Labor Year Book,* 1925, Table 72, p. 141.

3 See article by Judge Panken in the *Socialist World* (Chicago), Dec. 1924.

4 *Ibid.*

with the exception of the ailing Debs—the leaders of the Party: Morris Hillquit, Charney Vladeck, George Roewer, James Oneal, Otto Branstetter, Victor Berger and Seymour Stedman. It seemed, in these formative days of 1922 and 1923, as if American Socialism " would sacrifice its revolutionary myth to the realities of American economic life and—like the Independent Labor party in its relation to the Labor party of Great Britain—accept a place on the left wing of a farmer-labor movement." [5] In 1923, after the organization of the CPPA, the Socialists chose Morris Hillquit, Victor Berger and Mrs. Bertha Hale White as official delegates to the CPPA. At the same time, Eugene Debs outlined the terms upon which his party would join a labor movement, emphasising the hearty accord and co-operation which would be proffered such a movement, although the Socialist party was not yet ready to surrender its " identity and integrity " as a " revolutionary working-class party ".[6] Shortly afterwards, the Socialists moved officially to affiliate with the CPPA, by a vote of 38-12 of the Executive Committee.[7]

If the Socialists comprised the left wing of the CPPA, then the Committee of Forty Eight might be labeled its right wing. One man, J. A. H. Hopkins, its founder and Chairman, dominates the story of the Committee of Forty Eight. Mr. Hopkins had been one of the more prominent Bull Moosers in 1912, National Treasurer of the Roosevelt Executive Committee. A resident of one of the New Jersey suburbs, his close contact with well-to-do bankers and brokers in New York undoubtedly commended him for the position. Perhaps it is better to let Mr. Hopkins tell his own story of the origins of the Committee of Forty Eight: [8]

5 Sait, *op. cit.*, p. 187.

6 *Christian Science Monitor*, Apr. 22, 1923.

7 *New York Times*, May 21, 1923.

8 Correspondence, J. A. H. Hopkins to the author, June 12, 1923.

Back in the Nineties I became interested in independent politics but refused to associate myself with either of the old parties, realizing the necessity for a complete re-alignment along the lines of Social Development as opposed to political expedience. So when the Progressive Party was formed in 1912, I joined it, campaigned for it, and after the campaign, those of us who still held to our original principles continued the party organization. And in 1916 we held our convention in Chicago and nominated Theodore Roosevelt to run against Hughes and Wilson.

After Colonel Roosevelt broke his promise to us, refused the nomination, and betrayed the whole Progressive movement, we continued to function as Independents. We organized the remnants of the party and again met in convention at which I was authorized to turn over the assets and names to the first political re-organization conforming to our principles.

In 1918 we ran several state tickets in the name of the National Party, in Montana, Connecticut, and I think, South Carolina. But it gradually dawned upon me that while there were millions of people who wished to see a new party organised, most of them would not forsake their existing affiliations until the new party was definitely established.

Out of this grew the Committee of Forty Eight, which I purposely organized, not as a political party but as an organization pledged to create such a party. With this understanding we had little difficulty in obtaining membership and support and in 1920 we held a national convention in Chicago and endeavored to co-operate with the political movement amongst the labor element, who agreed to hold their convention at the same time and place.

The platform drawn up by the Executive Committee in 1920 reflects the " old-time " progressivism that had made such an appeal in 1912 to citizens who were far from revolutionaries. " Our purpose," the platform reads, " is the abolition of privilege, meaning by privilege the unjust economic advantage by possession of which a small group controls our national resources, transportation, industry and credit, stifles competition, prevents equal opportunity of development for all and thus dictates the conditions under which we live." [9] Here, alongside the Socialists within the CPPA, would be a group decrying the disappearance of competition!

The name of the organization was misleading. The " Forty Eight " was intended to refer to representation from all forty-eight of the states; not, as so many persons seemed to think, to a self-appointed and exclusive committee consisting of forty-eight members. J. A. H. Hopkins was Chairman; Howard R. Williams, Vice-Chairman; Allen McCurdy, Secretary; Charles H. Ingersoll, Treasurer. Included on the Executive Committee, among others, were McAlister Coleman, Will Durant, Arthur G. Hays, John Haynes Holmes, Frederic C. Howe, Horace B. Liveright, Robert Anderson Pope, Gilbert Roe, and Frank Stephens.[10] The Committee did not seem to lack for money, not a surprising fact in view of the financial status of some of its members.

The Chicago Farmer-Labor convention in 1920, sponsored by the militant labor organizations in Illinois, headed by John Fitzpatrick and Max Hayes, was a sad disappointment to the Committee of Forty Eight. The progressives went there determined to nominate Bob LaFollette for the Presidency and organise a third party. Before they had been around long, they realized that John Fitzpatrick and Ed Nockles, of the Chicago Federation of Labor, were trying to use them as pawns in their battle against Sam Gompers and that an " ultra-labor " group had seized control of the convention. The Committee of Forty Eight marched out. Arthur Garfield Hays remembers the disappointed Hopkins as " pale, unhappy and crushed as he saw the smashing of his dream ".[11] Senator LaFollette, with a keen

9 Committee of Forty Eight, " *Platform,*" Comm. of Forty Eight National Headquarters, New York, N. Y., 1920, (J. A. H. Hopkins paper).

10 Will Durant wrote " The Call to Action," national appeal made by the Committee of Forty Eight.

11 Hays, A. G., *City Lawyer,* p. 260.

prescience of Communist and anti-Gompers elements, refused to have any connections with the new party. Without LaFollette support and without the Committee of Forty Eight representation, the convention nominated Parley Christensen and Max Hayes for President and Vice President, respectively.

Allen McCurdy, in explaining why the Committee of Forty Eight withdrew from the Farmer-Labor convention, bitterly assailed the radicals who secured control and regretted the failure of a real liberal party to appear. " Unless this party is organised, the extremes of reaction in conflict with the extremes of radicalism will have the field to themselves, and in tearing each other to pieces, orderly process in America will be destroyed." [12] The above sentence sums up both the disgust of the Forty-Eighters with the Chicago 1920 convention and, perhaps unintentionally, reveals the essentially moderate political philosophy of the group. The prospect of revolution disturbed them no less than the possibility of reaction.

It is difficult to assay the political importance of the Committee of Forty Eight. It was always a small group. But what it lacked in numbers, it compensated for in other ways. The Committee was unusually vocal, and having members like Arthur G. Hays and Amos Pinchot and Allen McCurdy insured an ample supply of publicity and an intelligent presentation of its principles. The most tangible contribution that the Committee of Forty Eight made to the CPPA was the gift of the name " Progressive ". The Executive Committee of the Bull Moose Progressive Party had transferred the party name to the Forty-Eighters in 1919, authorized to turn over the name " to the first political reorganization " conforming to progressive principles. Hopkins exercised this authority by granting the right to use the name to the LaFollette-Wheeler movement in 1924.[13] This technicality was helpful to the Progressives

12 McCurdy, A., " The Forty-Eighters' Position," *Nation*, 111 :2874, July 31, 1920, p. 127.

13 *New York Post*, Sept. 23, 1924.

during the campaign, as, frequently, Republicans who had supported Teddy Roosevelt challenged LaFollette's use of the term.

All in all, the Committee of Forty Eight formed a kind of brain trust for the progressive movement, argumentatively and literately agile, but sometimes quite disarmingly unperturbed by practical political considerations. It included a fair quota, it has been noted, of those intellectuals who as amateurs " enjoy the higher exercise of politics but are too fastidious to get down to precinct work ".[14] The Forty-Eighters served as a balance wheel, within the progressive ranks, against the pragmatism of the labor men and the doctrinaire Marxism of some of the Socialists.

The first Conference for Progressive Political Action met in the Masonic Temple, Chicago, Illinois, on February 21, 1922, in response to an invitation sent out to liberal leaders throughout the nation by the fifteen standard railroad brotherhoods earlier in the year. Calling upon the progressive forces to co-operate effectively in this proposed plan for political unity and action, a committee of railroad men, consisting of William H. Johnston of the Machinists as Chairman, and Martin F. Ryan of the Carmen, W. S. Stone of the Lococotive Engineers, E. J. Manion of the Telegraphers, Timothy Healy of the Firemen and Oilers, and L. E. Sheppard of the Conductors, had invited various representatives of farm organizations, labor unions, and groups concerned with social problems or promoting liberal thought.[15]

The " call " for progressives to assemble read, in part : [16]

. . . . There has been no common understanding to bind the working of all walks of life together. For lack of this common understanding we have been divided and betrayed. To the end that there may be a beginning of that wisdom which

14 Lovett, R. M., " A Party in Embryo," *New Republic,* 83 :3, July 24, 1935, p. 366.

15 *Labor* (Washington, D. C.), Feb. 11, 1922.

16 *Ibid.*

comes only through understanding the fifteen standard railroad labor organizations, through the undersigned—their duly
authorized committee—invite you to attend a conference to
be held in Chicago, Illinois, February 20, 1922, at 10 A. M.,
Corinthian Hall, Masonic Temple, to which conference representatives of the progressive elements in the industrial and
political life of our Nation have been invited to discuss and
adopt a fundamental economic program designed to restore
to the people the sovereignty that is rightly theirs, to make
effective the purpose for which our Government is established,
to secure to all men the enjoyment of the gain which their
industry produces.

This is not an attempt to form a new political party. It is
an effort to make use of those constructive forces already in
existence and by cooperation bring about political unity.

This invitation, signed by Johnston and the members of his
committee, carefully refrained from making any political commitments. Its vague generalities were sufficiently alluring to
attract liberals and reformers without provoking the suspicion
that attendance would in any way bind them to a definite course
of action. The wording of the invitation must have whetted the
political appetite of many a liberal frustrated by post-war conservatism and inactivity and eagerly anxious to weld together
the forces of dissent and reform.

Brought together at the CPPA conference for the first time
was a host of labor men, farmers, progressives of all hues, some
associated with political and economic organizations, others
unattached to any group.[17] Three hundred were there, from all
walks of life and all sections of the country. Fifty international
labor unions were represented by their executives or official
delegates. Without doubt the most energetic of these was William H. Johnston, the President of the International Association
of Machinists, without whose efforts, as chairman of the railroad committee, the conference would probably never have been

17 See *Locomotive Engineers Journal,* (Cleveland, Ohio), 56:3, Mar. 1922,
p. 168 ff.

held. A large delegation of western farmers, including leaders of the Non-Partisan League, was there. The railroad brotherhoods had been generous—perhaps too generous—with their invitations. All sorts of organizations sent representatives: Single-taxers, The Committee of Forty Eight, the Socialist and Farmer-Labor parties, The Methodist Federation of Social Service, the Church League for Industrial Democracy, the Non-Partisan League, the National Catholic Welfare Council, with whom the heads of the railway labor organizations had little in common except a general resentment against existing conditions. These elements appearing at the February Conference ranged all the way from the railroad brotherhoods, whose conception of political action had long been the endorsement of friends of Labor on the Democratic and Republican tickets, to the Socialist party delegates who desired an immediate third party, independent political action and a revolutionary program of social and economic reform.[18]

The broad range of speakers at the first session of the CPPA gives a clue to its rich variety of representation. Morris Hillquit spoke for the Socialists. James Maurer, President of the Pennsylvania State Federation of Labor, one of the most politically active units of the AFL, called for direct labor participation. Out of the West came Jay G. Brown, Secretary of the Farmer-Labor Party, and H. F. Samuels, head of the Non-partisan League of Idaho, to pledge agrarian support. Richard Hogue, of the League for Industrial Democracy, and the Reverend Herbert Bigelow, of the People's Church in Cincinnati, voiced the feelings of the reformist wing. Here, beneath the broad canopy of the CPPA, diverse elements were finding a common meeting ground, brought together no so much by similar interests as by their willingness to experiment in group resistance to the economic and social classes in control of America's political authority.[19]

18 *Report of the Chairman*, W. H. Johnson, Chairman, to the Executive Committee of the CPPA, Washington, D. C., Mar. 15, 1922, p. 1 (Marsh papers).

19 *Labor*, Feb. 11, 1922.

Although the first day's session was largely occupied with the speeches of leaders of various organizations pledging their aid in the promotion of a progressive movement, two committees were appointed to report the following day. One of these was the Committee on Organization, the chairman of which was Frederic Howe. The Committee on Declaration of Principles—very similar to a committee on platform and resolutions—was headed by Basil Manly.[20]

The Committee on Organization was, of course, assigned the difficult task of mobilizing the inchoate bodies and organizations represented at Chicago into a compact political unit. In order to provide leadership for the conference, the Committee on Organization suggested that the CPPA appoint a Committee or Fifteen to co-operate with and assist the local organizations and to call a national conference on the second Monday of December, 1922. The Committee further specified that the organizations to be invited to the December conference should be: [21]

(a) Progressive organizations of farmers.

(b) Organizations of labor.

(c) Co-operative societies.

(d) The Socialist and Farmer-Labor parties, Singletaxers and other liberal groups.

(e) Such other organizations, bodies and persons as the Committee may invite; provided that such organizations or persons are in accord with the purposes of this conference.

The basis of representation to the December conference would be determined by the National Committee of Fifteen.[22]

The Conference adopted these suggestions of the Committee on Organization, establishing in the Committee of Fifteen its first duly elected executive body.

20 *Loco. Engi. Journal*, 55:3, Mar. 1922, p. 168.

21 *Report*, Committee on Organization, CPPA, Chicago, Ill., Feb. 20-21, 1922, (Hillquit papers).

22 See Appendix No. 2.

William Johnston was chosen as Chairman of the Committee, Warren Stone as Treasurer and Fred Howe as Secretary. Washington, D. C., was determined upon as national headquarters.[23]

The reason for the December conference was self-evident. By that time, the election of 1922 would have been held; and with the lessons of that election in mind, a national conference could determine whether the time was ripe for third party action.

The Committee on Declaration of Purposes faced a much more difficult task and immediately discovered that it would be impossible to agree on any program or even a declaration of principles which would be acceptable to all the delegates. So an " Address to the American People " was adopted, " mildly stating the criticisms of existing conditions and a plan of action which allows each organization to do exactly that which it would have done had the conference not been called." [24] Attacking monopoly, corruption, imperialism and special privilege, the " Address to the American People " was an indictment of " the invisible government of plutocracy and privilege."

There was nothing new or startling about this declaration of principles. There could not be. With so many disparate groups in attendance, it was an accomplishment to express any opinions whatsoever. The generalizations and the platitudes of the " Address to the American People " had to be couched in terms that would do nothing to alienate the groups which were so cautiously formulating a program of common action.

The accomplishments of the first Conference for Progressive Political Action were probably well summed up by the *Socialist World* in commenting upon the Chicago meeting: [25]

> On the whole, the Conference was a disappointment, so far as immediate results are concerned. The importance of the

23 *Loco. Engi. Journal, ibid.*

24 See Appendix No. 3 for the complete text of this declaration of principles.

25 *Socialist World*, Feb. 1922, p. 1.

Conference lies in the fact that representatives of both conservative and radical unions, farmer organizations and Non-Partisan League, Farmer-Labor party and Socialist party met together for two days, discussed conditions and remedies and adjourned without antagonism or resentment, with an increased respect and toleration for each other and each other's views, and a determination to get together in later conferences in an effort to establish closer understanding, and ultimately, if possible, secure united action on a common program.

At least there were some tangible fruits of progress. The progressives now had an organization, the Conference for Progressive Political Action.[26] A national committee, later to have offices in the Machinists' Building, Washington, had been appointed. Plans had been approved for a national conference, with delegates officially representing various bodies and groups, to meet on December 11. At Chicago, naturally, the delegates came only in their capacity as individuals invited to a meeting to discuss progressive political action. Finally, there was general agreement to conduct active campaigns on behalf of liberals in the general elections of 1922.

On the negative side, in this appraisal of the first conference, two facts stand out. Although—as the report of the Chairman ingenuously states—" the time was ripe for progressive political action," the organization of a new party had to await developments. This was the first of many disappointments for the Socialists and other left-wingers who wanted immediate action. The second negative feature of the Chicago conference was the mild and general statement of principles. At their first meeting, the progressives were facing the same dilemma that perplexes the old parties every time they draw up a platform—the risk of alienating some of the constituent parts of the amorphous, spineless creature known as an American political party.

26 The name, "Conference for Progressive Political Action," was suggested by Morris Hillquit, Socialist leader. See Hillquit, M., *Loose Leaves from a Busy Life*, p. 311.

Between February and December, the National Committee, with William Johnston as Chairman, directed the work of the CPPA. At a meeting of the executive committee in the spring of the year, it was decided to send Mr. Marsh to the West Coast and Mr. Holder to the Mid-West to co-ordinate and promote the CPPA activities. Plans to support friendly candidates in the ensuing elections were also approved.[27]

These were active months of achievement for the CPPA. Under the energetic leadership of Johnston and Holder, thirty-two state organizations were established, chiefly in the Northeast, Mid-West and on the Pacific Coast.[28] Some of them, of course, were merely skeleton frameworks upon which later a substantial political organization could be constructed.

Immediately after the Chicago meeting instituted the CPPA, Edward Keating, editor of *Labor,* the official organ of the standard railroad organizations, enthusiastically provided the new organization with much-needed press support. With a circulation in excess of 400,000 and enjoying a singular influence within the most powerful unions, *Labor* continued to be a source of invaluable assistance to the Progressives from start to finish of their campaign.

The second conference—held appropriately enough in the Brotherhood of Locomotive Engineers' Auditorium in Cleveland, Ohio, December 11 and 12, 1922—was preceded by a noteworthy gathering of progressives, many of them from Congress, at a dinner at the City Club in Washington on December 2.[29] This meeting was prompted and sponsored by Manly's People's Legislative Service. Robert LaFollette acted as chairman of this informal gathering of liberals, and among the speakers were Senators Norris, Brookhart, Wheeler, Shipstead and Frazier, Sam Gompers of the AFL and Samuel Untermyer

27 *Minutes,* Executive Committee of the CPPA, Meeting held at Washington, D. C., in May 26, 1922. (Hillquit papers).

28 *Report,* " The Executive Committee of the CPPA to the Second Conference," CPPA, Cleveland, Ohio, Dec. 11-12, 1922, p. 5.

29 *New York World,* Dec. 3, 1922.

of New York. Among those attending were Roger Baldwin, Herbert Croly, Fiorello H. LaGuardia, John Moore, legislative representative of the United Mine Workers, W. H. Johnston of the Machinists, Warren Stone of the Brotherhood and Herbert F. Baker, President of the Farmers' National Council. The unions and farm groups were well represented. Mellon and Daugherty were attacked in particular, the reactionary policies of the Administration in general. The group went on record as favoring a unity of progressives " for the purpose of bringing about the co-operation of progressives throughout the country to aid in the advancement of liberal laws and general reconstruction. . . ." [30] A resolution was passed favoring a model primary law in all the states and direct nomination of the President and Vice-President.

Oddly enough, this Washington meeting obtained more publicity than either of the 1922 meetings of the CPPA. The " big names " at the City Club meeting, the general acquaintance of the public with statesmen like Norris and LaFollette, made a first-page story out of this meeting of progressives. Without any formal or official connection with the CPPA, the progressive meeting at the City Club undoubtedly served to stimulate the interest of farm and labor groups in the formation of an independent political organization.

There was occasion for hope and anticipation at both the Washington dinner and the Cleveland conference. The 1922 general election was the cause of the joy. It was estimated, by the leaders of the CPPA, that 140 members of the new House were " progressive-minded." [31] Candidates endorsed by the CPPA had won in Oklahoma, Iowa, Nebraska, Kansas, Colorado and Arizona. Ninety-three undesirable members of the 67th Congress had been defeated. Among those defeated or forced into retirement were such outstanding conservative

30 *Ibid.*

31 *Proceedings,* Second Conference, CPPA, Cleveland, Ohio, Dec. 11-12, 1922, p. 7.

leaders as Cannon of Illinois, Fess of Ohio and Fordney of Michigan.[32]

Although the Republicans still retained their majorities in both houses of Congress—22 in the Senate, 169 in the House of Representatives—the advocates of independent political action were heartened. The defeat of such staunch supporters of the Esch-Cummins Law as Senators Frelinghuysen, McCumber, Poindexter and Pomerene, instilled a recovered confidence in the railroad brotherhoods. The smashing victory of La-Follette in Wisconsin, sweeping a progressive ticket into office with him, spearheaded the Progressive triumph. A correspondent for *Labor*, the official organ of the railroad unions, taking note of LaFollette's spectacular success in the election, started to refer to him as a " most formidable presidential possibility in 1924." [33]

After hearing a keynote address by Chairman William H. Johnston and the report of the National Committee, the second conference faced, for the first time, the question of accepting Communist support. The assembled delegates upheld Keating's motion not to accept credentials from representatives of the Workers' Party.[34] These delegates, C. E. Ruthenberg, H. Gannes, W. F. Dunne, C. Harrison and L. Lore, had not been invited but, in characteristic Communist manner, had come anyway. The number of delegates of the organizations invited to join the CPPA was apportioned as follows, by the National Committee :[35]

National and International Labor and Farm Organizations— 3 delegates each

State, Local and city Central Organizations of labor and farmer—1 delegate each

32 *Ibid.*

33 *Labor*, Nov. 11, 1922.

34 *Proceedings*, Second Conference, CPPA, p. 10.

35 *Ibid.*, p. 1.

National Co-operative Societies—3 delegates

State and Local Co-operative—1 delegate each

National Socialist Party—7 delegates

Farmer-Labor Party—5 delegates

Farmer-Labor Party of Minnesota—2 delegates

National Non-Partisan League—3 delegates

State Non-Partisan League—1 delegate each

League for Industrial Democracy—3 delegates

Single Taxers—3 delegates

State and Local Organizations for Progressive Political Action—1 delegate each

On roll call, national and international organizations were entitled to one vote for each 10,000 members, state and local organizations to one vote each as represented. This rule, for instance, gave the Brotherhood of Railway Clerks, with a membership of 125,000, a voting strength, on roll call, of thirteen. Twenty votes were allotted to the International Association of Machinists. With 500,000 members, the United Mine Workers were entitled to fifty votes. Political parties had as many votes as delegates were apportioned. This system of voting is mentioned here at length because, with certain minor revisions, it remained the basis for the apportionment of voting strength in the CPPA all through its three-year existence.

The chief issue at the second conference was the matter of organizing a third party at once. The Socialists, the left-wingers and the " intellectuals," in general, were in favor of some such move. The Brotherhood representatives, most of the labor men and farmers were less disposed to cross the Rubicon at such an early date. The Brotherhood was flirting with the idea of endorsing McAdoo in the forthcoming election if nominated by the Democrats. The farmers, subscribing to the strategy of the Non-Partisan League, were more anxious to capture primaries than launch third parties. The lively debate over this issue, portent of serious strife within the progressive ranks in the days to come, was provoked by a minority report of the Committee on Resolutions declaring for an independent political party of workers and farmers.[36] There followed the first of many debates on this issue. For the first time in a CPPA gathering, the lines were drawn with the conservative, cautious trade union and Brotherhood men on the one side, and the " third-party boys " on the other. After a discussion on the floor, during which the proposal was defended by Robert M. Buck and John Fitzpatrick, the Illinois labor leaders who had formed a Farmer-Labor Party in their state, the motion to launch a third party was defeated, 52-64.[37] The vote was close, but, as on so many subsequent occasions, the proponents of a definite third party were disappointed. Obviously, the Brotherhood men—who dominated these early conferences—were not ready to put all their eggs in one basket.

Even in the formulating of a platform was this precise caution of the union men in evidence. The Socialists, led by Morris Hillquit, were anxious to have the CPPA commit itself on a number of issues, including child labor, public ownership of power, war and imperialism, and nationalization of the coal mines. Once again these proposals were lost in a minority report. The platform adopted by the Conference at least had the virtue of brevity. The report, submitted by Edward Keating, as Chairman of the Resolutions Committee, was approved by the assembled delegates with certain minor concessions to the left-wingers.[38]

The six points incorporated in the platform submitted by the majority were as follows:

1—The repeal of the Esch-Cummins railroad law, and operation of the railroads for the benefit of the people. The public control of coal mines, water power and hydro-electric power in the interest of the people.

36 *Ibid.*, p. 28.
37 *Ibid.*, p. 29.
38 *Ibid.*, pp. 22-26.

2—The direct election of the President and Vice-President by the people and extension of direct primary laws in all States.

3—That Congress end the practice of the Courts to declare legislation unconstitutional.

4—Enactment of the Norris-Sinclair Consumers' and Producers' Financing Corporation bill designed to increase prices farmers receive, and reduce prices consumers pay for farm products, and the creation of an independent system of food producers' credits.

5—Increased tax rates on large income and inheritance, and payment of a soldiers' bonus by restoring the tax on excess profits.

6—Legislation providing minimum essential standards of employment for women; equality for women and men while improving existing political, social and industrial standards and State action to insure maximum benefit of Federal maternity and infancy acts.

The " post-card platform," as it was referred to because of its brevity, enabled the conservative union leaders to formulate the policy of the CPPA without antagonising too much the groups in favor of more direct and immediate action. The reluctance of the railroad unions to join in the formation of an active third party was more evident than ever before. Probably, the strategy of these " hold-back boys " of 1922 was to endorse a program of platitudes and generalities, awaiting the pleasure of LaFollette—or possibly McAdoo or Borah—to provide the leadership for an independent national ticket. If so, the plan worked. The second conference of the CPPA was effectively dominated—tactfully but confidently—by the railroad union leaders. The fact that this second conference was held in Cleveland, center of most brotherhood activities and comparatively distant from the agrarian agitation of the Northwest, perhaps significantly reveals the trend of the CPPA. It was moving away from the influence of both radical organizers and Northwestern Farm-Labor leaders into the well-ordered channels of railroad union domination.

Meanwhile, the ground work was being laid in the states. By the spring of 1922, fourteen states had established CPPA organizations.[39] As early as May, 1922, one of the leaders of the CPPA was professing his satisfaction with the progress of the state organization. But, as the Progressives were going to find out so well in the 1924 campaign, it made a lot of difference whether preliminary foundations had been securely laid. Fred Howe wrote to Morris Hillquit at this time: [40]

> I feel very well satisfied with the way things are going. The results are spotty. Some places there is every evidence of movements being permanently grounded on the right foundations; in other places they are ephemeral. Wherever the movement is a group movement and wherever the Non-Partisan League and the Socialists have done a lot of preliminary work, things are going amazingly well. This seems to be especially true in Texas, Oklahoma, Wyoming, North and South Dakota.

The tactics of the CPPA were well defined by the action taken in December, 1922, to defer consideration of a third party. The group intended to await developments and then, as the presidential campaign of 1924 approached, to consider a course of political procedure. Hence, 1923 was a year of watchful waiting, occasional meetings of the members of the Executive Committee and attempts—sometimes haphazard—to establish state organizations. When state CPPA's were established—in accordance with the expressed wishes of the delegates attending the first conference—the state organization was usually modeled after that of the national CPPA. A typical state CPPA was founded in New York State on July 29-30, 1923. As with the national CPPA, the " call " came from the Brotherhood rail-

39 *Labor*, April 1, 1922.

40 Fred Howe to Morris Hillquit, May 25, 1922, (Hillquit papers).

road unions. As in the case of the first national meeting at Chicago, the delegates who attended represented, in large part, diverse groups willing to try to arrive at some common ground in defense of liberal principles. The Albany meeting was presided over by Thomas E. Ryan of the Brotherhood of Locomotive Firemen and Enginemen. The diverse elements, from all parts of the country, attending a national conference obscured a rift in the ranks of the Progressives which was obvious in state meetings from the start. At Albany, the two most powerful groups, both in voting strength and political influence, were the members of the Socialist party and the members of the railroad brotherhoods. The two-day session was marked by continuous clashes between the moderate unionists and the more radical Socialists.[41] It is difficult to see how the New York CPPA made any contribution to the cause of progressivism. Mainly, it accentuated the fundamental differences in policy and procedure between the union men and the Socialist party. Several months after the Albany meeting, Mr. Hillquit still felt bitterly about the treatment accorded the Socialists. In writing Mr. Ryan, to complain of inaccuracies in the minutes of the Albany conference, Mr. Hillquit concluded with this sharp criticism of the men alongside whom the Socialists expected to fight in the 1924 political battle. " Perhaps some day the ' practical ' politicians within the ranks of organised labor will rise to the same plane of fairmindedness as their constituents usually display, and learn that there is a way of disagreeing with political opponents without grossly misrepresenting them." [42] Time and the common cause would never quite overcome this basic weakness in the progressive movement. The labor men always suspected the Socialists; the latter, in turn, reciprocated the distrust.

Perhaps if events had taken their normal course, the friction and disagreement among the splinter groups would have caused

41 *Proceedings,* New York State CPPA, held at Albany, N. Y., July 29-30, 1923, pp. 18-23, (Hillquit papers).

42 Morris Hillquit to Thomas E. Ryan, Oct. 1, 1923, (Hillquit papers).

the end of the promising experiment in political unity among farmers and workers. But, between 1922 and early 1924, both foreign and domestic events of great moment conspired to stimulate the interest and expectations of liberals in a third party movement.

The spectacular success of the British Labor Party had kindled hope among American progressives that the English labor movement could be duplicated on this side of the Atlantic.[43] Above all, the gains of British Labor seemed to be irrefutable proof that the trade unions and Socialists could work together for common victory. Furthermore, the speed and completeness with which Labour replaced the Liberal Party as one of the two great political organizations astounded the whole world. Nor was the success of third parties confined to England. If American labor could find comfort and inspiration in the achievements of Ramsay MacDonald's party, the farmers of the Northwest were no less delighted with the turn of events in Canada. For the first time, in 1921, the aroused farmers of Canada organised a party, the National Progressive Party, successful in winning thirty-seven seats in Parliament and disrupting the two-party system in Canada. The demands and purposes of this Canadian group " suggest a marked similarity with those of the farmers' Non-Partisan League which was spreading rapidly through the Northwestern states of the United States in this same period." [44]

If Ramsay MacDonald, the British Labor Party leader, and Robert Forke, the Canadian farm leader, were unknowingly playing their parts in the promotion of a progressive movement, here at home Harry Daugherty and William G. McAdoo were playing theirs most unwillingly. Daugherty, and all the other Washington politicians implicated in the numerous scandals of the Harding Administration, promoted a third party insofar as

43 The first resolution approved by the Third Conference, CPPA, was a congratulatory message to the British Labour Party. *Proceedings,* Third Conference, CPPA, held at St. Louis, Mo., Feb. 11-12, 1923, p. 24.

44 Wittke, C., *A History of Canada,* p. 361.

the public became aroused by the revelations of graft and as it became disgusted with the slim possibility of cleansing national politics without a thorough overhauling. McAdoo's unwilling and accidental role in the story of the progressive movement is merely an adjunct to his futile attempt to secure the Democratic nomination, discussed elsewhere.[45] But the revelation that McAdoo had been " retained " by the " oil interests " at a princely fee, shook the confidence of the labor men in their idol, the Director-General of the nation's railroads during wartime, whose friendly attitude towards labor had not been forgotten. Until he was " smeared " with oil, McAdoo seemed to be the ideal candidate of the unions, the railroad brotherhoods in particular. The intense disappointment of the railroad men in McAdoo was easily discernible when the third CPPA met at St. Louis, in February 1924.[46] Faced with a realization of the inacceptability of the aspirants within the old parties, the labor men, with renewed vigor, rekindled their interest in progressive plans.

On December 5, 1923, Chairman Johnston issued the " call " for the third conference of the CPPA, to be held at the Statler Hotel, St. Louis, Missouri, on February 11, 1924. Encouraged by the victories of labor abroad and stimulated by the disclosures of graft at home, the delegates were in an optimistic frame of mind. From Chairman Johnston's opening address the morning of the 11th until adjournment the next afternoon, the atmosphere radiated achievement and high expectations. The new spirit of hope and a refreshing desire to get things done were discernible to most of the delegates.[47] Johnston was happy and proud to report on the thirty-odd state organizations and the groundwork laid in 1923. He reported receipts of over $16,500, of which the largest contributions had come from the

45 See chapter V, pp. 99-105.

46 Thomas, N., " Progressivism at St. Louis," *Nation,* 118:3060, Feb. 27, 1924, p. 224.

47 *Ibid.*

Locomotive Firemen and Engineers ($3060), the United Mine Workers ($3000), and the International Machinists ($2778).[48]

Much of the work of the third conference consisted of ratifying plans of organization drawn up by the various committees. Perhaps the most significant of these endorsements was the official approval, given by the 200-odd delegates, to a declaration of the purpose of the Conference for Progressive Political Action.

As adopted by the St. Louis conference, the statement of purpose is as follows: [49]

> The Conference for Progressive Political Action is an organization created for the purpose of securing the nomination and election of Presidents and Vice Presidents of the Untied States, United States Senators, Representatives to Congress, members of State Legislatures and other state and local public officers who are pledged to the interests of the producing classes and to the principles of genuine democracy in agriculture, industry and government.

The highlight of the St. Louis conference was the decision to issue a call for a convention for the purpose of considering nominations for the Presidency. The call consisted of eight parts, specifying place and time, and determining representation and voting strength at the convention.

In view of its importance in the composition of the Cleveland meeting, the call is quoted here in full: [50]

> In view of the vital importance of the approaching presidential election and the unparalleled opportunity which it offers to organize and mobilize the progressive forces in American politics for united action in behalf of the wealth producers of the country, the Conference for Progressive Political Action in general meeting assembled, on the 12th day of February, 1924, resolves:

48 *Proceedings,* Third Conference, CPPA, p. 5.
49 *Ibid.,* p. 15.
50 *Ibid.,* pp. 18-19.

1—That the National Committee of this Conference be instructed to immediately issue a call for a convention of workers, farmers and progressives for the purpose of taking action on nomination of candidates for the offices of President and Vice President of the United States, and on other questions that may come before the Convention.

2—That the Convention shall be held in the city of Cleveland and open on the 4th day of July, 1924, at 10 a. m.

3—That invitations to participate in the Convention shall be extended to all bona fide labor organizations, progressive organizations of farmers, co-operative societies and progressive political parties and groups.

4—Representation at the Convention shall be on the following basis: Every national or international organization of labor, farmers, co-operative societies, and political parties shall be entitled to three delegates; state federations of labor, every state organization of the CPPA, every state legislative board of the transportation organizations and every state committee of a political party shall be entitled to two delegates; every general city central body of labor, and all local organizations of farmers and local co-operative societies in states in which there are no state organizations of such bodies, shall be entitled to one delegate. The National Committee shall be authorized to invite as delegates to the Convention such individuals as it may select, but such delegates shall have no vote in the Convention.

5—All motions and resolutions shall be voted on by viva voce vote or by a show of hands, except upon the demand of at least 50 delegates, the vote on any question before the meeting shall be taken by roll call. Upon a roll call vote, each national or international organization of farmers, workers, or co-operative societies shall be entitled to one vote for every ten thousand members in good standing or fraction of such number; every other organization shall cast as many votes as the number of delegates to which it is entitled.

6—The National Committee shall be authorized to call for voluntary contributions for the special purpose of enabling it to make all necessary arrangements for the Convention and to bring out the largest possible representation.

7—We recommend that the incoming National Committee invite the co-operation of the national arrangements committee of the Farmer-Labor Parties of the Northwest, consisting of William Mahoney, Dr. William A. Schaper, and H. G. Tiegan, in the arrangements for the Convention.

8—The next National Conference shall be held on December 8, 1924, at a place to be selected by the National Committee.

The Progressives marked time from February until June. The " call " for a national convention, scheduled for July 4, implied the readiness of the CPPA to endorse a liberal as candidate for President in the event of the nomination of unsatisfactory candidates by the old parties. Meanwhile, as the Progressives waited, events conspired to raise their hopes and impress upon them the virtues of LaFollette's candidacy. The nation was hearing the shameful story of wholesale corruption in the Administration; the oil which had smeared so many Republicans, playing no favorites, ruined the presidential chances of William G. McAdoo, LaFollette's most formidable rival as suitor for CPPA affections. In one of the earliest presidential primaries, that of North Dakota, LaFollette received the amazing total of 40,000 votes despite his refusal to permit his name to appear on the ballot.[51] In a poll taken by the Committee of Forty-Eight, LaFollette was the overwhelming choice of liberals throughout the nation to enter the race against the old parties.[52] In Illinois, the Farm Labor party., which had been suspicious of trade and railroad union motives, and intransigeant in its attitude toward the Progressives, finally accepted an invitation to collaborate with the CPPA.[53]

51 *New York Times,* Mar. 26, 1924.

52 *Ibid.,* Feb. 23, 1924.

53 *Labor,* Apr. 8, 1924.

The decks were cleared for action. The way was open to nominate Senator LaFollette, or some other acceptable liberal, as the candidate of the united forces of the progressive and reform elements. But before that promise of common action could be fulfilled the Progressives had to save their cherished dream of left-wing co-operation from a sinister kidnapping plot, as ingeniously conceived as it was skilfully manipulated. The Communists, of course, were at the bottom of it all. Antagonised by their frigid reception at CPPA gatherings and completely frustrated in their efforts to gain a foothold inside the new liberal organizations, the Communists sought to preempt the third party idea by gaining control of the Farm-Labor political machinery. The story of this craftily conceived strategy on the part of the Communists deserves some detail, not only because it came close to ruining the chance of independent political action in 1924, but also because it established a formula which the same group was to use more than once in gaining control over liberal organizations. The story of this flanking attack upon the CPPA, from the left, starts several years before its 1924 climax.

December, 1921, represents a turning point in the policies of the American communist movement. At a convention called for December 23 of that year, a " Workers Party of America " was founded. In this new organization were merged most of the underground Bolshevik groupings which for three years had fought each other almost as bitterly as they assailed the capitalists and the vested interests. The moderate tone of this new party was in marked contrast to the unrestrained cries of world revolution so prevalent in the years from 1918 to 1921.

It was more than coincidental that the Communists were changing their tactics and softening their tone just as Lenin retreated from his experiment in pure communism in Russia. Quite evidently the word had gone out from the Kremlin that more flies could be caught with molasses.[54] This was the first

54 See Gitlow, B., *I Confess,* ch. IV, for a detailed account of this reversal in policy.

Communist experiment in " united front " tactics. The way was now clear to break into the ranks of the liberals and labor unions. Within two months of its organization, the Workers party, in its ardent haste to apply " united front " methods, was courting the Conference for Progressive Political Action. The CPPA, which had met in Chicago as a result of the call of the Railroad Brotherhood unions, was prepared to consider the feasibility of establishing a political organization similar to the British Labour Party.[55] The Communists did not wait to be invited. The Central Executive Committee of the Workers party impatiently drafted a set of demands which would " furnish a common ground upon which every labor union and every political party of the workers can fight together ".[56]

Undeterred by the rebuff when the CPPA not only failed to accept the invitation to join forces but completely ignored the communication, the Workers party proceeded to send delegates to the second meeting of the CPPA, held in Cleveland in December, 1922.

Presentation of their credentials to the second conference precipitated an early decision within the CPPA concerning co-operation with the Communists. The delegates overwhelmingly supported Edward Keating's motion not to accept credentials of the Workers party—on the grounds that the Workers party did not truly represent the workers and that the movement represented by the Workers party was " un-American ".[57] The Socialists voted for the motion to keep the Communists out but for different reasons. The Socialists objected because of their dislike for the disruptive tactics of the Communists, revealed on so many unhappy occasions.[58]

Its complete failure, either by cajolery or stratagem, to get inside the doors of the CPPA perhaps encouraged the next

55 See above, p. 61.

56 Oneal, J., *American Communism*, p. 138.

57 *Proceedings*, Second CPPA, p. 10.

58 *Ibid*.

and most spectacular attempt of the Communist party to cap_
ture a worker-farmer organization. This opportunity presented
itself when the Farmer-Labor party issued a call for a national
conference of all groups with an interest in promoting an alliance of farmers and workers. The Farmers-Labor leaders
invited, among others, Socialists, Non-Partisan Leaguers, trade
unionists and, unaware of the fatal blunder being made, included the Workers party in the invitation.

The significance of the behavior of the Communists at the
Farmer-Labor convention in 1923 extends far beyond the mere
fact that they captured control of the organization. More than
that, it was the shape of things to come. Again and again, in
the years ahead, the Communists were to display the same disciplined tactics, obtaining for themselves an influence in left-
wing and liberal organizations out of all proportion to their
numbers.

" Packing " the convention turned out to be a ludicrously
easy matter. Delegates were seated from such organizations as
the " Lithuanian Workers' Literature Society," " Improvement Benefit Club," " Workmen's Gymnastic Association,"
"Sick and Death Benefit Societies," " United Workingmen
Singers," and even from an undecipherable and mysterious
" P.D. and P.H. of A." [59] The Communist plan to " pack " the
convention was facilitated by the error of the Farmer-Labor
credentials committee in accepting those invited to the general
conference as full-fledged delegates on the floor of the party
convention. The Communists who appeared at the convention
representing " innocent " organizations denied their party affili_
ation but they were all duly registered for a Communist caucus
of the convention, a caucus which included ninety percent of
the delegates present.[60]

Farm leaders from the Northwest and labor men like Fitzpatrick and Nockles of Chicago, motivated by a sincere desire

59 Oneal, J., *op. cit.*, p. 166.

60 Gitlow, B., *op. cit.*, p. 181.

to construct a genuine third party of liberal elements, were anxious to defer definite action on the formation of a party until the railroad brotherhoods and the CPPA had had time to formulate their policies. But the steering committee of the Communist caucus, consisting of Ruthenberg, Pepper and Foster, had things all their own way. As was to be demonstrated so many times again, the disciplined, well-oiled, compact machine of the Communists was able to dominate the proceedings. Gitlow succinctly describes what happened at Chicago. " The Steering Committee wanted to organise a labor party right away. It had the delegates present and they would do whatever the Steering Committee ordered them to do. They came for no other purpose. The Steering Committee also knew that if a labor party emerged from Chicago the Communists would control it. When the Communist steamroller flattened out Fitzpatrick and Nockles, they and their few supporters bolted the convention. Amid fanfare and wild enthusiasm the motion to organize a labor party was carried and the Federated Farmer-Labor party came into existence. The Executive Committee elected was dominated by the Communists, its Secretary being Joseph Manley, Foster's son-in-law, who had the unpleasant job of being the new party's wet nurse." [61]

But, without doubt, the Communists overplayed their hand in making off so boldly with the prize. The kidnapping was apparent for all to see. The New York *Times* remarked editorially upon the " borers from within " and the " bores from without " who marred the occasion.[62] A reporter present at the proceedings could not help noticing the tension, the recriminations, the frequent verbal clashes among delegates who obstensibly had arrived in Chicago to cement bonds of friendship among the liberal elements. To this observer, most of the trouble was due to the " rough-shod methods of the Com-

61 *Ibid.*, p. 183.

62 *New York Times*, July 5, 1923.

munists." [63] Truly " as once before when the sons of God assembled, Satan came with them." [64]

There was something pathetic about the unscrupulous manipulation of the grievances and discontent of these farmers and laboring men. It was more than bad manners on the part of the Communists. It was bad faith and a cruel, abrupt method of killing the brave hopes of men who were so conscious of injustice and exploitation. They were babes in the woods when brought face to face with the carefully planned and managed Communist strategy.

" The Farmer-Labor delegates were throughout in an impossible situation. When the program committee reported, there was nothing into which opponents of the Workers party could set their teeth. A federal law for the eight-hour day, a law providing compensation for unemployment, a child labor law, a living wages law, a compulsory education law, the soldiers' bonus, a workers' insurance law, a maternity insurance law— a law for everything and everybody. " Such a complete summary of ameliorative proposals that it reads like a satire. When the Farmer-Labor leaders tried to insinuate a fear of the red peril, the Workers party demanded to know what was red in giving a working mother a month's pay before and after childbirth." [65]

What considerations prompted the Communists to grace the occasion with such a *tour de force?* Obviously there was little to be gained politically in capturing such an inchoate organization. But to Foster and the other leaders of the CP, this was a back-door entrance to the labor unions. The small success of the party appeal to the trade unions had been a disappointment to the leaders of the Third International. The Communist party had not been able to penetrate the hallowed circle of trade

63 *Christian Science Monitor,* July 5, 1923.

64 Lovett, R. M., " The Farmer Labor Fiasco at Chicago," *New Republic,* 35 : 450, July 18, 1923, p. 198.

65 *Ibid.,* p. 199.

unionism. Moscow's approval of the new strategy led directly to the kidnapping at Chicago. " When the labor party policy was put into practice the Communist party was insignificant politically. Our total active membership was 6,862, of whom over two-thirds were not in the trade unions and the rest an insignificant minority there. We could make a lot of noise through our press and at meetings, but we were to all intents and purposes completely isolated from the main stream of organised labor. Through the Labor party we hoped to attract the workers and penetrate the trade unions." [66]

The Communist success at Chicago was a pyrrhic victory. One by one, the other affiliates withdrew or repudiated the new party, the Federated Farmer-Labor party. The Farmer-Labor party, at a rump convention, lost no time in announcing its refusal to support the new organization.[67] The Chicago Federation of Labor returned to the non-partisan " voluntarism " policies of Sam Gompers and disbanded its political vehicle, the Cook County Farmer-Labor party.[68] A flamboyant boast that the party represented 600,000 farmers and workers fell on deaf ears. William H. Johnston ignored a letter from Joseph Manly suggesting that a committee of the CPPA meet with a similar committee from the Federated Farmer-Labor party " in order to discuss ways and means for a nation-wide organization campaign among the workers and farmers." [69] Even the choice of a name for the party was ill-advised. It was too long to appear on many state ballots.[70]

Thus the curtain was rung down on the abortive attempt to start a real third party in 1923. Without accomplishing

66 Gitlow, B., *op. cit.*, p. 192.

67 Oneal, J., *op. cit.*, p. 171.

68 *The New Majority* (Chicago), May 24, 1924.

69 Leaflet of Federated Farmer-Labor Party, quoted in Oneal, *op. cit.*, p. 170.

70 Stolberg, B., " The Peter Pans of Communism," *Century Magazine*, 110:3, July 1925, p. 227.

anything for itself beyond a certain limited bargaining power for 1924, the Communists had almost succeeded in ruining any prospect of liberal political action. More than that, the fiasco at Chicago tended to reflect upon the serious and sincere efforts of labor leaders like Fitzpatrick to persuade the unions to adopt a policy of genuine political action. The pitfalls of Chicago seemed to reaffirm the fears expressed by Gompers and other adherents of the non-partisan policy.

The performance was to be repeated in 1924. The success of the Farmer-Labor party in Minnesota in electing Magnus Johnson to the United States Senate in 1923 encouraged the leaders of the state organization to issue invitations to a conference to consider the advisability of a national campaign in the coming presidential election. At the conference held in St. Paul in November, 1923, it was decided to hold a convention in the same city the following spring to which representatives of the various progressive groups would be invited.[71] In spite of the misapprehensions of experienced leaders like John Fitzpatrick, Robert Buck and Jay Brown, the farmers of the Northwest were going to repeat the mistakes of 1923 by inviting the Communists once more.[72]

Many of the Northwest farm leaders attended the February meeting of the CPPA (to which, of course, the Communists were not invited) and returned home enthusiastic over the prospects of a third ticket, comprising liberal, farm and union elements, and supporting LaFollette in the forthcoming presidential campaign. In light of the promising developments within the CPPA, these farm leaders moved to postpone the St. Paul convention altogether in order to throw their united support behind the CPPA effort.[73]

" The Communists who were excluded from the CPPA . . . maneuvered to prevent this and won Mahoney and Teigan over

[71] Fine, N., *Labor and Farmer Parties in the United States*, p. 435.

[72] Buck was editor of *The New Majority;* Brown was Gen. Secretary of the Farm Labor Party.

[73] See Fine, N., *op. cit.*, p. 435 ff.

to their point of view." [74] What Mahoney and the other leaders of the Farm-Labor movement did not know was that the Communists had received orders from Moscow to prevent LaFollette's endorsement or nomination under any circumstances.[75]

In the *International Press Correspondence* of February 28, 1924, a Communist publication printed in Vienna, Austria, appeared a prophetic account of the strategy of the Communists in the coming election. " By ruthless, merciless criticism of the third party and of petit bourgeois reformism the Communists will unmask its character. Though supporting the third party, they must be able to criticise it pitilessly. This is a strategy that the Communist parties of Europe and America are just learning to apply. It is a hard course but is the path of the revolution. The campaign in America will allow us to enter the third party, to form a left wing within it, and to split the left wing away from the third party." [76] With such a disingenuous plan in mind, the Communists did not fear too much simple Populists like William Mahoney. Once again, as in July, 1923, the stage was set. Once again the Communists, the invited guests, were going to make off with not only the ice cream but the dishes and silver as well.

On May 28, 1924, Senator LaFollette made public a letter he had written to his friend, Mr. Herman L. Ekern, Attorney-General of Wisconsin, making clear his attitude not only toward the Farmer-Labor party, but also toward the Communists.[77] LaFollette's complete, unreserved repudiation of Communist support and his indictment of the Farmer-Labor groups for affiliating with the Communists left no room for doubt. The letter came like a bombshell exploding the hopes of Farm Labor leaders to make LaFollette the candidate of their

74 *Ibid.*

75 Gitlow, *op. cit.*, p. 203.

76 Quoted by William Hard in *Nation*, 119:3078, July 2, 1924, p. 12.

77 *New York Herald Tribune*, May 29, 1924. The letter was dated May 25, 1924.

new third party. In light of what we now know about Communist activities during the past twenty years, the letter displays acute prescience on LaFollette's part in foreseeing Communist strategy. Some parts of the letter deserve particular attention.

> . . . . The communists have admittedly entered into this political movement not for the purpose of curing, by means of the ballot, the evils which afflict the American people, but only to divide and confuse the progressive movement and create a condition of chaos favorable to their ultimate aims. Their real purpose is to establish by revolutionary action, a dictatorship of the proletariat, which is absolutely repugnant to democratic ideals and to all American aspirations. The official declarations of the workers party show clearly that they are seeking to use the Farmer-Labor party of Minnesota and other progressive organizations that have lent their names to this convention as a means of advancing their own ends. . .
>
> . . . Reposing complete confidence in the soundness of the deliberate judgment of the American people, I have no apprehension that the communist party can ever command any considerable support in this country. I do not question their right, under the Constitution, to submit their issues to the people, but I most emphatically protest against their being admitted into the councils of any body of progressive voters. The communists stand for the substitution of the soviet form of government for the one we now have and propose to accomplish this change through a revolution with a class dictatorship as their ultimate aim instead of a democracy. To pretend that the communists can work with the progressives who believe in democracy is deliberately to deceive the public. The communists are antagonistic to the progressive cause and their only purpose in joining such a movement is to disrupt it.
>
> Not only are the communists the mortal enemies of the progressive movement and democratic ideals but, under the cloak of such extremists, the reactionary interests find the best opportunity to plant their spies and provocatory agents for the purpose of confusing and destroying true progressive movements . . .

. . . The approaching Democratic and Republican conventions will demonstrate to the people whether either of those parties can and will purge itself of the evil influences which have long dominated them. This cannot be accomplished merely by nominating some alleged progressive and filling the platform with misleading promises. It demands the elimination of monopoly control, the downfall of the corrupt political bosses, the adoption of truly progressive principles and the repudiation of those great campaign contributors who have in the past bought up both parties.

If this is not done, a long suffering and righteously indignant people will find in the coming campaign effective means, independent of both these old parties, to take back control of their government and make it truly representative . . .

The first paragraph quoted above reveals LaFollette's clear perception of the CP strategy. The second paragraph, enunciating so clearly LaFollette's personal feeling toward the Communists, helps to explain why Foster and the other Communists attacked LaFollette more bitterly than Coolidge or Davis in 1924. The last part of the letter, quoted above, must be interpreted as a broad hint, by LaFollette, that he was ready to accept an invitation to run for President, if such an invitation were to come from a truly representative liberal group. But the letter settled all lingering doubts about LaFollette's availability to the party holding its packed convention at St. Paul. He was going to have nothing at all to do with it.

When the St. Paul convention met, the Communist management and control were, if anything, even more complete than at the Chicago gathering. The correspondent for the *Christian Science Monitor* estimated that 99 per cent of the delegates were Communists.[78] Only five of the twenty-five members of the nominating committee were farmers. A disgusted veteran Populist from Nebraska reflected the opinion of most of the farm delegates when he accused the Party Line boys of " scrap-

78 *Christian Science Monitor,* June 20, 1924.

ing the whole United States " to get Communists to come to St. Paul to vote.[79]

Through it all, Mahoney, the veteran agrarian, rugged, unsuspecting Western Populist, remained a pathetic figure, stripped of his influence, suspected by his old friends, derided by the slick Communists who looked upon him as the personification of yokel shortcomings and credulity. Let a witness describe the scene of Mahoney's denouement: [80]

> Mahoney believed he could turn St. Paul into an impressive demonstration for LaFollette. Imagine his consternation when he found out that the communists were going to knife LaFollette! He soon discovered also what a stranglehold the communists had on the convention. About ninety percent of the 600 delegates at St. Paul were either communists or under communist tutelage. Outside of a few local unions and the Farmer-Labor Federation of Minnesota, the convention was practically nothing else than a conclave of the Communist forces in the labor movement. The millions of farmers and trade union workers, whose pressure was so glibly promised by us, were conspicuous by their absence. When the LaFollette question was raised, the Communist steam-roller went into action. I opened the fight on LaFollette by launching a tirade against him. The Communist faction under orders vociferously applauded every attack and at the end of my speech staged an anti-LaFollette demonstration that left the insignificant LaFollette minority at the convention almost speechless.

The Communists proceeded to choose their candidates: for President, Duncan MacDonald of Springfield, Illinois, and for Vice-President, William Bouck of Sedro-Wooley, Washington.[81] MacDonald had been a former president of the United

79 *Ibid.*

80 Gitlow, *op. cit.,* p. 208.

81 *New York Times,* June 20, 1924. It appears reasonably certain that these candidates were not themselves members of any Communist organization.

Mine Workers of Illinois and Bouck was a farm organiser and fruit grower in the Northwest. Neither had previous political experience.

The farm delegations, seeing in the forthcoming meeting of the CPPA the only hope of political unity among the liberal groups, strove to prevent a premature formation of a third party at St. Paul. Already their splendid idea for a conference of progressive leaders had grown into a Frankenstein. Here was the curious anomaly of the originators of the St. Paul convention desperately seeking to prevent the meeting from taking the action which they had proposed.

Apparently the moderates at St. Paul were able to wrest two compromises from the dominant Communists. Instead of outright establishment of a new party, the Committee on Organization reported in favor of a plan for a national committee to serve throughout the campaign with power to replace or withdraw candidates, and to negotiate for combination with other progressive groups. The second compromise lay in the choice of MacDonald for the office of President. It was understood before the nomination was made that MacDonald personally was prepared to withdraw in LaFollette's favor if co-operation could be arranged with the CPPA.[82]

The St. Paul convention is chiefly interesting because it sheds so much light on the relationship between the Communists and other left-wing groups. As in 1923, it was once again demonstrated that the Communists were quick to utilize every avenue of approach to the labor unions and to cultivate what appeared to be the most fertile fields for propaganda and proselyting. Both the Chicago and St. Paul Farmer-Labor conventions demonstrated that the Communists had perfected an amazing talent for parliamentary manipulation and organizational discipline. It was equally apparent by 1924 that the Communists had no intention of putting this gift at the disposal

82 Lovett, R. M., "The Farmer-Labor Communist Party," *New Republic*, 39: 500, July 2, 1924, p. 153.

of the other splinter parties. Progressives would have to pay a high price for Communist support, much higher than most of them were prepared to pay. As an observer put it, the Communists were not willing to do the kitchen work without being allowed in the parlor. But, we might add, the trouble with having Communists in the parlor was that everybody else had to live in the cellar.

But, fortunately for the CPPA, the full effects of the skilfully executed strategy of the Reds in seizing the Farm-Labor party had been averted by CPPA aloofness toward that organization and by the unequivocal language of LaFollette's letter. The Communists, to be sure, had made off with a baby carriage, but someone had already prudently removed the CPPA child to much safer surroundings.

CHAPTER V

" STRANGE ALL THIS DIFFERENCE
SHOULD BE "

THE Republican convention that met in Cleveland on June
10 to nominate a candidate for the Presidency exuded the spirit
of American business, and the men who came to Cleveland
were self-consciously proud of their business labels, flaunting
their roles as inspired protectors of the *status quo.* Coolidge
and his political advisors dominated the entire proceedings.
Almost nothing went wrong. Coolidge's " man " was there,
William Butler, authentic embodiment of the principles and
virtues of the acquisitive society. The " businessman's bloc "
had replaced the Senatorial clique of 1920. The most spectacular evidence that the old Senate crowd had passed into eclipse
was the ignoring of Senator Lodge when the committee ap-
pointments were made. Lodge had been warned of what was
in store for him, but went on to Cleveland to learn that no one
had proposed him for any place in the convention organization.
The new Massachusetts leader, William M. Butler, prototype of
the successful Babbitt, was now Republican leader of Massachusetts. It is not necessary to dwell too long upon this palace
revolution which had occurred within the Republican party
since 1920.[1] But its importance was considerable.

The proceedings were of the familiar steam-roller variety,
with little to break the monotony of the Coolidge control except
the occasional displays of independence by LaFollette delegates
from the Northwest.[2] As parsimonious as Coolidge was reputed
to be, the convention spent little time on extraneous matters,
not even allowing ample time for the prolonged applause and

1 A comprehensive account of this phase of the convention's proceedings
appears in Fuess, C., *Calvin Coolidge,* ch. XV.

2 See *Proceedings,* 18th Republican National Convention, held in Cleveland, Ohio, June 10-12, 1924.

92

demonstrations that are supposed to be such reliable indices of victory at the November election.

Only incidentally did the leaders relax in their vigilant, business-like control over proceedings. Of course, a certain amount of convention horse play, as patently artificial and preconceived as it always appears, was permitted. The last living survivor of the 1860 Republican convention was presented to the delegates amid thunderous applause, applause that must have served a useful purpose in awakening some of the more exhausted delegates. Later on, a similar show was presented for the crowd's entertainment when a quintet of Republicans from Coolidge's home town, Plymouth, Vermont, entertained with campaign songs. The fact that this quintet earned loud applause is perhaps an indication of how desperately starved the dele-gates were for any kind of relief from the monotony.

Theodore Burton of Ohio delivered an able, scholarly key-note address and in offering a tribute to the late President Warren G. Harding, nimbly avoided the pitfall of the oil scandals. Frank W. Mondell of Wyoming was made permanent chairman and Dr. Marion L. Burton, President of the University of Michigan and long-time Massachusetts friend and neighbor to Mr. Coolidge, was given the honor of presenting the nominating speech. Everything was proceeding according to plan. The delegates went on, respectfully listening to tributes to the great names of the party and impassioned oratory which, in typical, orthodox political style, pointed with pride and viewed with alarm. But, as William Allen White has observed, " the oration of the hour came when a frail, gray-haired wisp of a man rose in the Pennsylvania delegation waving some sort of a paper. Instantly the convention recognised Andrew W. Mellon, Secretary of the Treasury, known in the calendar of Republican saints as ' the greatest Secretary of the Treasury since Alexander Hamilton '. Here as Squeers would say, was richness, the richest man in the world. For the first time, the owners of America were appearing in Republican conventions."[3] Twice the Wisconsin delegation, during the proceedings, tried to resist the Coolidge steamroller. The first attempt, the minority report on the platform, merely indicated how hopeless the cause of the Wisconsin delegation really was. On Wednesday evening, June 11, after restlessly listening to the presentation of the LaFollette Progressive Republican platform, in the form of a minority report read by Mr. Henry Cooper of Wisconsin, the delegates, by voice vote, overwhelmed the small but courageous group of liberals from Wisconsin.[4]

Again, on Thursday, this time more vividly, the progressives displayed their obstinacy. On the roll call, after Dr. Burton had put Mr. Coolidge's name before the house and it had been seconded, they cast 28 votes for LaFollette.[5] In the final tabulation, 1065 votes were cast for Coolidge, 34 votes were cast for LaFollette (28 from Wisconsin and 6 from North Dakota) and 10 (from South Dakota) for Hiram Johnson.[6] A few LaFollette followers in the Wisconsin and North Dakota delegations offered the customary motion to make the nomination unanimous. A chorus of noes arose from that section of the convention. Non-plussed, the Permanent Chairman proved himself master of the situation with the following statement, which deserves some kind of recognition in parliamentary law as a classic paradox—" With the exception of a very few voices, the nomination of Calvin Coolidge is made unanimous."[7]

The Republicans had been waiting to find out whom the White House wanted for the Vice-Presidential nomination. If the skilfully managed Coolidge convention blundered at all, it must have been in attempting to make the selection for second

3 White, W. A., *A Puritan in Babylon*, pp. 299-300. By permission of the Macmillan Company, publishers.

4 *Proceedings*, 18th Rep. Nat. Convention, pp. 116-124.

5 *Ibid.*, p. 154. One delegate from Wisconsin, Thomas Scott, voted for Coolidge, after which he sat with the Pennsylvania delegation.

6 The North Dakota vote was split; 7 for Coolidge, 6 for LaFollette. In South Dakota, the division was 3 for Coolidge, 10 for Johnson.

7 *Proceedings*, 18th Rep. Nat. Convention, p. 165.

place. The delegates marked time as the Coolidge leaders evidently tried to induce either Senator Borah or ex-Governor Lowden to accept the place. Already the story has become legendary that Borah, upon being offered a position on the ticket, asked "in which place?" In a stampede on the second ballot, Lowden received a comfortable majority and nomination as Vice-Presidential candidate if he wanted it. But if it were the strategy of the Republican leaders to draft Lowden, the plan did not work. Dramatically, at this moment, an Associated Press dispatch was handed to the Permanent Chairman stating that Mr. Lowden had formally announced that he would not accept the honor. Rather awkwardly, with the bewildered air of a jilted swain, the convention wired Lowden for more information. After a recess of an hour or so, the answer came in the form of a telegram. It was still no.[8] And so on the third ballot, Charles G. Dawes of Illinois was chosen.[9]

In an atmosphere curiously suggestive of the weekly luncheon of the Kiwanis or Rotary, the Republicans had endorsed the *status quo* and ratified the act of Providence which had placed Calvin Coolidge in the White House. The "moving stairway" of politics had brought Mr. Coolidge a long way. But, with the exception of the dramatic elements present in that picture—so familiar to most Americans—of the honest, simple Vermonter taking the oath of office from his father by the light of a kerosene lamp, none of it had been spectacular. Nor was this convention, which had been a kind of mass embodiment of the Coolidge spirit and policy, endowed with the slightest degree of enthusiasm.

The Republican convention of 1924 was a tribute to the man "whose sheer honesty worked like a wizard's spell upon the debris of decency which was the Harding administration."[10]

8 White, W. A., *op. cit.*, p. 304.

9 *Proceedings*, 18th Rep. Nat. Convention, p. 190.

10 See White, W. A., *op. cit.*, ch. XXVII.

Only a short eleven months before this convention had assembled to pay homage to Calvin Coolidge, the Republican party was reeling under the relentless exposure of the venality and sordidness of the Harding Administration. Here it was now, cleansed and sanctified, at least in the opinion of millions of Americans, by the faith and honesty and simplicity of this " homely soul " who must have been inwardly dazed and bewildered by the course of events. In this strange, almost incredible story of Calvin Coolidge's success, the element of luck plays so fantastic a role that one is tempted not to seek any other explanation for the way Coolidge pulled the Republican party out of a desperate hole.[11]

Luck smiles on Coolidge—and incidentally, on the Republicans—all the way from that fateful August 2 when President Harding passed away right down until the election. Without violating the maxim *De mortuis nil nisi bonum* too crudely, we can state that luck was playing with the Republicans when Mr. Harding was so quickly and conveniently removed from the political stage. Without doubt, he had become their greatest liability, a most embarrassing liability as the party faced the inevitable decision in 1924 of endorsing or repudiating him. Mr. John W. Davis, who was to have more than a passing interest in the 1924 election, recalls vividly his reaction when he learned the news of Harding's death. Walking down a London street, he saw a bulletin board with the news of the death of the American President emblazoned. " How providential for the Republican party ! " he thought.[12]

If the study of politics were more scientific and if the necessary devices were available, we could measure—in terms of thousands of votes—how fortuitous were the circumstances under which Mr. Coolidge became President of the United States. The unforgettable scene, the plain New England farmhouse, the lamplight, the family Bible, the simple furnishings,

11 See White, W. A., *op. cit.,* p. 306 ff.

12 John W. Davis to author, May 24, 1943.

all of it became an indelible mind-picture for millions of Americans consciously repelled by the stench of the corruption of the slick politicians in Washington and sub-consciously yearning for the simplicity of days that were gone forever. Calvin Coolidge, to these people, was the embodied re-incarnation of principles and ideals that the 1920's had cast aside.

But once again the element of luck. As William Allen White so well describes this moment of dazzling good fortune: [13]

> Yet if that blood clot which closed Harding's life had only taken another turn in the artery—had delayed its course another day—the new President would have taken his oath under the glowing lights of Guy Currier's spacious parlors, surrounded by every bauble of sophisticated luxury that a millionaire's country palace could assemble, with one of the first score of America's veiled political prophets as the new President's host and sponsor. Knowing in his heart of this day's narrow squeak that might have spoiled his humble entrance to power and glory, how this sharp self-centered Yankee must have wetted his lips to throw surreptitious kisses to his Lady Luck for this good turn.

And so the convention honored Calvin Coolidge and his luck. And in doing so, it bowed down before Business and made the proper genuflections. With God in His heaven and Coolidge in his White House, the business of America was Business. The well-managed and extremely tractable convention obediently underlined this thought in its platform. The old familiar Amens run through the platform. It was a time to point with pride. Only the outlandish possibility of Democratic success could be viewed with alarm. Rigid economy . . . reduction in taxation . . . cherished traditions . . . we reaffirm our belief in the protective tariff . . . protection as a national policy . . . American standards of life . . . vigorous efforts of this Administration . . . a spirit of independence and self-reliance . . . private initiative . . . opposed

13 White, W. A., *op. cit.*, p. 243. By permission of the Macmillan Company, publishers.

to government ownership of public utilities . . . deep humiliation that our public life should have harbored some dishonest men . . . respect for law . . . unyielding devotion to the Constitution . . . [14]

It all sounded so familiar and yet, to the Republican delegates in 1924, its platitudes had a deep fervency. It was the Creed of Business and they were repeating it after Calvin Coolidge. All the demands of liberals and labor unions and agrarians had been dexterously avoided. The platform had gone on record as in favor of the Constitution and as opposed to poison gas and submarines. But little else. Years later, a brilliant analyst of the post-war era was to remark that Mr. Coolidge apparently broke his health and brought himself to the grave prematurely with the intensity of his inactivity.[15] In similar vein might as well be said of the Republican convention at Cleveland that its silence on the issues of 1924 was deafening.

The unrestrained enthusiasm which Democrats so often display in springing at each other's throats, both figuratively and literally, whenever one of their national conventions takes place, has long been a subject of serious consideration to students of American political behaviour. An experienced observer of many a party gathering, Arthur Krock, has sought an ethnological explanation for their odd antics. He believes the disproportionate percentage of Irish from the cities, and Scotch-Irish from the South endows the party with its contentious nature. With perhaps oversimplification, H. L. Mencken has blamed the bad manners of the Democrats on the singularly degenerative effects of the low-grade liquor they consume at their quadrennial gatherings. Others, likely to be Republicans, disinclined to trust in any transparent explanation, merely agree with Thomas Reed that the Democratic party is just " a hopeless assortment of discordant differences as incapable of positive action as it is capable of infinite clamor."

14 Excerpts from the platform of the Republican Party in 1924 as published in the *Proceedings*, 18th Rep. Nat. Convention, pp. 98-114.

15 Webb, W., *Divided We Stand*, p. 196.

The Democrats confirmed almost all the slanderous allusions as one of the most bizarre pages in American political history was written at old Madison Square Garden from June 24, 1924, until July 10, 1924. In those seventeen days the assembled Democrats succeeded in ruining whatever prospects—and they had been reasonably good—the party had had for success in November. The " curious readiness " (as one puzzled member of the party has put it) with which Democrats divide on a moral issue swelled into a torrent of political fratricide. Before long, the psychopathic behaviour of the Democrats had moved an unusually restrained observer to indulge in grave misgivings about American civilization. To Mrs. Anne O'Hare McCormick, the crowd at Madison Square Garden was " sullen, angry, passionate." Even more disturbing to her was the thought that " intolerance so primal and menacing could boil under the skin of America." [16] Indeed, the meeting of the Democrats at New York in 1924 was, without question, a shameful indictment of American political behaviour, tawdry in its vulgar display of exhibitionism, irresponsible and helpless as emotions overcame reason and respect gave way to suspicion.

The story of the debacle at the Garden is more than just the account of Smith and McAdoo deadlocking the convention for 103 ballots. Much more than personalities was involved. Two great and deep forces in the Democratic Party met head-on. Ever since the days when Tom Jefferson went on his botanical excursion along the Hudson River, these two forces have been evident in the Democratic party: one, the old, established, propertied agrarian element from the South and West; the other, the newer, more alien and urban Democratic vote of the cities. In 1924, the national feelings about the Ku Klux Klan and Prohibition intensified these differences of opinion. Unquestionably, scores of the delegates from the South and West were members in good standing of the KKK. On the other hand, the alien groups and first and second generation Irish,

16 *New York Times,* July 6, 1924.

Italians, etc. provided the votes for the city machines in places like New York and Chicago. In seven of the important and pivotal states of the East and North Central sections, the Democratic boss was a Catholic.[17] The Brennans and the Taggarts, the Hagues and the Olvanys were much in evidence. A strange study in contrasts, the convention brought together, though not in harmony, bourbons from the deep South, many of them in wing collar and with flowing moustache, rough-hewn Irish bosses from the Northern cities, ranchers from the West, discontented farmers from the prairies.

These two antagonistic elements within the Democratic party broke sharply on two issues, the Ku Klux Klan and Prohibition. Looking back upon the performance of the Democrats, one is forced to smile at the picayune and trifling matters over which the enraged delegates almost bled a party to death. The convention represents a nadir in the whole story of American conventions. Bryan, living out his last few days, personifies the degradation of the Democrats. " When the man who had fought stormily for noble principles in every Democratic convention for thirty years found nothing better to talk about than Prohibition, no one better to support than McAdoo, a time of petty politics was at hand." [18]

There were only a few brief moments during this seamiest and most tragic of conventions when someone was inspired to noble heights of political idealism. One such occasion came when Newton D. Baker bravely and sincerely renewed his pledge of devotion to the Wilsonian vision of a brave new world.[19] The convention promptly adopted a craven declaration which, in effect, evaded the League issue by favoring a referendum.[20]

17 Illinois, Indiana, Maryland, Massachusetts, New Jersey, New York, and Pennsylvania.

18 Agar, H., *The Pursuit of Happiness*, p. 342.

19 *Proceedings*, Democratic National Convention, 1924, pp. 259-270.

20 See *Democratic Campaign Book*, 1924, pp. 40-41.

Another opportunity for bravery and the re-affirmation of Jeffersonian principles came when a delegate, Andrew Erwin of Georgia, made an unexpected attack upon the Klan. But even in its noblest moments, the convention displayed its penchant for malappropriate action. As the northerners staged an impromptu demonstration for Mr. Erwin, someone struck up "Marching Through Georgia" on the organ! [21]

The unprecedented bitterness, the passions aroused by the fight over whether the platform should denounce the Klan by name, insured the ruination of party success in November. The whole sordid affair was just as illogical and unreasonable as the fact that, in the course of the debate over whether the Klan should be mentioned by name, speaker after speaker should mention it. The final, dramatic roll-call vote of 543-3/20 —542-7/20 against mentioning the Klan settled nothing.[22] It merely served to accentuate the fact that the Democratic party had been cracked in two on a highly emotional question packed with political dynamite.

The hisses and boos that came from the Tammany ward-heelers, the city boys, in the galleries as Bryan pleaded for the majority report were audible proof of Democratic disunity. Here was the three-time leader of his party speaking on the most important issue before the convention; and every time he finished a sentence, it was drowned out in a thunderous expression of disapproval from the gallery.

Without in the least condoning the attitude of the old-time Democratic chieftains from the West who were flirting with the Klan, it is difficult not to adjudge the behaviour of the gallery and Madison Square Garden as one of the rudest, most shameful displays of civic discourtesy in American history. It is a source of wonderment that a realization of New York's position as host city did not temper the uncouth incivilities of the gallery rowdies. These camp-followers of Tammany, subject

21 *Proceedings*, Dem. Nat. Convention, 1924, p. 298.

22 *Ibid.*, p. 310.

only to the discipline of a district leader, were to overplay their hand and hurt their idol, Al Smith, much more than anything they ever did to benefit him. The most shameful day of a shameful convention must have been the day of the debate and vote on the Klan issue. Tempers reached the boiling point. A strange and sinister sense of impending violence pervaded the whole Garden. One of Smith's biographers has well described those inglorious moments:[23]

> So thin was the veneer of civilization, so black the thoughts in the minds of the delegates that it was a terrifying thing for onlookers to behold . . . only the presence of husky Irish patrolmen, who would as cheerfully have knocked in the head of a pugnacious Catholic as of a Protestant Klansman, prevented rioting.

The convention, exhausted by the platform battles, limped on to the selection of a candidate. It is not necessary, in this study of the Progressive movement, to enter into a protracted discussion of the famous deadlock between McAdoo and Smith. It must suffice to say that McAdoo had well been on his way to the candidacy until the spring of 1924. McAdoo was favored by several factors. His able administration of the railroads during the war had established his national record, commending him especially to the Railroad Brotherhood who appreciated his efforts on behalf of the establishment of a Railroad Labor Board.[24] With the solid support of the Brotherhood and substantial support from the trade unions, McAdoo was far out in front of the other candidates until an unexpected turn in the oil exposures began to smear his political chances.

Edward L. Doheny, the oil magnate who, of course, had been involved in the oil exposures conducted by the Senate, revealed that he had "retained" W. G. McAdoo at $25,000 a year, for legal services after the latter had retired from the

23 Pringle, H. F., *Alfred E. Smith*, p. 308.
24 See McAdoo, W. G., *Crowded Years*, p. 447 ff.

cabinet. Although from a legal point of view, and perhaps as well, from an ethical point of view, Mr. McAdoo was justified in accepting a fee for his legal services, the effect upon the public, failing to distinguish too well between the service that McAdoo performed for Doheny and the " service " that men like Albert Fall had been performing, was instantaneous. McAdoo asked for and received a hearing before the Senate Committee but, in spite of his forthright explanations, the damage was done.[25]

His friends, and leaders of the party, advised him to withdraw. Obviously the slightest taint of oil on its own candidate would vitiate much of the forthcoming Democratic offensive against Republican responsibility for the scandal. Mr. Keating, editor of *Labor*, official organ of the Railroad Brotherhood, was among those who advised McAdoo to quit.[26]

McAdoo's embarrassment was Smith's opportunity. As Pringle has pointed out, it is not improbable that Smith was scheduled to be used merely to block the nomination of McAdoo or any other dry.[27] Smith had been used similarly in 1920. Another possible explanation—this one presented by a Western Democrat opposed to Smith—was that the city bosses and vested interests wanted to effect a stalemate so that a conservative could be chosen.[28] In any event, the Smith candidacy, quite suddenly, in the spring of 1924, began to take on serious proportions. The Doheny relationship did infinite harm to McAdoo.[29] Smith's political sun was rising. Along came unex-

25 *New York Times*, Feb. 11, 1924. See also Mark Sullivan's *Our Times*, Vol. VI, " The Twenties " pp. 335-337.

26 Edward Keating to the author, June 17, 1943. But many Brotherhood leaders continued to support McAdoo. See *Railway Maintenance of Way Employee Journal*, June 1924. The leading editorial is most laudatory in sketching McAdoo's ability and qualification for high office.

27 Pringle, *op. cit.*, p. 302.

28 Mullen, A., *Western Democrat*, p. 245.

29 Mark Sullivan is of the opinion that it prevented McAdoo's nomination in 1924. Sullivan, *op. cit.*, p. 337.

pected victories in the primaries in Wisconsin and Minnesota. Governor Smith was visibly astonished by his victory in the western primaries. When informed of his victory in Wisconsin, he exclaimed, " Why, I don't even know anybody 'way out there ! " [30]

As the balloting began, there were three points distinctly in McAdoo's favor. First, he had the support of the Railroad Brotherhoods. Second, he had the support of the Drys. Third, he was Bryan's choice for the office. Smith, on the other hand, had the Wet, Catholic, city delegates backing him.

Along with all that, Al Smith, the " city kid who made good," who came up from the city streets, with his urban mannerisms, his New York East Side peculiarities of speech, his ungrammatical but very democratic lapses of tense and diction, was making a new kind of appeal in national politics— a frank, unconcealed appeal to the millions of industrial and urban workers and voters.

For nine weary, hot and uncomfortable days the balloting continued. Neither candidate had a serious chance of success. McAdoo's real strength was about 420 delegates; the Smith vote never more than 300. It was evident, as the roll calls were taken, that McAdoo and Smith were not losing delegates to each other. When a fluctuation occurred, the votes might go to a dark horse candidate, but never to the enemy.[31] Under these circumstances, it was folly for Smith and McAdoo to carry on their feud for more than a week. Obviously, the Smith men would never vote for McAdoo and the McAdoo men never for Smith. It was Lowden and Wood all over again, with a bitterness far in excess of that of the 1920 Republican convention.

Since—as William Allen White has remarked—a Democratic convention has to smell the blood of a death struggle before it can decide whom it will honor, one hundred and three wearisome ballots were necessary to convince the delegates that

30 *New York Times,* Apr. 11, 1924.

31 *Proceedings,* Dem. Nat. Convention, 1924, pp. 338-969.

neither McAdoo nor Smith could be nominated.[32] Belatedly making amends for its ludicrously bizarre behaviour, the convention chose John William Davis, of West Virginia and New York, whose dignity and highmindedness of conduct contrasted so sharply with the exhibitionism and vulgarities of so many of the Democrats at the Garden.[33] John W. Davis, without doubt, was the best possible choice the Democratic party could make after coming so close to political suicide. Equipped through his legislative and judicial experience at home and his diplomatic activities abroad, Mr. Davis, at the time of his nomination, had had a wider range of training for the Presidency than either Cleveland or Wilson. Although his campaign managers had skillfully guided his political fortunes by having him, like Brer Rabbit, lie low and remain benevolently neutral toward both leading candidates, his selection by the Democratic party to be its presidential nominee was a personal tribute, a recognition of the sterling qualities, a judicial temperament, a brilliant legal career, a creditable record of faithful and diligent service, usually in a legal or diplomatic capacity, for his country. Above all, Mr. Davis was the gentleman in politics, a kind of Jeffersonian Elihu Root. Able, educated, urbane, Mr. Davis subscribed to that brand of old-fashioned yet hearty liberalism which believes that the ideal government is the least government consonant with the preservation of law and order. With a respect for the dignity of the individual nurtured by his family's long allegiance to Democratic principles, Davis' political philosophy rejected governmental paternalism, as embodied in protective tariffs and " special-interest " legislation as unreservedly as it rejected the radical panaceas of the Socialists.

In the course of a distinguished career characterised by devotion to duty and diligent application to the work at hand, Davis had never become the spectacular type of personality. His chief contributions while in Congress seem to have been

32 White, W. A., *Politics, The Citizen's Business*, p. 56.

33 See Stone, I., *They Also Ran*, pp. 321-339.

careful and judicious reports on tariff schedules and compensation laws.[34] As Solicitor-General, under President Wilson, Davis was able to make fuller use of his legal talents. Arguing more cases before the Supreme Court than any other lawyer in its history save one, Wilson's Solicitor-General compelled attention through the brevity and logic of his arguments. Chief Justice Taft expressed the opinion that John W. Davis was the best all-around lawyer who had ever appeared before him.[35] Chief Justice White is said to have remarked to a friend that "the Court thinks so much of John Davis' learning and character that when he appears for the Government, the other side really doesn't get due process of law."[36] As Solicitor-General, Davis presented the Government's brief in such important cases as those involving the validity of the Adamson Act, the Child Labor Law, and Selective Service.[37] In the second year of America's participation in the World War, President Wilson appointed Davis a member of a commission sent to Berne, Switzerland, to confer with German government representatives over the disposition and exchange of prisoners. The commission had scarcely organised when Walter Hines Page resigned as Ambassador to England and Davis was appointed to succeed him. With distinction and success, Mr. Davis remained at the Court of St. James until the Harding Administration, of course, brought Republicans into the diplomatic posts.

Some members of the Democratic party had recognised his talents and abilities as early as the national convention in San Francisco in 1920. At that time he received considerable support for the Presidency. Returning to this country to campaign

34 ————, "John Davis, Democrat," *World's Work*, 48:6, Oct. 1924, p. 608.

35 *The Literary Digest*, 82:4, July 26, 1924, p. 36.

36 ————, "John Davis, Democrat," *World's Work*, 48:5, Sept. 1924, p. 497.

37 *The Literary Digest*, 82:4, July 26, 1924, p. 36.

for Cox and Roosevelt, he wholeheartedly supported the proposal that America join the League of Nations at once. When he retired from his diplomatic post in 1921, John W. Davis joined the New York law firm of Stetson, Jennings, and Russell.

There can be little doubt that John W. Davis was one of the most distinguished, intellectually and morally, and impeccably honest candidates ever nominated by an American political party. Why was he unacceptable to the progressive element? Obviously, his political philosophy, restricted by horizons of individualism and made cautious by suspicions of ready-made panaceas and inroads upon free enterprise, was much too conservative for the ardent reformers who looked upon such a philosophy as merely a device for concealing the evils of *laissez faire*. But, from a political viewpoint, a more serious liability in the candidacy of John W. Davis was his association with a law firm which had, on occasion, served great corporations and powerful financial houses. Worst of all, the firm had acted as counsel for J. P. Morgan. This fact, of course, was going to provide a campaign stereotype. Davis would be denounced again and again as a " Wall Street lawyer," a charge manifestly unfair to a man whose background, environment and political behaviour vouched for his integrity and highmindedness. But the damage was done. A lawyer whose firm had advised J. P. Morgan and whose handsome residence was in Locust Valley, Long Island, could hardly convince rebellious Mid-West farmers of his sympathy and good intentions. But the Wall Street label was probably not fatal; the fatal blow to Davis' candidacy had already been delivered— by the internecine follies of the stormy sessions at Madison Square Garden. After the election, one of his close friends said, " He was the finest race horse that ever started on a political track, and he got the worst ride." [38]

38 Kent, F. B., *The Democratic Party*, p. 501.

One historian of the Democratic party states that the principle blunder the Democrats made at the 1924 convention was nominating Charles W. Bryan for the Vice-Presidency. Of course, the political strategy was obvious. First of all, it was a way of placating William Jennings Bryan, Charles' big brother in more ways than one. The Great Commoner had denounced Davis during one of the acrimonious sessions of the convention, declaring that with Davis as nominee the Democrats would not be able to carry a state west of the Alleghenies.[39] Healing the breach between the 1924 nominee and the three-time leader of the Democratic party became the pressing business of the Democrats. In addition, Charles Bryan met the three requirements of a running-mate who, from the point of view of political expediency would "balance the ticket" with John W. Davis. The Vice-Presidential candidate had to be a resident of the agricultural section of the West; he had to be progressive; and, finally, he had to be a "Dry." Charles Bryan, Governor of Nebraska and long-time partner to his brother in business and newspaper publishing, met these requirements.[40] Davis approved of Bryan's nomination as his running-mate after Senator Walsh had declined the honor.[41]

But the strategy of the Democrats boomeranged. It was too obviously a Dr. Jekyll-Mr. Hyde combination. Many persons looked upon the Bryan nomination as a kind of political bribe to keep the more famous member of the family quiet. Unquestionably, the incongruity of a radical agrarian running on the same ticket with an urbane New York lawyer provides American political history with one of its most ironic pages and contributes no small part to the gayety of political lore. With both a sense of humor and political intuition, J. N. "Ding" Darling portrayed the dignified Davis and the bucolic Bryan

39 *New York Times,* July 2, 1924.

40 Bryan, W. J., "My Brother Charles," *World's Work* 48:5, Sept. 1924, p. 548.

41 John W. Davis to author, May 24, 1943.

seated on the same battered sofa alongside a bewildered donkey after a cyclone had destroyed the Democratic household.[42] Apparently all that the two candidates had in common was a middle initial and the ill fortune to be chosen as the national candidates of the Democratic party after the carnage at Madison Square Garden. Of that poor, exhausted donkey, pommeled by the cyclone in the Garden, it appeared truer than ever before that he had neither pride of ancestry nor hope of posterity.

42 *New York Herald Tribune,* July 15, 1924.

CHAPTER VI
BORN TO SET IT RIGHT

In the same municipal auditorium where, just three weeks before, Coolidge had received the proper blessings from the Republicans, the Progressives gathered on July 4, 1924. The delegates to the Republican meeting had been cast in the familiar mold; to them eccentricity consisted of failing to vote a straight Republican ticket. But now, like a refreshing and unexpected breeze—out of the four corners of the compass—came these men who had visions of a brave new world; who had heard the rumblings of thunder on the left. About a thousand had come, " broad-shouldered men and earnest women." [1]

The informal, enthusiastic nature of the CPPA convention should not obscure the fact that much planning and organization had anticipated the event. The great majority were there as chosen representatives of some liberal group or society. In addition to the delegates representing the labor organizations, the farm-labor units, the Socialists, and the Committee of Forty-Eight, (the four most influential parts of the CPPA), there were duly accredited delegates acting for such organizations as the National Unity Committee, the Food Reform Society of America, and the Davenport, Iowa, Ethical Society; organizations hardly calculated to frighten the managers of the Republican and Democratic campaign.[2]

The necessarily elastic rules under which the status of a delegate would be determined put a heavy strain upon the credentials committee. With a perspicacity lacking in many of his liberal colleagues, LaFollette was keenly aware of the dangers of Communist infiltration. Perhaps recalling the fiasco of

1 *Cleveland Plain Dealer,* July 5, 1924. About 1000 persons attended but not all were delegates. See *Proceedings,* CPPA Convention held at Cleveland, Ohio, July 4-5, 1924 (M. G. Johnston papers), for roster of delegates. See also *Locomotive Engineers Journal,* 58:8, August 1924, p. 571.

2 *Proceedings,* CPPA Convention, Vol. II, pp. 168-169.

the Farmer-Labor party in 1920, or remembering the Communist predilection to kidnap political orphans, a predilection so evident a few weeks earlier at the Chicago Farmer-Labor convention, the LaFollette managers made sure that there would be no repetition of any such capitulation to the Reds. The credentials committee, headed by Chester Thorpe of the Brotherhood of Locomotive Engineers, scrutinised the delegates so carefully that the roll of the convention was delayed a whole day. One hundred husky sergeants-at-arms were recruited to prevent any possible intrusions from Moscow.[3]

Cleveland must have presented a colorful picture that Fourth of July in 1924 when the independents gathered to organise the forces of discontent. It was different in so many respects from the stereotyped convention.[4] One of the members summarised his reaction by stating that " the Republican convention was a gathering of Babbitts, the Democratic a meeting of Southern gentlemen and Northern sportsmen and politicians. This is a gathering of students." [5] The delegates were mostly serious— dead serious—and their earnest visages contrasted with the light-hearted, indulgent attitude of so many of the members of a convention of one of the old parties. They were young too. One observer estimated that the majority of them were under forty.[6] Undergraduates flocked in, one of the largest groups coming all the way from Columbia University. Other student pilgrims came from such institutions as Yale, Harvard, Dartmouth, Barnard, Vassar and Union Theological Seminary. The political clubs of some colleges had sent accredited delegates to the convention.[7] LaFollette's crusading zeal and flamboyant dis-

3 *New York Herald Tribune*, July 4, 1924.

4 John M. Baer, Non-Partisan League delegate and former Congressman from North Dakota, recalls the bouyant atmosphere of the convention and the enthusiastic nature of those in attendance. Mr. Baer assisted in broadcasting some of the sessions. John M. Baer to the author, Nov. 15, 1943.

5 *New York Herald Tribune*, July 4, 1924.

6 *Ibid.*

7 *Proceedings*, CPPA Convention, Vol. II, pp. 168 ff.

regard for conservative sensibilities made much the same appeal to socially-conscious youth that Norman Thomas was to make in 1932. In wealthy Yale, LaFollette's popularity had prevented the mock election of Calvin Coolidge.

The mechanical precision, the sophisticated formalities of the Republican convention that had nominated Calvin Coolidge were absent. Even the *New York Times,* unfriendly as it was to LaFollette, had to admit that there " was nothing artificial " about this gathering.[8] Probably the delegates and visitors who attended the CPPA Cleveland convention represented the most diverse pot-pourri of our body politic that ever convened for the purpose of selecting a presidential candidate.

It was a strange and timeless admixture of old and new. Old " General " Jacob Coxey was there vainly hoping to take the floor on behalf of his proposal to abolish all interest. The self-designated " last of the Populists," John J. Streeter, editor of the *Vineland* (N. J.) *Weekly,* was more in evidence than the other octogenarians because of the length and thickness of his whiskers. Mr. Streeter had taken an oath, in the Nineties, not to cut his beard until Populism triumphed. Eighty-three-year-old Robert Springer, who had witnessed the nomination of Abraham Lincoln and felt sure that LaFollette's nomination would be equally historic, had ingeniously borrowed enough money from a Republican to make the trip to Cleveland from the Old Soldiers' Home in Milwaukee. As forthright in his willingness to speak for the veterans of all wars, including the Indian campaigns, as he was in his conviction that he was going to live to be 140, Springer was good-naturedly applauded by the assembled delegates.[9]

At the other extreme were the young crusaders like the " Yipsils," the members of the Young People's Socialist League, ready to remould this sorry scheme of things. They came from New York by hitch-hike, arriving tired but content

8 *New York Times,* July 5, 1924.

9 *Proceedings,* CPPA Convention, Vol. II. p. 226.

in the thought that the railroad companies had made no profits on their trip. Soon there were facetious remarks about the large number of walking delegates at the CPPA convention.[10]

Still there was a poignancy about the faith of these reformers at Cleveland. Back of all their grumbling and denunciation was a solid allegiance to the American system of government. Their grudge was not against America; it was against those who held America in bondage. Quixotic they might have been; but never cynical. Again and again during the proceedings the Declaration of Independence and the Gettysburg Address were read. Portraits of American heroes were prominently displayed. Their awareness of American history was doubtless far more acute than that of the delegates who had heard the Republican speakers conjure up visions of Washington and Lincoln.

To be sure, the meeting had its quota of the lunatic fringe. Some of the delegates were hardened convention-trotters, inexorably attracted by the roar of a crowd or the expostulations of a political harangue. There were people there with all kinds of panaceas. The procurers of nostrums naturally gravitate to a place that offers such promise of a receptive hearing. " Men and women with every conceivable prescription for the relief of suffering humanity are in Cleveland, but nine-tenths of them will cool their heels outside this convention." [11]

Typical of the light touch of ridicule employed by the conservative press to discredit both the CPPA convention and Senator LaFollette is the following account in the *St. Paul Pioneer-Press* of the arrival of a delegate from New York:[12]

> Miss Elizabeth Goldstein, who says she lives in Greenwich Village, and looks as if she did, walked in all alone. She started last Saturday morning and arrived Tuesday afternoon. 'I'm like LaFollette, I don't need a party,' she re-

10 *New York Herald Tribune*, July 5, 1924.

11 *Ibid.*

12 *St. Paul Pioneer-Press*, July 4, 1924.

marked when asked why she didn't come with the rest of the crowd.

It was one member of this noisy and irrepressible minority who caused the greatest disturbance of the two-day session. James Francis Murphy, claiming to represent " The Migratory Workers of America," tried to work his way to the platform, obsessed with a plan to nominate himself for the Presidency. A husky delegate from one of the railroad unions interfered with his dreams of greatness by planting him securely in a chair with a force and directness audible throughout the convention hall. There, under the watchful eye of the union delegate, he was held *incommunicado*. His self-appointed custodian would not even allow him to receive the gentlemen of the press. In order to learn his story, the newspapermen had to write to him as he spent the rest of the session in his peculiar kind of solitary confinement.[13]

Some of those who did manage to get inside the doors were perhaps not so far over on the lunatic fringe as their contemporaries thought. There was a delegate, from Boston, bearing credentials from the Committee of Forty Eight, who offered a plank to the resolutions committee compelling Klansmen to wear their hoods and sheets twenty-four hours daily. This delegate, affectionately known to his friends as Old Sock Joe, also offered a resolution providing for a national referendum on the question of whether the Volstead law should be suspended for ten days each year.

"That," said the delegate, "would give the Drys plenty of fresh arguments for abstinence every year and the Wets a chance to express their true sentiments." [14]

Throughout the proceedings, the strong humanitarian instincts of these reformers assembled to tilt against the enormous odds of Coolidge Prosperity and the callous materialism of

13 *Cleveland Plain Dealer,* July 6, 1924.

14 *New York Herald Tribune,* July 5, 1924.

the 'Twenties, gave rise to spontaneous cheers and applause for leaders of causes, some lost and some yet to be won.

Reddened by his fluency and vigorous in his gestures, the patriarchal Edwin Markham evoked applause from the crowd by reading his long laudation " Lincoln, the Man of the People." It was to be a convention where the man with the hoe would not only be heard, but listened to. Edwin Markham was followed by Representative Fiorello H. LaGuardia, who, after enthusiastically prophesying LaFollette's election, explained that he had come " to let you know there are other streets and other attitudes in New York besides Wall Street. I speak for Avenue A and 116th Street, instead of Broad and Wall." [15]

The contrast between the Republican and Progressive conventions extended beyond the political views of the speakers. Although Villard noticed less of the revivalist sentiment than at the Bull Moose gathering of 1912, " Onward, Christian Soldiers" and special " LaFollette Hymns," written for the occasion, remained popular and evoked lusty, full-throated singing.[16] On the stage, fifty men and women—called the " choir " —led the singing. The convention could be stirred with a spontaneity that must have been the envy of the managers of the Republican show. Peter Witt—one of old Tom Johnson's protegés from Cleveland—brought the Progressives to their feet with a pungent denunciation of the Republican Babbitts. Aroused to a fighting pitch, the crowd implored Witt to go on at the conclusion of his speech. The social conscience of the convention was aroused again when William Pickens, a Negro graduate of Yale, arose to read a message from the National Association for the Advancement of Colored People.[17]

15 *Ibid.* It is interesting to note that a few days after this speech was made by Mr. LaGuardia, the Democrats nominated for President a lawyer whose office was located at Broad and Wall Streets, in New York City.

16 *Nation,* 119:3078, July 16, 1924, p. 63. The New York Public Library, in its Scrapbook of the 1924 Presidential Campaign, possesses a collection of these campaign songs written expressly for the 1924 campaign.

17 *Proceedings,* CPPA Convention, Vol. II, p. 228 ff.

Above all, it was a refreshingly enthusiastic assemblage, long on spirit if short on cash. The zealous crusading fervor, so patently contrived in major party conventions, was here in abundance. No band had been hired but an impromptu fife and drum corps was organised within a few hours. With no state standards—there was economic rather than geographic representation—the audience seemed to mingle more and more in a friendly, uninhibited atmosphere. During lulls in the Democratic balloting at Madison Square Garden, the CPPA preceedings were broadcast locally by Station WJAX. For the first time in their lives, many of the speakers faced a microphone. Some of them, like Edward Keating, jokingly confessed their fright.[18] Young girls, passing the contribution plate, collected more than $3,000 to help defray expenses.

A consideration of the heterogeneous nature of the people who came to Cleveland for the meeting of the Progressives would lead one to think that its sessions were aimless and unguided. This was far from true. Left to their own devices, the delegates would doubtless have arrived at an endorsement of LaFollette; but the National Committee was taking no chances. The leaders of the labor unions, with McAdoo unavailable because of his connections with Doheny, had long since decided that LaFollette would be the only possible third party leader with any reasonable chance of success. They were going to endorse him, but neither the labor leaders nor LaFollette wanted to burden themselves with the organization of a third party before the election. That—the birth of a new party—could wait upon the developments of the election.

Hence it was apparent, even before the convention opened, that experienced leaders had worked out a scheme of political strategy. Clinton Gilbert, on the scene, sensed it right away. " There is little organization and no machine, but there is a sort of self-imposed discipline." [19] Although Gilbert noted that

18 *Ibid.* Vol. I, p. 40.

19 *New York Post*, July 5, 1924.

" there is none of the slavish loyalty to LaFollette here that there was to Colonel Roosevelt in Chicago," anyone who had planned to come to Cleveland to prevent or obstruct the La-Follette candidacy was soon disillusioned. Robert Pointer, candidate for President of the old Ford organization in Michigan, was refused a seat on the rather ironical grounds that his organization already had a presidential candidate. The real test of the strength of the LaFollette-labor union leadership came when William Mahoney, member of the national committee and Chairman of the St. Paul convention, was denied his seat by the credentials committee. It was evident that the leaders of the convention were not even going to flirt with the Communists. Unable to voice their protests in person, the Communists had to content themselves in the distribution of pamphlets which denounced the convention as " the most reactionary " held this year.[20] They found that, in contrast to the meeting at St. Paul, they had been left out in the cold. The blunt, forthright disposal of Mahoney left no doubts as to the Progressive policy toward the Communists and fellow travelers. Mahoney's misfortune in becoming enmeshed in the Communist web at St. Paul was to cost him a place in the Cleveland convention. Not a Communist himself, he had been sacrificed by the strategy of the directors of the Workers party. He was a victim of forces which were probably unintelligible to him and his friends.[21]

The convention was organised and directed with a deft hand. The three well-knit elements in the convention were the railroad labor unions, the LaFollette machine from Wisconsin and the Non-Partisan and farm-labor people of Minnesota and the Dakotas. They co-operated with no evidence of friction. What disagreements were to arise would come between these groups, reluctant to commit themselves to third party organization, and the Socialists and other relatively unorganised groups impatient to get along to the construction of a new party.

20 *New York Herald Tribune,* July 6, 1924.

21 See above, pp. 85-89. See also Gitlow, B., *I Confess,* p. 209.

The first indication of the extent to which LaFollette would dominate the proceedings came with the announcement, on the eve of the gathering, that the National Committee had asked the Senator to run for the Presidency. William H. Johnston, Chairman of the National Committee, was authorised to send a telegram to LaFollette to accept the Presidential nomination from those assembled. The following is the text of the telegram as sent to LaFollette: [22]

Hon. Robert M. LaFollette, United States Senate, Washington, D. C.

The national committee of the Conference for Progressive Political Action have met and carefully considered the national political situation. They are convinced that the time is ripe for decisive action. The Democratic and Republican parties have both forfeited all claims to public confidence. Under the recent administrations of both of them, there have been grave scandals and flagrant betrayals of the public trust.

At their recent conventions both parties have shown no disposition to meet the public demand for fundamental reform. The Republican party has nominated reactionary candidates upon a platform that is repugnant to every progressive mind. In our opinion, it is unnecessary to await the outcome of the apparently endless battle now being waged by the Democratic bosses over the nomination of candidates. No genuine progressive could or would run on the meaningless, hypocritical platform that has been adopted in New York.

We have inferred from your public addresses that if the Democratic and Republican parties failed to purge themselves of the evil influences that now dominate them, and unless they offered the people sound hopes for substantial relief, you would consent to become a candidate for President and thus give the people an opportunity to express their deep desires for clean progressive government.

---

22 *New York Times*, July 4. 1924.

Recognising you as the outstanding leader of the progressive forces in the United States, we ask, therefore, whether you will, under present conditions, become a candidate for President of the United States. We should also appreciate a message from you setting forth your view of the present political situation.

This request is presented by the unanimous action of the national committee.

William H. Johnston, Chairman.

This unusual procedure of picking the candidate before the convening of the delegates sheds some light on the strategy of the labor leaders and the LaFollette advisers. Anticipating the endorsement of Senator LaFollette this way was a clever strategem to avoid a formal nomination from the floor with its implications of third party organization.

Socialists and Farmer-Labor groups had come to the convention fully prepared to organise a new party. The battle—perhaps the most important issue at the Cleveland convention—was largely restricted to committee. Overt conflict between the party organisers and the labor union men was signaled by the LaFollette letter of acceptance on the afternoon of July 4th—first day of the convention. Immediately after the declaration that LaFollette would run, H. E. Wills, grand chief of the Brotherhood of Locomotive Engineers, obviously deeply moved by the letter, rushed to the platform and moved that the delegates endorse Mr. LaFollette's candidacy. This motion was immediately challenged by Morris Hillquit, leader of the Socialists, who called attention to the fact that the committees on credentials and resolutions had not as yet reported and that no real binding action could be taken until the delegates duly authorized to attend the convention had been selected.[23]

Here the issue was joined. The Socialists would not tolerate any precipitate action. The sharpest acrimony of the entire proceedings followed before the Socialists won their temporary point.

23 *Ibid.*

Other Socialists, opponents of LaFollette because of his antipathy to a third party campaign, sought the floor. Delegates were arising in all sections to propose new motions and amendments. A half-dozen crowded the passage-way between their section and the press seats. It appeared for a moment that forceful 'Bill' Johnston, the chairman, might find himself with a maverick convention on his hands.

But seizing his gavel, he pounded down the disorder with biceps made mighty in a machine shop.

" The delegates," ordered Mr. Johnston, " will all take their seats."

The delegates did. Mr. Johnston obviously meant what he said and 100 sergeants-at-arms were on hand to carry out the will of the chairman.

" Is this a steam roller? " inquired one little delegate with a fiercely bristling moustache as he resumed his seat. Mr. Johnston looked at him calmly but meaningly and the little man hurried his retreat.

When quiet was restored, Chairman Johnston recognised Municipal Judge Jacob Panken, of New York. Judge Panken arose to a point of order.[24]

Mr. Johnston adjudged the point well taken and ruled the motion to endorse LaFollette out of order. Throughout the demonstration, the Socialists sat silently, not because of any lack of enthusiasm for LaFollette, but because they were anxious to proceed with the organization work which seemed to them as important as the selection of a presidential candidate.

The second and final day of the CPPA convention completed the business of the occasion. While the Democrats in New York wearily moved through a seventy-seventh ballot, with Smith and McAdoo still hopelessly deadlocked, the Progressives rapidly and pointedly concluded their gathering. At the afternoon session, LaFollette was endorsed for President of the United States and a platform, embodying the recommenda-

24 *New York Herald Tribune,* July 5, 1924.

tions in the LaFollette speech delivered the previous day by Bob, junior, was adopted.[25] Both the endorsement and the platform were made by acclamation. The National Committee was authorized to select a candidate for the Vice-Presidency. There was some slight opposition to the proposition vesting this authority in the National Committee, but it was feeble and unimportant. A correspondent for the *New York Times* estimated that perhaps only a dozen voices were raised in opposition to it.[26]

The LaFollette endorsement was proposed to the convention by Chairman Manion of the Organization Committee. The resolution recommended " that this convention endorse the candidacy of Senator Robert M. LaFollette for President of the United States upon the platform submitted by him." [27] Short seconding speeches were made by Morris Hillquit, speaking for the Socialists; George W. Lefkowitz, on behalf of the Farmer-Labor party; Mrs. Harriet Stanton Blatch, speaking for the women progressives; and William Pickens, one of the Negro delegates.

With Senator LaFollette endorsed, and the platform agreed upon, the final hour was used to dispose of various resolutions.[28] The convention went on record in favor of immediate and complete independence for the Philippines. It also favored a pay increase for postal employees. The CPPA assured the Irish people of its sympathy " for the aspirations of the Irish people for freedom and independence." It opposed exploitation in Haiti, Santo Domingo and Nicaragua. A resolution favoring recognition of Soviet Russia was tabled.

Various speeches, delivered by all kinds of personalities, punctuated the routine business of the last day's session. Senator Lynn Frazier denounced the return to " abnormalcy "

25 See Appendix # 4.

26 *New York Times,* July 6, 1924.

27 *Proceedings,* CPPA Convention, Vol. II, p. 263.

28 See *Proceedings,* CPPA Convention, Vol. II, pp. 281-304.

which had caused the farmer to endure so much suffering since 1920. W. T. Rawleigh, who was to be LaFollette's chief financial supporter, explained the need for a free and truly competitive market. Herman Ekern, LaFollette's close friend and adviser in Wisconsin, to whom LaFollette had written the letter intimating his willingness to run as an independent, sounded the keynote of the LaFollette campaign with the charge that the great issue before the American people was control of industry by private monopoly. The Progressives were to repeat it many times during the subsequent months.

When the delegates prepared to return home, there was much they could rightfully feel had been accomplished. In two days a candidate and a platform had been adopted. The disparate liberal and progressive groups, so hopelessly confused a few years earlier, had been able to agree upon a program without apparent friction or the dissensions and withdrawals which characterised the attempt at a third party in 1920. Concealed by their common devotion to LaFollette and a common cause against the old parties, the basic differences of the CPPA groups hardly came to light at Cleveland. But the bitter fight in the Organization Committee of the CPPA, not settled until young Bob LaFollette told the recalcitrant members that his father would run only as an independent and not as a candidate of a third party, presaged the difficulties ahead.[29] The Socialists, reluctantly in private committee meetings, but loyally on the floor of the convention, had agreed to go along with LaFollette and wait upon the later formation of a third party.

As they departed, many of the delegates were convinced that they had witnessed the birth of a great movement; that they had been present at a significant occasion in American life. They cared little if the conservative press remarked that the free railroad passes of the members of the Brotherhood accounted for the good attendance, or if others sneered at "the lunatic fringe."[30] Even the local diversions could not distract

29 *New York Times,* July 6, 1924.

30 *St. Paul Pioneer-Press,* July 5, 1924, remarked upon the free railroad passes.

them. Down the street a boisterous convention of Rotarians was dutifully proving its good fellowship. Clevelanders less interested in seeing history made in their midst than in listening to the brawl at Madison Square Garden gathered about loud-speakers to hear Alabama, again and again, cast twenty-four votes for Underwood. But the Progressives were aroused. They had their candidate now, and their platform. Soon, perhaps, they would even have a party! With more flair for hyperbole than regard for historical perspective, one ebullient delegate flamboyantly described the most dramatic moments of the gathering in the following words: [31]

> There are moments in human history which shape the destiny of nations and of mankind. Columbus pleading for the support of Queen Isabella, Caesar plunging across the Rubicon, Constantine crossing the Milvian bridge, Luther facing the prelates at Worms, Cromwell picking up the mace of power from the Speaker's table, and Hancock placing his signature upon the Declaration of Independence—the men who witnessed these epochal events gained fame and honor from the occasion. And so with us as we listened to Robert M. LaFollette, junior, read the great document in which his father pledged his fidelity to the people's cause and consented to take the leadership in a political crusade to regain the " freedom and prosperity and happiness of the American people." Privileged and fortunate were we who heard the thrilling message, which historians of the future may record as the turning point in American democracy.

That the convention was no turning point in history was certainly not the fault of these earnest folk at Cleveland who stood, with St. George, ready to slay the Dragon.

The choice of this convention to lead its good fight against the forces of evil and reaction had remained in Washington, far from the tumultuous applause which greeted every mention of his name. Far removed from the scene as Senator LaFollette

31 Albert F. Coyle, Editor, writing in the *Locomotive Engineers Journal*, 58:8, Aug. 1924, p. 572.

was, the persuasive forcefulness of his personality dominated the convention from start to ending. The entire proceedings had been a series of tributes to the man who, during the generation he had occupied a seat in the United States Senate, had emerged as the chieftain of the progressive forces in America. The cohesive nature of their common faith in LaFollette's integrity of character and strength of leadership enabled the Progressives assembled at Cleveland to overlook many a minor difference of opinion in their greater devotion to the captain of their cause. LaFollette's personality was so dynamic that often the movement or idea with which he was associated seemed pallid by contrast. Whether it pleased him or not, the Progressive campaign in 1924, under the impact of LaFollette's powerful personality, became more and more " LaFollette's campaign " and the Progressive movement was increasingly (and mistakenly) referred to as " LaFollette's party."

Any attempt to portray LaFollette is fraught with all kinds of difficulties. His was the kind of character whose manifold traits refuse to be reduced to simple terms of black and white. In evaluating his achievement another difficulty lies in the mass of prejudice and opinionated thinking which distorts almost any word picture his contemporaries drew. One was either " for " LaFollette or " agin " him. With the possible exceptions of Teddy Roosevelt and William Jennings Bryan, Robert LaFollette provoked more emotional thinking and irrational attacks than any American statesman of his time. There is no one today, unless it be Franklin D. Roosevelt, who has this fine faculty for being simultaneously hated and loved.

The coloring, consequently, in a picture of Robert Marion LaFollette has to be intense. He hated and, in turn, was hated. He enjoyed a fight and there were many willing to fight him. He was as convinced of the righteousness of his cause as his critics were of his folly. To his supporters he was a crusader; to his enemies he was demagogue.

Watching and hearing LaFollette in action on the Senate floor must have been one of the privileges of the last generation. Whenever he spoke, one could depend upon a good show. His brand of oratory is fast disappearing in these days of radio broadcasting. One of the paradoxes about the man is that, for all the novel ideas he proposed, he represented something that was essentially of America's past. His fear of "big business," his political methods, his oratory belonged to an America which had not yet turned the corner into the complexities of the twentieth century.

Robert Marion LaFollette was a son of that Middle Border which had nurtured so many righteous causes and ardent crusaders. His background and early training belonged, as John Chamberlain has noted, to a "pre-technological" age, while "his roots went back into that agricultural America which was dear to the heart of Jefferson." [32] John LaFollette had established the family in this country about the middle of the eighteenth century when, faced by the choice of so many French Huguenots had to make, he decided to leave his own country whose reckless and sadistic persecutions were making life unbearable for so many Protestants.[33] Jesse LaFollette, grandfather of Senator LaFollette, owned a farm in Hardin County, Kentucky, adjacent to that of Thomas Lincoln, father of the Civil War President. It is interesting to record that Jesse LaFollette and Thomas Lincoln were joint defendants in an ejectment suit which resulted from some of the faulty surveying so prevalent at the time.[34] The suit was probably the principal reason for both LaFollette's and Lincoln's leaving Kentucky. Another reason was doubtless their antipathy—as strong in one family as in the other—to slavery.[35]

32 Chamberlain, J., *A Farewell to Reform*, p. 246. By permission of Reynal and Hitchcock, publishers.

33 Warren, L. A., "The Lincoln and LaFollette Families in Pioneer Drama," *Wisconsin Magazine of History*, 12:4, June 1929, p. 362.

34 *Ibid.*, p. 368.

35 *Ibid.*

Of Huguenot pioneer stock, of a family so close to the grass roots of America, with family associations linking his name and fortune with that of Lincoln and the hardy adventurers who conquered the prairies, LaFollette, appraised in terms of political availability, had many of the attributes so necessary to a prospective presidential candidate. To make the picture almost perfect, LaFollette was born in a log cabin—a log cabin in the small township of Primrose (whose name so belied the turbulent course of life LaFollette would lead!) in Dane County, Wisconsin, on June 14, 1855.

Forced to endure the hardships of poverty as a youth, La-Follette learned to be resourceful and to compensate for his lack of money by an abundance of intelligence and diligence. Working his way through college, he embraced—never to renounce them—the two great affections of his life.[36] One was the University of Wisconsin, which inspired in the young LaFollette an unquenchable intellectual curiosity and respect for the truth, a debt which in turn was repaid by Senator LaFollette through his untiring and eminently successful efforts to make the institution one of the great centers of learning in America. No alumnus ever served his college more faithfully, more abundantly. The other great affection of Robert LaFollette's life was, of course, his wife, Belle Case, classmate at the University. His inseparable companion during a life of mutual devotion and respect, his constant and vigilant nurse during so many days of physical tribulation, she fully deserved the frequent references, the numerous recognitions of her services, which the Senator included in his autobiography. Highly intelligent and endowed with an appreciation of political realities, Mrs. LaFollette joined veteran campaigners as a member of the select group whose counsel her husband valued.[37] " My wisest and best counsellor " Senator LaFollette called her.[38] Undoubt-

36 See LaFollette, R., *LaFollette's Autobiography*, pp. 6-32.

37 *Ibid.*, p. 180.

38 *Ibid.*, p. 314.

edly his tender and felicitous relations with the women in his life—his mother, sister, wife and daughters—their priceless influence in shaping his career, all help to explain his life-long, consistent espousal of women's rights.[39]

After being admitted to the bar in 1880, the young LaFollette announced his candidacy for the office of District Attorney of Dane County in opposition to the ticket proposed by Boss Keyes. After a spectacular campaign during which his college friends rendered invaluable aid, LaFollette was elected by a narrow margin and his political career had begun. Four years later, in 1884, he was elected to the House of Representatives, youngest member of the 49th Congress.[40] In the fall of 1890, after serving three terms in Congress, LaFollette was defeated for re-election as the Democrats swept Wisconsin as the result of state issues, the " Bennett Law " in particular. Back in Madison, Wisconsin, resuming his private practice, LaFollette broke completely with the Republican bosses like Senator Sawyer and Senator Spooner. Launching a program of reform directed against boss-controlled politics and the domination of the " vested interests," LaFollette in the years from 1893-1900 rallied the latent forces of Populism and liberalism. LaFollette captured the nomination as Republican candidate for Governor in 1900 and subsequently won the election. With the "Stalwarts"—or conservatives—in control of the State Senate and " Battling Bob " in the Executive Mansion, the fight was on.

In formulating a broad program of reform, Governor La-Follette not only carried the fight to his enemies; he became a national figure as prominent writers and political authorities haled his " Wisconsin Idea." [41]

39 See LaFollette's views on women's rights, LaFollette, *op. cit.*, pp. 311-318.

40 LaFollette, R., *op. cit.*, p. 49. Unless otherwise noted, the facts in La-Follette's political career are taken from his autobiography.

41 See McCarthy, C., *The Wisconsin Idea.*

Simply expressed, LaFollette's program was as follows: [42]

(a) a system of direct-primary nominations protected by law

(b) an equalization of taxation on corporate property with that of other similar property

(c) the regulation of charges by railroads and other corporations to ensure fair play and to prevent them from passing on their taxes to the public

(d) the erection of commissions of experts for the regulation of railroads and for other public interests

The Old Guard was no match for LaFollette. Sustained by his "mystic faith" in the people, he called upon the voters to endorse his program of reform. These were the people he understood: the people he had met at county fairs and talked to at Chautauqua gatherings. LaFollette was re-elected twice and his program was almost wholly adopted. The progressive legislation did not stop there. The state insurance laws were recodified; the state banking laws were overhauled; civil service was extended; a long-range program of conservation was instituted.

In 1905, LaFollette resigned as Governor to take a seat in the United States Senate. Three times he was to be re-elected to that body. His career in the Senate has become an American saga. It is not necessary to retell the entire tale here. He brought from Wisconsin with him his strong convictions about railroad control and valuation, his devotion to the cause of conservation, his deep-seated suspicion of party bosses and party regulars although, paradoxically, in doing so, he often appeared to his contemporaries to be as tyrannical and ruthless as his enemies. Often morose, usually serious, undoubtedly egotistical, he baffled his friends perhaps as much as he confused his enemies. [43] Chamberlain, with his masterly ability to

42 Paxson, F., "Robert M. LaFollette," *Dictionary of American Biography*, Vol. X, p. 542.

43 See Stoddard, H. L., *As I Knew Them*, ch. LXVIII.

sketch the meaningful elements of a character, has described
LaFollette this way: [44]

> His personality was not one of easy winsomeness; he
> didn't appeal to voters in any baby-kissing, glad-hand way.
> After the World War, with most of the Progressive program
> lying about in shattered debris, he showed his disappoint-
> ment; he was at times bitter. But bitterness is sometimes an
> index of the original faith of a man. This was certainly true
> in the case of LaFollette; he had given a great deal, and had
> seen it all swept away. It is silly to call a man egotistical in
> a tone of reproof; what person who believes in himself and
> is willing to fight for the prevalence of his beliefs is not self-
> centered?

With what might be called " obvious subtlety " Chamberlain
touches upon the ubiquitous LaFollette-Roosevelt comparison.
" The business of dismissing LaFollette as a demagogue has
persisted, even as the habit of regarding Roosevelt as an effective President still persists." [45]

LaFollette had discovered, in his early days in Wisconsin
politics, that sincerity and crusading zeal were powerful
weapons against bosses. As candidate for prosecuting attorney,
representative, governor and senator, he had amply demonstrated that the old-line machine could be challenged by some
one with fight and energy and conviction.[46]

But the reasons for the lasting impression LaFollette had
made upon the American political stage lay in more than just
his aggressive and forceful personality. His political and economic views had become a *bête noire* to the reactionaries
from Maine to California. They looked with concern upon this
" agitator " beside whom " Bryan, in his palmiest days, was a

44 Chamberlain, J., *op. cit.*, p. 243. By permission of Reynal and Hitchcock, publishers.

45 *Ibid.*, p. 241.

46 Paxson, F., *op. cit.*, p. 542.

cooing dove." [47] LaFollette had come out of the West with a well-formulated program of Populism. He was for the direct primary; he was for woman suffrage; he was for rigid trust legislation and regulation. He was against Republican-Wall-Street tariffs; he was against the railroad companies. To La-Follette there was always a conflict going on between the People and the Special Interests. Unconsciously, he looked upon himself—as Bruce Bliven has put it—as a St. George slaying the dragon of Special Privilege.[48] He felt that the corporations and the trusts, through their very bigness, had secured positions of influence out of all keeping with the welfare of the country. LaFollette looked back, with a nostalgic longing, to the days of little business and individual responsibility. In this respect, LaFollette was an agrarian rather than a radical. As Paxson so well says, " He was no Socialist, but feared for democracy if it did not develop agencies to overcome the selfish power of wealth." [49] LaFollette had an abiding faith in the inherent goodness of the " People."

Never deviating from his conviction that the unholy alliance of greedy monopolists and corrupt politicians threatened the welfare of the nation, he looked upon himself as spokesman for the voiceless multitude. One paragraph of his autobiography summarises the creed to which LaFollette remained steadfastly loyal: [50]

> Within the changing phases of a twenty-five year contest, I have been more and more impressed with the deep, underlying singleness of the issue. It is not railroad regulations. It is not the tariff, or conservation, or the currency. It is not the trusts. These and other questions are but manifestations of one great struggle. The supreme issue, involving all the

47 *The Literary Digest,* 44:2, Jan. 13, 1912, p. 12.

48 Bliven, B., "LaFollette's Place in Our History," *Current History Magazine,* 22:5, Aug., 1925, p. 716.

49 Paxson, F., *op. cit.,* p. 544.

50 LaFollette, R., *op. cit.,* p. 760.

others, is THE ENCROACHMENT OF THE POWER-
FUL FEW UPON THE RIGHTS OF THE MANY. This
mighty power has come between the people and their government. Can we free ourselves from this control? Can representative government be restored? Shall we, with statesman-
like and constructive legislation, meet these problems or shall
we pass them on, with all the possibilities of conflict and chaos,
to future generations?

As champion of the cause of the Plain Man, LaFollette had
become a presidential possibility long before 1924. In 1908 he
had received a score of votes at the Republican convention.
Much happened during his first term as Senator to make him a
prospect for the Presidency. Before Roosevelt returned from his
travels to throw his hat in the ring, LaFollette had been the
first choice of the 1912 Progressives. The story of the estrange-
ment of Roosevelt and LaFollette needs no repeating here—
suffice it to say that " Roosevelt reaped where the tireless La-
Follette had sown " after the ex-President had been induced to
run again for office, thereby checking the LaFollette candidacy
just as it had gathered momentum.[51] LaFollette, by 1912, was
already a famous progressive. The enthusiasm of reporters like
Steffens for "the Wisconsin idea" had brought LaFollette
favorable comment from the nation's liberals and reformers.[52]
LaFollette's fight in the Senate for equitable railroad rate
legislation, his last-ditch opposition to the Aldrich Currency
Bill (which he and many others saw as a sell-out to the financial interests) and his stand against protectionism had made
him a recognised leader of the people opposed to domination by
Wall Street, the industrial bosses and the reactionary leaders of
the Republican party. His opposition to American involvement
in the World War endeared LaFollette both to those Americans
suspicious of imperialism and to those who, because of blood-
ties or sentimental attachments or pacifistic beliefs, had no approved our entry into the Great War.

51 Binkley, W. E., *American Political Parties*, p. 345.
52 See Steffens, L., *Autobiography*, ch. XIV.

As the black reaction of Harding's normalcy settled upon the land, LaFollette, indefatigable and dauntless, stood like a beacon of liberalism in the Senate. Steadily his stock, among the Progressives, climbed. In 1922 he was the only prominent American politician invited to address the American Federation of Labor. The exposures of corruption in the Republican Administration provided him with an unprecedented opportunity to lash out, with all his old-time leonine ferocity, against the mischievous forces within the government. As the oil exposures widened to engulf William G. McAdoo, LaFollette's preeminent position among the Progressives was assured. In January, 1924, a group of prominent liberals asked LaFollette to lead a third party.[53] When the Committe of Forty Eight, in the spring of 1924, conducted a poll of the nation's liberals to determine their choice for an independent candidate, LaFollette was an overwhelming choice.[54] Most progressives would probably agree, as the perspective of the passing years established dimensions for the American political leaders of the first quarter of the twentieth century, that LaFollette had been " the ablest of all the progressive Senators; a tireless worker, bold and fearless and reckless as a fighter, giving nor asking favor or 'quarter'." [55]

LaFollette's death within the year after the 1924 election gave rise to the belief in some quarters that he had run for the presidency that year because it was a case of " now or never." In his *Farewell to Reform,* John Chamberlain subscribes to this theory. " LaFollette's last phase," Chamberlain says, " was rather pitiful. . . . in 1924 LaFollette was getting old; his time was growing short. He had seen the dying Penrose, a flabby thing of skin and bones, come back to power with the accession of Harding. Perhaps the time had arrived—at last!—for a

53 *New York Times,* Jan. 14, 1924.

54 See correspondence between J. A. H. Hopkins and M. Hillquit (Hillquit papers). See also *New York Times,* Feb. 23, 1924.

55 Joseph L. Bristow to C. B. Kirtland, Mar. 20, 1909, quoted in Hechler, K., *Insurgency,* p. 84.

third party movement. . . . So LaFollette swallowed the bait of the Conference for Progressive Political Action and headed a third party ticket." [56] Ickes feels the same way. Referring to 1924, he says " that was the year that Senator Bob LaFollette of Wisconsin decided that it was then or never for him." [57] Donald Richberg speaks of LaFollette's " getting in shape for one last battle." [58] The implication is hardly fair to LaFollette. If anything, LaFollette's health might have dissuaded him from making the attempt in 1924.[59]

The " now or never " explanation implies that an inordinate degree of self-interest motivated LaFollette's decision to run for the presidency in 1924. Moreover, such a theory is based on the assumption that LaFollette seriously expected to win the election and to move into the White House next March. It is difficult to find any evidence—outside the extravagant claims made in campaign speeches and press releases—that LaFollette, or the other responsible CPPA leaders, anticipated outright victory at the polls. Most of them looked upon the campaign of 1924 as an opportunity to establish a basis for future farmer-labor political action; some planned, no doubt, to deadlock the Electoral College; but few were so sanguine as to entertain any hopes that LaFollette would become President of the United States.

With the realization that the sands of his time were running out, LaFollette may have looked upon the 1924 campaign as a fitting climax to his long and consistent career as a champion of progressive causes. It is even more likely that the battle-scarred warhorse, recovering from a siege of sickness, once again smelled gunpowder and—restless and impatient—welcomed the call to combat.

56 Chamberlain, J., *op. cit.*, p. 261.

57 Ickes, H. L., *Autobiography of a Curmudgeon*, p. 252.

58 Richberg, D., *Tents of the Mighty*, p. 132.

59 Raney, W. F., *Wisconsin, A Story of Progress*, p. 303.

Conjectures about LaFollette's running mate began even before the Cleveland delegates decided to place the authority to select a vice-presidential candidate in the hands of the Executive Committee. In the days following LaFollette's endorsement at the CPPA convention, rumors came thick and fast. It was reported variously that Representative Huddleston of Alabama, William H. Johnston of the Machinists, and George Berry of the Pressmen would be the second-place choice of the Progressives. Persistently appeared the report that Justice Brandeis had been asked to run as LaFollette's partner.[60] It is impossible to determine whether some effort was made to secure the liberal spokesman on the Supreme Court. It was obviously to the advantage of the old parties represented by the press to suggest that some great leader like Brandeis had been asked to accept if events later proved that the third party men would have to content themselves with a lesser light. Three days before the Executive Committee met in Washington to decide upon its candidate, the news of Burton K. Wheeler's bolt from the Democratic Party made the headlines. Wheeler was the first Democratic congressman—and first prominent Democrat, one could say—to announce publicly his support of LaFollette. In declaring his support of the Progressives and his desertion of Davis, Wheeler emphasized his distaste for his party's connections with Wall Street. The punch line in the announcement of his bolt was the vigorous " I can not support any candidate representing the house of Morgan." [61] Wheeler was making it sufficiently clear that he was not going to vote for Davis. At the same time he carefully explained that he would diligently campaign for the Democratic ticket in Montana (because there, he believed, it was truly progressive), especially for the re-election of Tom Walsh to the United States Senate.

By Friday, July 18, the day of the Executive Committee meeting to choose a vice-presidential candidate, it was a fore-

60 *New York World,* July 17, 1924.

61 *New York Times,* July 17, 1924.

gone conclusion that Wheeler would be invited to accept the position as running mate to LaFollette. The only question was whether he would accept. The Committee did not disappoint, and neither did Wheeler. At the meeting of the Committee, with John Nelson and Gilbert Roe representing the LaFollettes, the CPPA endorsed Wheeler and sent a committee consisting of Johnston, Nelson, Mrs. Costigan, Manly and Hillquit to call upon Wheeler and ask him to accept the honor. The next day this select committee performed its function and Wheeler, accepting, had cast in his lot with the CPPA.

The offer of the nomination had come as no surprise to Senator Wheeler. Earlier in the week, LaFollette, accompanied by his son, Bob, and son-in-law, Ralph Sucher, had visited Wheeler and, speaking frankly, had discussed the prospects of the campaign and proffered the second-place nomination to the young Montanan. Although, in his own words, he was "frightened" as he envisaged the almost insuperable problems of such a campaign, Senator Wheeler decided to get into the fight alongside his friend and counselor from Wisconsin. Wheeler having thus assured LaFollette privately, the visit of the nominating committee was just a formality.[62]

In accepting the nomination the new candidate left no doubt of his opinion of Davis Democrats:[63]

> In this situation I find myself unable to support either the Republican candidates, who frankly admit their reactionary standpat policies, or the Democratic candidate who may claim in well-chosen phrases that he is a progressive but whose training and constant association belie any such pretension. Between Davis and Coolidge there is only a choice for conservatives to make.

Later on—and this is important insofar as it shows a reluctance, even in the midst of such a strong excoriation of Davis, to make a final break with his party:

62 Burton K. Wheeler to the author, Mar. 27, 1944.
63 *New York Times*, July 20, 1924.

In accepting this call, I do not abandon my faith in the democracy of Thomas Jefferson; I am a Democrat but not a Wall Street Democrat. I shall give my support and whatever influence I may possess to those candidates for office who have proven their fidelity to the interest of the people, wherever they may be found, but I shall oppose every man on whatever ticket he may appear who bears the brand of the dollar sign.

Wheeler's break with his party was never so complete and definite as LaFollette's. When the campaign was over, Wheeler—to the chagrin of some Progressives—resumed business immediately at the old party stand.

What kind of a man was this candidate for the vice-presidency, who, less than a year before, had had to be lectured on the etiquette of not smoking in the Senate Chamber; who in the first third of his first tenure as junior Senator from a frontier state would receive five million votes for the office of Vice-President?

Years later, newspaper men would talk of the "paradox" of Burton Wheeler; his opinions and loyalties would defy analytical dissection; arguments would rage over whether the Senator from Montana was fascist or liberal.[64] Whatever judgment one might render here in the 1940's, one must admit that, in more than a number of respects, Wheeler's career has been singular and spectacular. Wheeler was the first Senator to come out for Franklin Roosevelt. Wheeler is believed to have been the model for the popular motion picture, "Mr. Smith Goes to Washington."[65] Certainly the adventures of the junior Senator from Montana during his first term of office have a quality about them hard for even Hollywood to reproduce. But his whole career leading up to the Senate had been as stormy and vigorous. He was an unpredictable combination of New Eng-

64 Cf. "Potomacus," "Wheeler of Montana," *New Republic*, 108:13, Sept. 20, 1943, pp. 390-392.
65 *Ibid.*, p. 391.

land heredity and Montana environment, born in Hudson, Massachusetts, not far from Boston, in 1882, of a long line of New Englanders. There was nothing to indicate his subsequent attachment to the West, not, at least, until he was graduated from high school and decided to complete his education at the University of Michigan. Not from choice, but from necessity, he followed the prescribed American political formula and worked his way through the law school washing dishes and selling books. But his doctors advised him, by the time he had finished his course, to go West. He suffered from asthma and was threatened with tuberculosis. Quite by accident, he decided to settle down in Butte, Montana, where life was " red and dripping " — in the words of one of Wheeler's biographers —and soon was well enough established to return to Illinois to marry the farmer's daughter he had met while selling that household companion, *Dr. Price's Recipes.*[66]

The town where Wheeler had settled was, of course, one of the greatest mining towns in the world, rough, uncouth, still retaining most of the evidences of frontier existence. The place was dominated by the great Anaconda Copper Company. Wheeler, fresh from the genteel environment of a New England village and a college campus, was shocked by some of the policies of the copper bosses. When the county attorney began to give him assignments in defense of offenders—often miners who had no counsel of their own—he came in closer contact with conditions which appeared to be even more disturbing. By 1910, he was in the State Legislature, put there by the Democrats and the votes of men he had befriended and to whom he had given legal advice. " When, in the legislature, he proposed bills to abolish the ' fellow-servant ' and ' contributory negligence laws ', through which such companies customarily escaped

66 Tucker, R., and Barkley, F., *Sons of the Wild Jackass,* p. 278. This biographical material on Sen. Wheeler is in large part derived from Tucker and Barkley, *op. cit.,* Wheeler's biography in the *LaFollette-Wheeler Campaign Text Book,* and various newspaper and periodical accounts, in addition to information supplied by Senator Wheeler himself.

damages sought by injured employees, he became a radical in corporate eyes." [67] Wheeler carried on the challenge by a last-ditch fight to send Tom Walsh, long-time enemy of Anaconda, to the United States Senate. Montana, at this time, was still employing the legislative method in choosing United States Senators. Walsh, two years later chosen by the people in Montana in a direct election to the Senate, remembered Wheeler's loyalty and, through his recommendation, President Wilson appointed Burton K. Wheeler as United States Attorney for the District of Montana.

In his new position, Wheeler was able to strike at the widespread corruption which had long been part of the Montana political picture. Wheeler displayed more enthusiasm and vigor for the extermination of graft in high places than for the prosecution of workers who were allegedly pro-German and seditous because they insisted on striking in war-time. This was annoying to the corporations which " had always looked to the Federal law enforcement agencies as valiant and ready accessories in putting down strikes and other threats to their feudal sovereignty." [68] In 1918 they sent word, through the Democratic machine, to Washington that Wheeler's resignation would be the price of Walsh's reelection. To save his old friend, Wheeler resigned. He stayed in Montana to carry on the fight.

> His term as federal attorney was marked by a spate of prosecution for all the kinds of corruption that flourish in a frontier society dominated by powerful absentee industrialists. It was a period of germination for the causes and antipathies that were to govern his future political life. He started out by smashing the practice of using decoys to catch saloon-keepers in the act of selling fire-water to the Indians and ended up fighting against the manner in which the war-time espionage laws were being applied. He repeatedly refused to indict Wobblies as such and spoke out boldly against the persecution of German-Americans. He made no secret of his

67 Tucker and Barkley, *op. cit.*, p. 279.
68 *Ibid.*, p. 282.

opposition to American entry into the war and was rash enough to advocate, in a mining state, government owner- ship of natural resources and the railroads. Small wonder that his bid for the governorship in 1920 was greeted with the show of bloody hands.[69]

In 1920, endorsed by the rapidly-growing Non-Partisan League, Wheeler won the Democratic nomination for Gov- ernor. There ensued one of the stormiest state campaigns in American political history. War-time passions were aroused; the old shibboleths were dusted off and trotted out; the press whipped up the feeling until violence and terrorism swept the state. All but one of the Democratic papers supported the Republicans. " Wheeler himself, the candidate for governor of the state, was refused the right to speak in the city of Dillon and was later surrounded in a way-station by a mob which was kept at bay by a veteran of the World War with a rifle, who declared he would shoot the first man who attempted to cross the railroad track. After a four-hour siege, the mob retired." [70] Wheeler was defeated by about 33,000.

Two years later, Wheeler was again a candidate, this time for the United States Senate. The war hysteria had subsided. The progressive tide of 1922 carried him into office with a comfortable margin. So it was that, in 1923, at the age of forty-one, this singularly dynamic figure, who had been plum- meted from the serene atmosphere of the New England countryside into the hurly-burly of frontier-town politics; the young man who had accepted a position as a stenographer with a Boston firm after graduation from high school, found himself in the midst of a mining country thousands of miles away, " sprawling, brawling Butte," with its card sharps, Saturday night sports and dance-hall girls. But, most of all, with its crowd of poor, perhaps ignorant miners, dominated by great Anaconda.

69 Bendiner, R., "Burton K. Wheeler," *Nation*, 150:17, Apr. 27, 1940, p. 533.

70 *LaFollette-Wheeler Text Book*, p. 22.

When Wheeler ran for the Senate in 1922, it was difficult for the Republicans to find an issue. Two years before, they had insisted that the mines would close if Wheeler were elected; Wheeler lost, but the mines closed anyway.

In the Senate it did not take Wheeler long to establish the same kind of a reputation for what his biographers like to call " brash pugnacity." On his third day in the Senate—when, most certainly, Senators should be seen rather than heard— Wheeler challenged the party whips successfully on the reappointment of the conservative Cummins as Chairman of the Interstate Commerce Commission.[71]

Three months later, Wheeler embarked upon what was to result in one of the most dazzling and incredible exposures in American history—the investigation of the Department of Justice under Attorney General Harry Daugherty.[72] Acting as prosecutor for a congressional investigating committee, Wheeler savagely revealed the sordid tale of Administration corruption. The story was not completed until some of the men Wheeler was investigating had gone to a federal penitentiary and others had committed suicide, " and the easy going President of the United States had died in an odor that could hardly be called one of sanctity." [73]

" The Little Green House on K Street " became familiar to most Americans. Sensation followed sensation. Relentlessly Wheeler pinned the evidence on the men about the Attorney General. The drama of the investigation was heightened by the mysterious death of Jess Smith, Daugherty's intimate associate and alleged go-between. This was the Jess who, Wheeler would recall, had been offered the post of Comptroller of the Currency. " But he patriotically preferred to work for the Government for nothing—there was more money in it." [74]

71 New York Times, Dec. 11, 1923, and Jan. 10, 1924.

72 New York Times, Mar. 1, 1924.

73 Bendiner, R., op. cit.

74 Quoted in Tucker, R., and Barkley, F., op. cit., p. 287.

To strike back at their tormentor, the Ohio Gang, using the good offices of the Department of Justice and the Secret Service, scrutinised the Wheeler record back in Montana to get something—anything—which would discredit him. Finally the charge was made that Wheeler had accepted a fee to use his influence as a Senator to secure government oil concessions for a client. The Government obtained an indictment against Wheeler in Montana in April, 1924. The case was not decided until the trial a year later when the jury took two ballots— " one to go out to lunch and one, after thirteen minutes' deliberation, to acquit Wheeler." [75]

Their apparent willingness to resort to crude devices in order to discredit Wheeler is a fair indication of the effect of the Wheeler prosecution on the Administration's corrupt elements. It is difficult, especially now, to understand how the honest men within the Administration could condone such obvious persecution tactics. Still the records indicate that Harlan Stone, whom Coolidge had appointed as Attorney-General, implacably continued the case. In August, 1924, in private correspondence, a prominent American newspaperman, Mr. Gilson Gardner of Scripps-Howard, was expressing himself as " shocked " by Mr. Stone's desire to see Wheeler convicted.[76]

The hard feelings between Wheeler and Stone engendered by this case gave way to friendship years later as both gentlemen came to appreciate the extent of distortion and misunderstanding manipulated by less scrupulous persons eager to persecute the Senator and willing to misinform the Attorney-General.[77]

The selection of Burton K. Wheeler was indubitably a logical choice for the Progressives. In the pragmatic terms of practical politics, he could " balance " the ticket. LaFollette had the

75 Bendiner, R., op. cit.

76 American Civil Liberties Union, " Departments of Justice, Labor and State," Cases, 1924-1925, No. 27, p. 142 (American Civil Liberties Union papers).

77 Burton K. Wheeler to the author, Mar. 27, 1944.

advantage of age and long experience. Wheeler could comple-
ment LaFollette's contributions with his own youthful vigor
and aggressive ideas. Both physically and temperamentally,
Wheeler was equipped to swing around the circuit; and the
news accounts of the savage prosecution of Daugherty had already provided advance notices of his ability as a public speaker.
Through his singular accomplishments as a freshman Senator
and his meteoric rise within a few months to a position of
recognised leadership among the Western Democrats, Wheeler
was newly established as a kind of LaFollette of the Democrats,
a bold, crusading liberal whose forceful, withering offensives
against the intrenched interests provided a common ground for
action on the part of the Progressives against the old-line
politicians. Upon two spectacular occasions—the revolt against
Cummins and the forced resignation of Daugherty—Wheeler's
tactics had already paid off in rich political dividends.

CHAPTER VII
THE CAMPAIGN GETS UNDER WAY

By comparison with the platforms presented by the old parties in 1924, the Progressives offered a model of concise and cogent statements.[1] The platform was perhaps not more than one-third the length of the major party platforms. It was couched in language that in no way revealed the constant compromising and conceding that go on in the room where the committee on resolutions meets. The Democrats began their platform by paying respect to the memory of Woodrow Wilson. The Republicans bowed their heads in reverent remembrance of Warren G. Harding. Regardless of the appropriateness of these respectful gestures, they imparted, from the beginning, a negative quality to the platforms that became more and more apparent as the old parties sought to keep all sections and segments contented.[2] In striking contrast is the first sentence of the Progressive platform. " The great issue before the American people today is the control of government and industry by private monopoly." There were no reservations in this assertion, no intentional chance of misunderstanding nor ambiguity by design.

The outstanding planks in the platforms were clearly defined by the Progressives, planks which had been concealed by evasive or platitudinous language in the old party platforms. Perhaps the most striking were the proposals that Congress be given the power to overrule the Supreme Court, government ownership of railroads, abolition of the use of injunctions in labor disputes, direct nomination and election of the President, amending the Constitution to extend the initiative and referendum to the Federal government, and provision for a popular referendum in the event of war.

1 See Appendix No. 4.

2 The three platforms may be conveniently compared in Kirk Porter's *National Party Platforms*, pp. 476-522.

The Progressive platform, instead of turning out as an amorphous document with loose ends and contradictory statements, so frequently the case with party platforms, can stand comparison with such able—and rare—statements of policy as the Democratic platform of 1932. Both of them were startlingly concise; both of them were logically presented. The able platform in 1924 belonged to a losing party. The able platform in 1932 belonged to a victorious party. Progressive experience in 1924 supports the often-expressed opinion that, after all, platforms do not make so much difference on Election Day.

After a short exposition listing the ills of American society, a result—according to the Progressives—of the methods employed by the monopolists, the platform pledged a " covenant with the people " consisting of twelve points. First of all, a thorough house-cleaning of the corrupt Administration in Washington was promised. Eventual public ownership of the nation's water power and railroads was pledged. The Mellon tax plan was repudiated. The Great Lakes waterway plan was endorsed. Immediate tariff and freight rate reductions would be made. The Supreme Court was to be curbed in two ways. Its judges were to be elected for fixed terms not exceeding ten years. Its decisions could be overridden by act of Congress. The Progressives promised Labor that its rights to organise and bargain collectively would be recognised and that injunctions in labor disputes would be abolished. Prompt ratification of the Child Labor Amendment was urged. The platform went on record in favor of the " soldiers' bonus " and increased salaries for postal employees.

In a mood reminiscent of the vibrant democratic faith of other, earlier liberal movements, the Progressives enthusiastically pledged such implementations of the principle of popular sovereignty as the direct election of the President, use of the initiative and referendum, and a popular referendum in the event of war, except in case of actual invasion.

Its plank on foreign affairs came tagging along at the end, like some half-forgotten afterthought. With an ambiguous indefiniteness, the platform called for "revision of the Versailles Treaty," along with the abolition of conscription and reduction of armaments.

Several comments on this platform may be made. First, it is worth noting the almost nostalgic call to do battle against "special privilege" and monopoly. Almost pathetically, the platform states that "monopoly has steadily extended its absolute dominion to every basic industry." Did these leaders of the Progressives—LaFollette in particular—have any feeling that they were much like Canute seeking to hold back the tide? If they were aware of any such inevitable trend of concentration in American business, there is no indication in the platform. Undoubtedly, the Socialists within the Progressive ranks recognised this fact far better than most of the leaders of the party.

The unusually long appeal to the American farmer is also worthy of note. No similar appeal was made to any other group. Like the attack upon the privileged and monopolistic groups, the section devoted to the farmer is another evidence of the indigenous nature of the progressive movement. There might be Amalgamated Union men within the ranks; there might be editorial support from the New York parlor pinks, but, basically, the movement was stemming from the West. There was something of the frontier about it. If true individualism had been exalted at all in 1924, it certainly did not occur in the steam-rollered Republican convention nor in the shameful spectacle at Madison Square Garden. These men of the CPPA had a deep and abiding faith in the omniscience of popular sovereignty. More than political buncombe accounts for the reference to Jefferson in the Progressive platform.

Like the major parties—but to a lesser degree—the Progressives were not without their dilemmas in resolving some of the intra-party dissension regarding parts of the platform. The discussion with reference to the formation of a new party we shall reserve for another chapter.[3] But occasionally even the

3 See pp. 197-205.

platform reveals a concession made, a balance struck. The moderates hesitated on going along with the Socialists on public railroad ownership. The Socialists had their way but at a price. They had to agree to the insertion of a clause assuring that the government ownership would have " definite safeguards against bureaucratic control." It is amusing to perceive this similarity between the language of the Progressives of '24 and of critics of the New Deal in 1944, perturbed by the growth of bureaucracy.

Foreign affairs, especially the question of international cooperation, presented a problem to the Progressives. Within the progressive movement were large numbers of Northwestern isolationists skeptical of proposed international organization. On the other hand, the Eastern intellectuals, magazine support like the *New Republic,* and large segments of labor were distinctly pro-League. The latter were headed by William H. Johnston, who wanted the CPPA to go on record in favor of the League of Nations. Henrik Shipstead was generally conceded to be the leader of the anti-League, isolationist forces.[4] Tactfully, no mention of the League was made although the strong language used in calling for a revision of the Versailles Treaty was, in effect, a condemnation of the League which had been created at Versailles.[5] The preoccupation of the American public with domestic issues in 1924 prevented much active discussion of this problem although Oswald Garrison Villard kept pressing LaFollette to speak out more strongly on foreign affairs and against war.[6] Any evasion of the issue by the Progressive platform-makers might be partially condoned in view of the cowardice displayed by the Democrats in avoiding a commitment and the callous attitude of the Republicans in re-

4 *Nation,* 119:3083, Aug. 6, 1924, p. 143.

5 See *Proceedings,* CPPA Convention, July 4-5, 1924, (M. G. Johnston papers).

6 O. G. Villard to R. M. LaFollette, Sept. 13, 1924 and Sept. 25, 1924, (Villard papers).

fusing to accept "any obligations under the covenant of the League."

Like both old parties, the Progressives were silent on the Klan. Perhaps, as some of the Progressives pointed out, they were justified in ignoring it because—unlike the major parties —the Klan was without representation within its ranks. The Klan was the exclusive headache, perhaps, of the old parties. In any event, the whole issue was completely clarified by La-Follette's courageous letter to Scripps on August 8 in which he unqualifiedly denounced the Klan and all it stood for.[7] The LaFollette letter to Scripps accomplished more than the mere clarification of progressive feeling. It smoked out both the Democrats and Republicans who had, with amazing political agility, avoided any direct reference or offense to the Klan up until this time. Within a few weeks both John W. Davis and Charles G. Dawes followed LaFollette in direct and uncomplimentary references to the Klan. Throughout the entire campaign, Calvin Coolidge, of course, remained too overwhelmed by the pressure of business in the Executive Office to get an opportunity to mention the Klan by name.[8]

It is evident that the Progressive strategy was to make monopoly the great issue of the campaign. That the strategy failed may be ascribed either to the indifference of the American public to a live issue or to the effectiveness of the Republican counter-propaganda, which utilised to the fullest extent the inner fears of many good Americans that Bolshevism was waiting to take over. In either case, it must be admitted that the Progressives had neither the time to educate the American electorate sufficiently to the dangers of monopoly nor the organization with which to promote the LaFollette campaign. If the strategy ("monopoly is the supreme issue") was wrong, what alternative was there? Mr. Basil Manly, Washington director

7 *New York Times,* Aug. 9, 1924.

8 See pp. 214-217 for a discussion of the Ku Klux Klan as a campaign factor.

of the Progressive campaign, in looking back, has suggested an alternative.[9] At the beginning of the campaign, Mr. Manly wanted the Progressives to concentrate on one issue—" thou shalt not steal." That might have forced the Republicans onto the defensive. A further virtue of such a campaign would have been that such a simple issue, involving little more than the question of moral behaviour, would have been comprehended better than all the intricacies of monopolistic practice. Without the benefit of much schooling in economics, the average American in 1924 was unable to share the Progressives' disquietude over the appearance of Big Business. Not understanding their apprehensions, he came to view the Progressives with suspicion. Their cries of monopoly perhaps concealed a plan to wreck American enterprise.

The early days of the 1924 campaign augured well for the new movement. In spite of the Herculean tasks ahead, the enthusiasm around headquarters was a sufficicent tonic to buoy up the hopes and expectations of the staff. The rather inchoate and heterogeneous group which had gathered at Cleveland on July 4 was beginning to show signs of organization and planning. Out of several Washington conferences among the Progressive leaders emerged a compact yet representative Joint Executive Committee whose responsibility it would be to guide and direct the campaign.[10]

The dependence of the progressive movement upon three main groups—farmers, Railroad Brotherhood and Socialists—was accentuated by this selection. Congressman Nelson, young Bob LaFollette and Senator Frazier were, of course, first and foremost, Northwesterners. Robertson, Wills and Keating were

9 Basil Manly to the author, June 16, 1943.

10 The members of the Joint Executive Committee were as follows: John M. Nelson, Wisconsin, Chairman; Robert M. LaFollette, Jr., Wisconsin, Vice Chairman; Mrs. Edward P. Costigan, Washington, D. C., Secretary; Lynn J. Frazier, North Dakota; Morris Hillquit, New York; William H. Johnston, Washington, D. C.; Basil M. Manly, Washington, D. C.; D. B. Robertson, Ohio; Rudolf Spreckles, California; Edward Keating, Washington, D. C.; Herman E. Wills, Washington, D. C.

from the Brotherhood, the latter, as editor of *Labor,* in an unusually advantageous position to publicize the campaign. Morris Hillquit represented the Socialists. Later Norman Thomas of New York was added to reinforce the movement in New York where he was running for Governor on the Socialist and Progressive tickets. Her intimate association with the liberal movement in Colorado, her husband's record of progressivism in the Senate, and her gifted ability as a women's leader, all justified Mrs. Costigan's appointment. Mr. Spreckles' financial and newspaper influence on the Coast made him a logical representative in the Far West. Mr. Johnston's tireless efforts to organize a third party and his position as president of the Machinists assured him, of course, a place on the Joint Executive Committee.

The influence of LaFollette and the Northwest was further demonstrated by the organization established to direct the campaign. Headquarters were opened in both Chicago and Washington, with no clear definition or demarcation of authority. But Westerners were in charge in both places—Mr. John M. Nelson having charge in Chicago and Mr. Basil Manly, a resident of Illinois, in Washington. Mr. Manly was director of the People's Legislative Service in Washington. Mr. Gilbert Roe, long-time law partner of Senator LaFollette, was made director of New York headquarters. In general, the efforts of Chicago were directed toward the farmers of the Northwest. Washington headquarters took care of developments in the Capital and, in New York, the New England and Middle Atlantic plans were formulated.

With practically no cash on hand and little prospect of much unless the union members responded, Darwin Meserole of New York was chosen for the difficult and thankless job of Chairman of the Finance Committee. Plans for fund raising, chiefly through the already-established channels of the Brotherhood unions, and by direct appeal to the public, were immediately devised.

One of the first developments of the 1924 campaign was the official endorsement which the American Federation of Labor, in early August, bestowed upon LaFollette and Wheeler. Inasmuch as this unprecedented action revised campaign plans even before they were put into effect, it would be well to glance at the role Labor was playing in 1924. Chagrined by its postwar legislative and judicial reverses, rebuffed again and again by old-party politicians, the American Federation of Labor was finally prodded, by a series of political disappointments, into supporting the Progressive ticket.

Cheered by the victories of 1922 and by the prospects of a political alliance with rebellious farm groups, labor leaders in 1924 plotted their political strategy. True to its policy of non-partisan political action, the American Federation of Labor proposed to present its demands before all the political parties and await results. To provide the machinery for this strategy, the Executive Council of the AFL, before the conventions had been held, assigned to the American Federation of Labor Non-Partisan Campaign Committee the task of formulating a brief statement of AFL political aims and presenting it to the political parties. This "Non-Partisan Political Campaign Committee" consisted of Samuel Gompers, Frank Morrison, James O'Connell and Matthew Woll.[11] Of course, this plan in no way deviated from the traditional Gompers-AFL program of non-partisan action. But the plan does suggest that the hope of the capture of one of the old parties still survived, for Labor's confidence in William G. McAdoo, already noted, persisted in spite of the oil disclosures and the emotional stress of the Democratic convention. Paradoxically, Labor was almost as trusting in Alfred E. Smith, McAdoo's adversary in the convention. His labor record in New York State was quite as inspiring as McAdoo's in Washington. Perhaps this persistent hope of successful co-operation with the Democrats, dashed by the disappointments of Madison Square Garden, was instrumental

11 *American Federationist*, 31 :7, July, 1924, pp. 554-555.

in forcing an endorsement of LaFollette as Labor began to understand how completely it had been ignored.

Dutifully the AFL Non-Partisan Committee presented its statement to the Resolutions committees of the major parties. It was presented, in the case of the CPPA, to the committee in charge of selecting a vice-presidential candidate.[12]

The demands incorporated in the statement sound quite mild today.[13] In general, they formed a presentation of the political goals toward which the American labor movement had been working for years. They were fairly definite, but hardly radical. It was obvious, of course, that the Republican party could not endorse them; but they were sufficiently innocuous for the Democratic party to have accepted without adding to party disunity.

The demands of the AFL included restriction of the use of injunctions in labor disputes, ratification of the Child Labor Amendment, repeal of the anti-trust laws detrimental to labor unions, more comprehensive workmen's compensation laws, membership in the League of Nations and the World Court, a constitutional amendment empowering Congress to re-enact by a two-thirds vote any measure declared unconstitutional by the Supreme Court, and the recognition of the right "to bargain collectively" through a union and representatives freely chosen, to work and to cease work collectively, and collectively to withhold or bestow patronage.

The labor leaders had no illusions about convincing the Republicans so the presentation of the statement at Cleveland in June was merely a formality. But the high expectations of winning Democratic support began to flicker out as the Democrats turned their backs on Labor's demands and Labor's candidates. After the Democrats had ignored his published entreaties, Samuel Gompers, ill at the Lenox Hill Hospital in New York, began to realize the hopelessness of the situation. A measure

12 *Ibid.*

13 *Ibid.*

of Gompers' personal reluctance to depart from the non-partisan tradition can be gained by his remark after the Madison Square Garden delegates had rejected a pro-labor platform plank. " It looks as if we are forced to turn to LaFollette," he said sadly.[14] After the nomination of the unacceptable John W. Davis, Gompers reiterated this curiously negative reaction. " There is no other way," he commented.[15] Preoccupied with his illness, an illness that was to prove fatal before the year was out, and saddened and disappointed by the behaviour of the Democrats, Sam Gompers was unable to devote to the campaign the personal attention that might have been infectious enough to arouse enthusiasm for the Progressive cause during the campaign. As it turned out, the sick and preoccupied Gompers almost embodied the defects of the AFL campaign to elect LaFollette and Wheeler.

Rebuffed by the Republicans and ignored and disappointed by the Democrats, the American Federation of Labor, for the first time in its history, abandoned its traditional non-partisan activity during a presidential election to endorse LaFollette and Wheeler. The report incorporating this change of policy— temporary as it was to be—was submitted by the AFL Non-Partisan Committee to the Executive Council of the Federation on August 2, 1924, at Atlantic City.[16]

The report explained at length the reasons for the action: [17]

> The Republican convention nominated candidates unacceptable to labor . . . The Democratic convention nominated candidates unacceptable to labor . . . There remain the candidacies of Robert M. LaFollette and Burton K. Wheeler, the first an independent Republican, the second an independent Democrat running as such . . .

14 Thorne, F., Epilogue, " His Last Year," in Gompers, S., *Seventy Years of Life and Labor,* Vol. II, p. 537.

15 *Ibid.*

16 *American Federationist,* 31 :9, Sept. 1924, p. 708.

17 *Ibid.*

. . . . Co-operation hereby urged is not a pledge of identification with an independent party movement or a third party, nor can it be construed as support for such a party, group, or movement except as such action accords with our nonpartisan political policy. We do not accept government as the solution of the problems of life. Major problems of life and labor must be dealt with by voluntary groups and organizations of which trade unions are an essential and integral part. Neither can this co-operation imply our support, acceptance or endorsement of policies or principles advocated by any minority groups or organizations that may see fit to support the candidacies of Senator LaFollette and Senator Wheeler.

The report was not entirely negative. LaFollette and Wheeler were commended and approved for having " throughout their whole political careers, stood steadfast in defense of the rights and interests of wage earners and farmers." Their platform met the economic issues of the day " in a manner more nearly conforming to Labor's proposals than any other platform."

The nervous-Nellie attitude displayed by the AFL when it finally made the great decision to support LaFollette and Wheeler can not be fully understood without an appreciation of Gompers' faith in non-partisan activity coupled with his repugnance for any American labor party and his suspicious attitude toward the Socialists. In his autobiography, Gompers comments on the " philosophic and economic short-comings " of socialism and wonders if it—Socialism—has not been manipulated by " sinister influences." [18] Twelve times in its history, starting back in 1885, the American Federation of Labor has refused to entertain resolutions in favor of a third party. In 1923, a motion favoring the formation of a labor political party was overwhelmingly defeated after a short debate.[19] Pamphlet after pamphlet came off the AFL presses during the presidency of

18 Gompers, S., op. cit., Vol. II, pp. 378-380.

19 Proceedings, 43rd Annual Convention, AFL., held at Portland, Oregon, Oct. 1-12, 1923, pp. 284-285.

Sam Gompers justifying the policy of " voluntarism " and non-partisan activity. The members in the American Federation of Labor were admonished, by paper and pamphlet, to " stand faithfully by our friends and elect them. Oppose our enemies and defeat them whether they be candidates for Congress or other offices; whether executive, legislative or judicial." [20]

The wording of the endorsement made by the American Federation of Labor on August 2, 1924, must be noticed to understand fully what stand the organization was taking. La-Follette and Wheeler were endorsed as *independent* candidates for the offices of President and Vice-President, respectively. There was no commitment whatever to the Progressives or to any third party and, further, no promise of future co-operation or commitment. In fact, the AFL seemed to find comfort in LaFollette's and Wheeler's affiliations with the old parties. LaFollette, to the AFL, was " an independent Republican " and Wheeler " an independent Democrat." It is almost as though the magic words " Republican " and " Democrat " lent respectability to the Progressive candidates! The false statement that the American Federation of Labor endorsed the Progressive party in 1924 is a recurrent error in histories of the 'Twenties. To begin with, there was no Progressive party to join or support. In the second place, the American Federation would never have endorsed it. It did not support the progressive movement. It merely supported the personal candidacies of LaFollette and Wheeler.

Gompers must have feared that, after the vacillations and reservations in the report endorsing LaFollette and Wheeler, there might still be someone within the AFL rash and reckless enough to promote a third party or possibly apply for membership in the Socialist party. To forestall such a possibility, President Gompers devoted his editorial in the September

20 See *AFL pamphlets,* " Should a Political Labor Party Be Formed? ", an address by Samuel Gompers, New York, Dec. 9, 1918, " Non-Partisan Successes," et al., AFL Library, Washington, D. C.

Federationist to a further dissertation on what the AFL endorsement did not mean.

" I want to emphasize the fact," he wrote, " that our support of Senator LaFollette does not in any way, or to any degree, identify us with or commit us to doctrines advanced by any other group that may be supporting the same candidates. These candidates have the support of minority groups, in themselves of no great importance, but with which we are and have been in the sharpest kind of disagreement. We shall continue to oppose those doctrines at all times. . . . "[21]

Some members of the American Federation of Labor must have been confused and bewildered after perusing that September, 1924, issue of the *Federationist!* Some, indeed, must have resolved at once to vote for Coolidge rather than to comfort, in any possible manner, the anonymous and sinister " minority groups " to whose doctrines Gompers was pledging unalterable opposition!

But, in spite of the hedging, the AFL endorsement of La-Follette and Wheeler represented a substantial initial victory for the Progressives. Although far below its top membership figure of four million (in 1920), the Federation still constituted an organization of 2,865,979 workers with paid-up dues.[22] If they, and their families, supported LaFollette—and the old parties had no way of knowing that they would not—Labor could swing the election. After all, was not a Labor government in power in England? Without doubt, the AFL action quickened—and possibly revised—political strategy within the old parties and heartened immeasurably the Progressives as they prepared for the campaign. The skies looked blue to the Progressives in August, 1924.

In one sense, the campaign was opened when Senator La-Follette—breaking the precedent long before Franklin Roosevelt flew to Chicago in 1932 to accept the nomination—notified

21 *American Federationist,* 31 :9, Sept. 1924, p. 742.

22 *American Labor Year Book,* 1925, p. 50.

the CPPA immediately that he would run for the presidency. But the formalities of a campaign have to be observed, and it was not until mid-August that Mr. Davis and Mr. Coolidge were formally notified of their nominations. On August 11, amid his boyhood surroundings at Clarksburg, West Virginia, Mr. Davis accepted the Democratic nomination. The unprecedented downpour which accompanied his speech was a portent of Democratic fortune in November. Three days later, in a much drier atmosphere, Calvin Coolidge accepted the Republican nomination in Memorial Hall, Washington. The LaFollette campaign began in earnest on Labor Day when the Senator, after arrangements had been made, broadcast on a nation-wide hook-up, perhaps the first political speech so delivered in American history. Senator LaFollette, Junior, who was in charge of the arrangements with the radio stations, recalls the troubles encountered, in view of the technical obstacles, in obtaining a national broadcast and further recollects a sense of futility that there were not enough receiving sets in America to justify the expense incurred! [23]

The campaign for the Progressives was slow in getting under way. John W. Davis had delivered a host of speeches before Senator LaFollette launched his campaign. Offices had to be rented; plans had to be made; strategy had to be formulated. In spite of all that, LaFollette might have been expected to begin his speech-making campaign before the 6th of October. For anyone acquainted with " Fighting " Bob's love of battle, some explanation has to be sought. On the day that LaFollette began his campaign—October 6—a *Herald-Tribune* correspondent wrote from Washington that LaFollette headquarters were not concealing the fact that the delay had been caused by lack of funds.[24] According to this source, the financial efforts of the Progressives had been such a dismal failure that there

23 R. M. LaFollette, Jr., to the author, June 17, 1943.
24 *New York Herald Tribune,* Oct. 6, 1924.

were insufficient funds to carry the candidate's train beyond St. Louis. Hence, at the outset of the campaign, the dismal threat of financial exhaustion hung like the sword of Damocles.[25] Nothing was better calculated to dampen enthusiasm for the cause. Another possible contributing factor in the delay might have been Senator LaFollette's health. The elderly Progressive leader had just recovered from a protracted illness. As we have seen, his heart was not in perfect condition. Before the campaign began, Carter Field was wondering how much effect the consequences of his illness would have upon Senator LaFollette's campaign.[26] According to Field, LaFollette had not fully recovered from his illness; most certainly he was not the old-time LaFollette, fountainhead of tireless energy and ceaseless campaigning. It is possible that his speaking schedule was curtailed on account of the fear that his heart would be unable to stand the strain.[27] It is possible that a projected tour which would have taken LaFollette to the west coast was called off because it was felt that the trip over the Rockies would be too great a demand upon his heart. Perhaps the announcement by Progressive headquarters that LaFollette, cheered by reports, had changed his itinerary and was going to come east instead of continuing to the Pacific Coast concealed the true reason for the change. If so, Robert LaFollette, Jr. does not recall. He remembers his father standing up well under the strain and recollects no revisions or curtailments caused by his father's health.[28]

The LaFollette campaign itinerary divided into three trips: the first journey launching the campaign with speeches in the

25 In conversations with the author, many persons associated with the LaFollette campaign, such as O. G. Villard, Basil Manly and Mrs. Gilbert Roe, have verified this statement.

26 *New York Herald Tribune,* Aug. 10, 1924.

27 Raney, W. F., *Wisconsin, A Story of Progress,* p. 303.

28 R. M. LaFollette, Jr., to the author, June 17, 1943.

East; the second, a trip through the Mid-West and, finally, a return " invasion " of the East.[29]

Starting from Washington, LaFollette travelled to Rochester to open his campaign on October 6. At Rochester he pointed to the Republican graft and promised a thorough house-cleaning. In promising reform, he endorsed the domestic part of the P·ogressive platform. It was not an auspicious occasion. The crowd was neither very large nor very enthusiastic.[30] At Scranton, the next evening, LaFollette found, among the miners, the kind of whole-hearted campaign support that he needed. At Scranton, the speech was largely devoted to an attack on the " slush fund " financing of the Republicans. At Newark, as he completed his first eastern tour, LaFollette attacked monopoly and " Big Business."

The great swing around the Mid-West started as LaFollette returned from the East and stopped over in Detroit and Cincinnati to deliver speeches. No doubt mindful of Cincinnati's racial composition, the Senator devoted his talk to war and imperialism, reaffirming before a crowd that must have included hundreds of first-generation Germans, his war-time views. Of his ten speeches in the Mid-West, four dealt with problems whose major theme was the farmer's plight. At Kansas City, LaFollette criticised the Administration's farm policy; at Des Moines, he criticised the " anti-farm " policies of the Federal Reserve System. At Sioux Falls and Omaha, the railroads and middlemen were denounced for stealing from the farmer.

29 The LaFollette itinerary was as follows:

Oct. 6—Rochester, N. Y.	17—Sioux Falls, So. Dak.
7—Scranton, Penna.	20—Omaha, Nebr.
8—Newark, N. J.	21—Rock Island, Ill.
9—Detroit, Mich.	22—Peoria, Ill.
10—Cincinnati, Ohio	23—Syracuse, N. Y.
11—Chicago, Ill.	27—Baltimore, Md.
13—Kansas City, Mo.	28—Brooklyn, N. Y.
14—St. Louis, Mo.	29—Schenectady, N. Y.
15—Des Moines, Ia.	30—Boston, Mass.
16—Minneapolis, Minn.	Nov. 1—Cleveland, Ohio.

30 *New York Times,* Oct. 7, 1924.

The final phase of the Progressive campaign began on October 23 when LaFollette " reinvaded " the East for five speaking engagements. The most important of these were delivered at Baltimore, where LaFollette raked the Republican tariff; and Brooklyn, where the Eastern tour was completed with an attack upon the forces of imperialism and Republican mesalliance with international finance. Back in Cleveland, the city of Peter Witt, the Railroad Brotherhoods and progressive traditions, where the CPPA had held its convention, LaFollette gave his final address of the campaign.

It is significant, in analyzing the LaFollette campaign strategy, to note that, of the twenty major speeches delivered by LaFollette during the campaign, four were almost entirely devoted to LaFollette's favorite theme—that monopoly was the supreme issue.[31] Every one of the twenty contained some references to this menace to America. Just as " monopoly as the supreme issue " had been trumpeted by the Progressive platform, so LaFollette continued to stress its importance through the campaign.

Adjusting their campaign methods to Calvin Coolidge's temperament and personality, the Republicans decided to use Dawes for the swings around the circuit. This served a double purpose. Dawes, with his picturesque—and perhaps carefully nurtured—mannerisms and vigorous language, could meet Davis and LaFollette in rough-and-tumble campaigning. Moreover, by letting Dawes do the work, the Republican managers heightened the effect of Calvin Coolidge earnestly attending to the pressing business of the nation while his more irresponsible and less sober-minded contemporaries engaged in the banalities of campaigning. Coolidge, with this initial psychological advantage, did not have to deliver many speeches. Only as some state occasion warranted, did Calvin Coolidge speak. The occasion itself lent prestige to the speech. On September 24, at Philadelphia, Coolidge spoke, as President of the United States,

31 The speeches at Newark, Chicago, Brooklyn and Cleveland.

upon the observance of the 150th anniversary of the First Continental Congress.[32] By happy coincidence, Coolidge's attack that evening upon those who would undermine the Constitution seemed to corroborate the charges which the Republican high command had been making against LaFollette. When, two weeks before election, the President of the United States graciously spoke before the United States Chamber of Commerce, he was attending to his business as Chief Executive and standard-bearer for his party, both at once. Subscribing to this kind of campaign behaviour gave the Coolidge campaign an effortless grace and unchallengeable dignity. The burden of proof was on Davis and LaFollette. Yet, the more they attempted, through their campaigning, to submit proof of Republican unfitness, the more they heightened the contrast between their political activities and Calvin Coolidge's attention to duty. It was the perfect campaign pose for the " strong, silent man " in the White House.

General Dawes, who willingly bore the brunt of the task of campaigning for the Republicans, welcomed the opportunity to challenge LaFollette on the issue of monopoly. To begin with, it probably diverted public interest from the scandals of the Harding Administration. More than that, Dawes sensed an opportunity to use a political weapon against the Progressives. Dawes seized upon what he considered to be the most vulnerable part of the Progressive creed—the suggestion for curbing the Supreme Court.

In Dawes' own words, " In my speech of acceptance I announced the constitutional issue precipitated by Senator LaFollette as the dominant one. Chairman Butler was adverse to this course, feeling that the issue of economy should be the one to be stressed. I sent my speech before delivery to President Coolidge, who returned it without suggestion as to change, except that he substituted " an important issue " for " the predominant issue " as a caption to that portion of my address

32 *New York Times,* Sept. 25, 1924.

devoted to the LaFollette position on the Constitution. From the time of delivery of the acceptance speech ... until the end of the campaign, during which I travelled fifteen thousand miles in a special train and made one hundred and eight speeches, I endeavored to keep that issue in the minds of the people." [33] Dawes became so completely the spearhead for the Republican campaign strategy, that sometimes it appeared that LaFollette, Davis and Dawes were the respective presidential candidates. There is no evidence that General Dawes did not relish his uniquely prominent position. Becoming accustomed to the headlines during the campaign, General Dawes did not relinquish them even on Inauguration Day in 1925, when his speech attacking Senate rules attracted more attention than President Coolidge's platitudes about the virtues of American commerce.

33 Dawes, C. G., *Notes As Vice President*, pp. 19-20.

CHAPTER VIII
REPUBLICAN STRATEGY
TAKES COMMAND

THE Republicans did not fail to capitalize upon LaFollette's record of opposition to American participation in the war and his outspoken and repeated reflections upon the motives of imperialists and " Big Business " during the war days. There was wide distribution of Roosevelt's wartime statement about LaFollette. " He (LaFollette) is showing himself the worst enemy Democracy now has alive, and if I were at this minute a member of the United States Senate, I would be ashamed to sit in that body until I found some method of depriving him of his seat in that chamber which he now disgraces by his presence there." This remark was included in a printed pamphlet reflecting upon La Follette's patriotism.[1] Handford Mac-Nider, prominent member of the American Legion, headed a special " Republican Service League " to " scotch LaFollett-ism." These vigilant protectors of the Constitution, complete with ladies' auxiliary, called upon the men who had offered their lives for their country in 1917 and 1918, to rally again to the defense of " their native land." [2] The convention of the 35th Division Association condemned LaFollette's candidacy because " six years ago, LaFollette was an enemy to the country, a foe of the army and navy." [3] The stories about LaFollette's lack of loyalty were so disquieting to many of his lieutenants that they continued to suggest instituting libel suits. The Steuben Society, embittered by some of the aspersions cast upon LaFollette's wartime speeches, complained after the election that " all the old machinery of the notorious Creel Information Bureau was dragged out of its obscurity and set up

1 Leaflet among collection in Frank P. Walsh papers.

2 *New York Herald Tribune*, Oct. 9, 1924.

3 *New York Times*, Sept. 24, 1924.

anew to belch forth an avalanche of vituperation and mendacity about the Progressive cause and its candidate." [4]

But attacking LaFollette's war record was not a guarantee of political success. The risk of alienating German voters was always involved; and, moreover, the war was six years distant and apathy, if not disillusionment, was already the attitude of many Americans toward the great crusade. Bolshevism, in 1924, was much more alive than the issues of the Great War, and so the inevitable charge of world revolution was brought against the Progressives. Moreover, a campaign against Russian Bolshevism would be doubly effective. It would serve to discredit LaFollette and, at the same time, frighten rich Republicans into contributing to what might otherwise be a lethargic campaign. The party leaders must have had in mind Oscar Ameringer's remark that it is the business of the old party politician to get campaign contributions from the rich and votes from the poor on the grounds that he will protect one from the other.

While various veterans' organizations sought to stem the tide of un-Americanism by passing resolutions condemning the effrontery of a man who aspired to be President of the United States after refusing to make the world safe for democracy, nervous patriots became haunted by weird dreams of the Kremlin and by ugly visions of world revolution spreading out from Madison, Wisconsin. Perhaps the neatest trick of the campaign was the Republican success in tagging LaFollette as a radical. Of course, the Supreme Court issue, more than anything else, was responsible for the ease with which the Republicans convinced a large segment of the American voting population of the imminent danger to the Constitution. Not even the Liberty Bell emblem and the generous display of American flags at CPPA meetings could offset the damage when General Dawes began to discern in the Progressive movement, as early

4 Steuben Society of America, New York, N. Y., " The Republican Victory Analyzed," *pamphlet*, Nov. 15, 1924, p. 2.

as August, " a heterogeneous collection of those opposed to the existing order of things, the greatest section of which, the Socialists, flies the Red Flag." [5] The Democrats could but helplessly deny the implication when Dawes referred scornfully to their party as lying between the two great armies, one of radicalism, the other of " progressive conservatism." [6] The Democrats were being crowded into the class of non-essential neutrals in this Armageddon which was to determine the fate of the Star-Spangled Banner!

The charge that Russian money was supporting LaFollette was occasionally made, although rarely by those responsible for the conduct of the Republican campaign. Dawes never made the charge directly, although his speeches were usually replete with innuendoes. More irresponsible leaders, like T. V. O'Connor of Buffalo, often professed to see a direct link between Moscow and Progressive headquarters. In the middle of the campaign, O'Connor made the sensational charge that Russian money, coming by way of Mexico, was being used to finance the La-Follette campaign. " How much money has been sent here by Soviet Russia to win this fight? " asked O'Connor without providing any sort of answer.[7] Misleading inferential questions of this type were a favorite device employed by the anti-LaFollette forces. Congressman Lineberger of California " discovered " that the twenty-five cents charged as admission to LaFollette-Wheeler meetings was a crafty camouflage to conceal the Soviet slush funds which financed the Progressives.[8] Over the signature of its president, Mr. E. Bliss, the Regal Shoe Company employed its half-page advertisement in the metropolitan press on October 25, 1924, to reveal the extent of Soviet penetration:

5 *New York Times,* Aug. 20, 1924.

6 See *New York Times,* Sept. 20, 1924, for account of Dawes' speech on " radicalism."

7 *Washington Post,* Oct. 16, 1924.

8 H. M. Harden to J. M. Nelson, Oct. 16, 1924, (Walsh papers).

"I like Silence and Success better than Socialism and Sovietism. Brains mean more to Business than a Brainstorm. They produce results without making so much noise."

"I prefer Coolidge to Chaos, and according to the present political situation, there isn't any other choice in this election."

The threat to American institutions brought a quick response from a DuPont of Delaware. General Coleman DuPont, the former United States Senator, in an interview, denounced the slackers who would stay away from the polls in such a crisis, failing to see in the possibility of a LaFollette victory "an opening wedge, a beginning to tear down our Constitution."[9]

Cyrus Curtis, whose ancient dislike for LaFollette had ripened into passionate hatred, was the publisher of the Philadelphia morning and evening *Public Ledger,* the *New York Evening Post,* the *Saturday Evening Post,* the *Country Gentleman* and the *Ladies Home Journal.* All of these publications became vehicles for Republican strategy, especially the *Saturday Evening Post* and the *Country Gentleman.* Although credited with only a $1000 contribution to the Republicans, Mr. Curtis may have spent hundreds of thousands of dollars in advertisements of a political character aimed at LaFollette. For instance, on August 28, 1924, the *Country Gentleman* ran a full page in daily newspapers in practically every large city in the nation, entitled "How Would Government Ownership of Railroads Affect Business?" This (which had been an editorial in the *Country Gentleman*) was also published on the back of a menu card for the Pennsylvania Railroad. General Atterbury, President of the Railroad, stated that it reached 30,000 patrons daily.[10]

The Curtis charges against LaFollette became most extreme in an article which appeared in the heat of the campaign. This article, "Let X = LaFollette," prepared by Samuel G. Blythe, veteran Curtis political correspondent, was publicized by a

9 *New York Times,* Oct. 21, 1924.
10 Memo on Cyrus Curtis, (Walsh papers).

nation-wide advertising campaign asking Americans to make
sure to read the *Post* article. When the story appeared, on
October 18, 1924, the reader soon realized that Mr. Blythe and
the *Post* strongly suspected that X stood for Communism. To
faithful readers of the *Saturday Evening Post,* it might have
come as conclusive evidence of LaFollette's Moscow connections, the language being so strong and convincing. In part,
it stated: [11]

> Recent surveys of the activities of the Reds in this coun-
> try show that however much Senator LaFollette may deny
> his association with men of this type, he seems powerless to
> prevent their association with him. Numerous of the leading
> members of the Workers' Party, which is the William Z. Fos-
> ter party, are now actively canvassing for LaFollette.
>
> In any event, his motley collection of Socialists, Reds,
> committees, blocs, half-baked parties, combined with the dis-
> satisfied Republicans and Democrats, is in a position to work
> havoc with the chances of President Coolidge and Mr. Davis,
> with our two-party system, with our economic situation, with
> our American theory and practice of government and, ulti-
> mately, with our Constitution.

The same article called LaFollette the candidate of the " Reds,
the Pinks, the Blues and the Yellows."

As the campaign reached its final stages, the Republican
press became more reckless in its charges of an alleged Soviet-
Progressive united front. When the *Cincinnati Enquirer* discovered that 213 college professors had indicated their support
of LaFollette, it called editorially for the discharge of these
teachers " attached to recognised heresies." It added that the
country and the government would be safer " if they are
relieved from all duties as instructors of the youth of the
nation." [12] With eloquent rhetoric, the *Herald-Tribune* was

11 *Saturday Evening Post,* Oct. 18, 1924, p. 193.
12 *Cincinnati Enquirer,* Nov. 15, 1924.

asking, as the election drew near, " shall the Eagle's eye be dimmed? Shall its nest be turned into a laboratory for mad experiment? " [13] At the same time, out in Illinois, Mr. Dawes was bringing the campaign to a climactic finish by conjuring up the spirits of '61 (Dawes reminded his audience that his father had been one of the men in blue) once more to preserve the Union.[14] Apparently Dawes had given up hope of carrying the solid South!

The complicated nature of our cumbersome machinery for electing a President presents the old parties with an issue to use against any third party which appears in the field against them. The bogey of a " deadlocked " electoral college—with considerable justification—can always be raised. That this was especially true in 1924 was in part due to the infelicitous choice of a vice-presidential candidate made by the Democrats. Charles Bryan, in the eyes of most Easterners and all conservatives, represented all the sinister implications of " Bryanism " without his brother's redeeming qualities of political experience and stature. And still the possibility existed that he would become Chief Executive of the United States if enough votes were cast for the third party to deadlock the Electoral College. This, according to the Constitution, would throw the election into the House of Representatives.[15] But the Progressive bloc would prevent either Coolidge or Davis securing the majority necessary for election. Then the Senate—with Progressives and Democrats voting for Bryan—would choose the Vice President, who would automatically succeed to the Presidency, no President having been elected.[16] On paper, such a contingency

13 *New York Herald Tribune,* Oct. 26, 1924.

14 *New York Times,* Nov. 1, 1924.

15 Article XII, Federal Constitution.

16 " And if the House of Representatives shall not choose a President whenever the right of choice shall devolve upon them, before the fourth day of March next following, then the Vice President shall act as President, as in the case of the death, or other constitutional disability of the President." —from Art. XII, Federal Constitution.

did not seem unlikely. After all, according to the leading straw polls, LaFollette appeared to have enough strength to " throw the election " into the House. In the lame-duck House, with the unit rule observed in presidential balloting, the Progressives would be in a position to prevent election of Coolidge or Dawes if they wished to risk the consequences of adverse public judgment. And it was possible—just possible—that the Progressives and Democrats would join in the Senate to vote for Bryan rather than for Dawes.[17] With more ardent optimism than good political judgment, some Progressives unintentionally aroused misapprehensions by reckless predictions that the election would be thrown into Congress.[18]

Of course, the most effective way for a conservative Democrat to prevent the bleak eventuality of Bryan in the White House, as Mark Sullivan was eager to point out, was to vote for Coolidge. It became a case of " Coolidge or Chaos," both Bryan and the manner of electing him being synonymous with chaos.[19] Reputable members of Mr. Coolidge's official family— especially those with legal and constitutional knowledge— explained apprehensively to the American electorate the tortuous and sinister route by which Bryan might become President. Attorney General Stone, already highly esteemed as a valuable member of the Cabinet, soon to be appointed to the Supreme Court, emphasized the danger of electing Bryan in his speeches on behalf of Coolidge. The Secretary of War, Mr. John W. Weeks, concluded his campaign radio address—an expensive novelty in those days—by warning the voters not to throw the election into Congress, electing a man " for whom you would not vote as a Democratic nominee for the Presidency." [20] A

17 See Merz, C., " If the Election Is Deadlocked," *New York World*, Oct. 5, 1924.

18 e.g., Gilson Gardner's article, " Our Next President," *Nation*, 119:3087, Sept. 17, 1924.

19 George Harvey coined the expression, " Coolidge or Chaos," in an editorial in the *North American Review*, 220:824, Sept., 1924.

20 *New York Times*, Oct. 22, 1924.

bankers' committee in New York sought to inform the electorate of the dire consequences—the election of Bryan—of a deadlocked Electoral College. To assist in preventing this, bankers and their friends were urged to contribute to the Coolidge campaign chest. This appeal was made on the letterhead of a prominent New York bank.[21]

It is interesting to note that in all this clamor over the possibility that Bryan might become President, no constructive suggestion was advanced to revise or amend the electoral process. Without the fears and emotions aroused by campaign techniques, it would be logical to expect the widespread discussion over this shortcoming of the electoral system to reinforce the arguments of the Progressives in favor of direct election of the President and Vice President. There is no indication that it helped in the least. On the contrary, the misapprehensions of the conservatives that a Bryan would find his way into the White House, via the back door, were sufficient, no doubt, to switch many votes from Davis to Coolidge and, perhaps, even from LaFollette to Davis or Coolidge.[22]

The Republican professions of fear in regard to a deadlocked election were probably more sincere and substantial than some of the other campaign stratagems. The tide did not start to run strongly in Coolidge's favor until October; until then, he was an unknown factor as a campaigner. The Administration scandals had smeared the Republicans. The farm and labor endorsement for the Progressives contained great potential. The *Literary Digest* and Hearst polls showed LaFollette leading Davis.[23] It all conjured up a terrifying picture to many conservatives. Most of them had a vague acquaintance, through

21 Appeal made by George W. Simmons, on behalf of the Bankers' Committee for Coolidge and Dawes, Oct. 9, 1924, (Walsh papers).

22 Mr. Davis concurs in this opinion. Conversation with the author, May 24, 1943.

23 On Oct. 2, 1924, *The Literary Digest* inserted, in many newspapers, a quarter-page advertisement whose heavy type proclaimed, " LaFollette Cutting Down Coolidge Lead."

the pages of a school text, with the electoral crises of 1800, 1824 and 1876.[24] They were convinced that LaFollette would stop at nothing to obstruct orderly processes of government. There is some evidence—though inconclusive—that Bascom Slemp was anticipating the need for good will in Congress in the event of the election being thrown into the House. He was thought to be assisting congressmen in close elections whose vote he felt Coolidge could depend upon in case of the election being held in the House of Representatives.[25]

The amount and extent of intimidation, social, economic and even physical, in the 1924 campaign raises the question whether it should not be included with such notorious campaigns in our history as 1828 and 1896. Sometimes the disturbances bordered on physical violence. Intimidation was greatest around factory towns and industrial centers where the Socialists and Progressives had made inroads or were active in campaigning. Often, in these places, the police authorities and the courts would be friendly to the business interests and antagonistic towards any display of "radicalism." Louis Budenz, editor of *Labor Age* and an active Progressive in New Jersey politics, described one such attack, made upon him at his home in Rahway, N. J. Late in the evening a mob of about a thousand headed by a group of men in military uniform, carrying a flag-draped casket, descended upon his residence, clamoring and calling out, " Kill the Socialist! " and " We'll drown the rat." The police made no effort to disperse the crowd.[26]

In Darien, Connecticut, the Reverend George O. Richmond, speaking for LaFollette and Wheeler, was removed from his platform by two constables, haled before a justice of the peace, lectured " for insulting the people of the United States," and

24 This fear was also expressed in 1860. See Fite, E. D., *The Presidential Campaign of 1860*, p. 223.

25 Walsh *Memo*, Oct. 27, 1924, (Walsh papers).

26 Statement made by Louis Budenz, sworn to and notorized, Mar. 28, 1924. *American Civil Liberties Union Cases*, No. 263, 1924, pp. 233-235.

ordered to leave town. Referring to this case, the *St. Louis Post-Dispatch* sarcastically remarked in its editorial that " evidently Mr. Dawes' agitation for the Constitution had not got across to his own people." [27]

The Democrats sometimes joined the Republicans in these frontal attacks upon the enemies of two-party government. An elector on the Progressive ticket in North Carolina, the Reverend Tom P. Jimison, was requested to give up his pastorate by the Western North Carolina conference of the M. E. Church South " because of his activity in politics." [28]

One of the favorite devices of the local authorities to thwart third-party activity was to interfere with and obstruct planned meetings and rallies. This could be done by refusing permission to hold the meetings or by breaking up the meetings as " disturbances of the peace." Various complaints about this sort of predicament came to the American Civil Liberties Union during the campaign. In Pasco, Washington, for example, a Socialist was arrested and fined for speaking on behalf of LaFollette. When he complained of such an unconstitutional procedure, the police chief sneeringly said, " Maybe LaFollette can get you out of this." [29] Usually by the time such miscarriages of justice were rectified, the campaign was over. Occasionally, self-appointed protectors of the Existing Order, sometimes dressed as ex-service men, would attack Progressive speakers, sometimes the automobiles they were driving. In Meriden, Connecticut, a group of rowdies, dressed in the uniforms of a veterans' organization and led by two officers of the World War, forcibly attacked the car in which J. A. H. Hopkins, the head of the Committee of Forty Eight was riding. Hopkins' automobile was halted and its American flag removed. The police, instead of dispersing the crowd, referred the La-Follette party, already late for a speaking engagement, to the

27 *St. Louis Post-Dispatch*, Nov. 4, 1924.

28 *Washington Post*, Oct. 18, 1924.

29 *American Civil Liberties Union Cases*, No. 267, 1924, p. 197.

Prosecuting Attorney who was glad to take "the whole matter under advisement." [30] Young Bob LaFollette, attending a meeting in Des Moines at which an organised effort to embarrass and to intimidate the Progressives was made, was convinced that the behaviour of such hecklers was much more remunerative than spontaneous.[31]

In all elections where the class lines are sharply drawn, in 1936 when the New Deal was the issue, in 1896 when Populism appalled the middle class, another—and familiar—type of intimidation appears. Workmen are frightened into voting to maintain the *status quo*. 1924 was no exception. Employees were told to look out for their jobs if LaFollette won. Prosperity and employment depended upon Coolidge. No part of the campaign harbored more resentments when Election Day was over than this kind of appeal. Typical was the case reported by the *Advance*, organ of the Amalgamated Clothing Workers. One worker explained that his foreman had told him that good times were conditioned on a Coolidge victory. "My God," he exclaimed, "it's hard enough now to make both ends meet, and we can't afford to take a chance of being thrown out of work, even for two weeks." [32] Frank Walsh, as counsel for Senator LaFollette, collected evidence of employees contributing to the Coolidge fund to keep their jobs, of prominent American corporations using trade letters to distribute Republican campaign slogans and literature. A machinist employed by a Midwest railroad was fired because he posted a LaFollette clipping on a bulletin board used for general purposes where there was already Coolidge-Dawes literature! [33] In at least one city, notes taken on the purchase of automobiles had a clause

30 *New York World*, Oct. 4, 1924.

31 See telegram, R. M. LaFollette, Jr., to Mrs. R. M. LaFollette, Sr., Oct. 15, 1924, (Walsh papers).

32 The Advance, Nov. 21, 1924, p. 7.

33 Signed affidavit by Ivan Bell, Danville, Ill., Oct. 27, 1924, (Walsh papers.)

inserted to the effect that there would be no renewal in the event of a LaFollette victory.[34]

McAlister Coleman found shocking conditions of economic servitude and police terrorism in West Virginia when he went there, heading a joint committee of the American Civil Liberties Union and the League for Industrial Democracy, to report on conditions in the mining towns.[35] An angry Progressive, reporting on conditions in the Northwest, complained that the farmers were told that workmen would lose their jobs if Coolidge were not elected. Consequently farmers would not get so much for their products. The same reporter described how women went about, often in tours, spreading the story to some that LaFollette was a Catholic, and to others that he was a Unitarian and Socialist.[36] Roger Baldwin, close observer of the campaign in his own state of Connecticut, believed that two reasons accounted for LaFollette's defeat in that state. First, the conservative Democrats were " scared " into voting for Coolidge; second, foremen told workers they would lose their jobs if they did not vote for Coolidge.[37]

As in the case of evaluating the charge of radicalism and the election-deadlock bogey, it is extremely difficult to state, with any degree of assurance, how much intimidation, ranging from quiet persuasion to vigilantism, affected the outcome. Probably some voters, resenting a campaign of innuendo and compulsion, actually cast their ballots for LaFollette as a kind of protest against unfair tactics. Undoubtedly thousands of employees— perhaps the same workers who wore Landon buttons in 1936 —listened dutifully to their bosses explaining the merits of " Keeping Cool with Coolidge " and then voted for LaFollette

34 Dr. J. E. Engstad, Grand Forks, North Dakota, to LaFollette Headquarters, Chicago, Oct. 15, 1924, (Walsh papers).

35 *American Civil Liberties Union Cases,* No. 268, 1924, pp. 175-186.

36 Alan Bogue, Parker, S. D., to R. M. LaFollette, Dec. 1, 1924, (Confidential Source).

37 Roger S. Baldwin to the author, Aug. 24, 1943.

regardless of the threatened consequences. It might be observed that the apathy of many Americans to political issues is so complete that even the dreadful visions of economic catastrophe and social disaster pictured by the alarmists leave them unperturbed. Consequently it is an exaggeration to say, as the New York *American* did immediately after the election, that " the Progressives lost millions to Mr. Coolidge because LaFollette's program was successfully misrepresented." [38] Those millions were probably safe for Coolidge because America was comfortable and complacent in 1924 and did not care particularly what kind of a program LaFollette espoused and was not unduly concerned whether it was misrepresented or not. Intimidation was part of the political picture in 1924, not because the politicos were more unscrupulous than in other elections, not because resort to desperate methods was necessary, but rather because, economically, socially, even temperamentally, the times were right for such tactics. America was prosperous—workmen could be frightened with thoughts of upsetting the *status quo*. Bolshevism was a hideous nightmare, a constant threat to all our social institutions. All " radicals " were suspect. The vigilantism of the KKK, the contempt for law and order engendered by the rise of gangsterism and failure of prohibition, the post-war cynicism and materialism, all provided fertile soil for the kind of political tactics that would have met with general disapprobation in times of better sense and fuller values.

38 *New York American*, Nov. 5, 1924.

CHAPTER IX
THE ODDS AGAINST THEM

THE campaign revealed basic weaknesses in the third party movement, serious shortcomings which would probably accompany any liberal political crusade organized on short notice. The most glaring of these defects were: faulty organization, the difficulty of complying with state election laws, insufficient funds, and inadequate supporting tickets.

The faulty organization was inevitable. With a party established on such short notice and with such a temporary basis, it was almost impossible to set up a smooth-functioning machine to compete against the experienced and confident Democratic and Republican organizations. The geographical magnitude of the United States works against a third party. The soundest construction of the CPPA would have required organizing the local election districts throughout the nation, approximately 120,000, including on the average, 350-400 voters. Although some state headquarters had been established in 1922 and 1923, the major portion of the task remained when LaFollette was endorsed on July 4, a few months before election. Money had to be collected; plans had to be formulated and approved; state and local directors had to be appointed.

With the National Executive Committee co-ordinating the whole effort, campaign headquarters were set up in both Chicago and Washington. Congressman John Nelson of Wisconsin was made national campaign manager for LaFollette, although it was understood that he and his office would concentrate on winning the West while Basil Manly, in charge at the Washington headquarters, would watch the East.[1] Later, additional Eastern headquarters were established in New York City, under the supervision of Gilbert Roe, LaFollette's law partner. This division of authority was regrettable. It often led to duplication of effort and frequently one office was unaware

1 Basil Manly to the author, June 16, 1943.

of what another was doing.[2] As late as September 26, La-Follette leaders were discovering that there were only seventeen peakers in the field and only fifty more available.[3]

The attempts to establish local Progressive organizations failed for a variety of reasons. The Progressives never quite made up their minds whether they wanted functional or geographical units. The Brotherhoods worked out an ambitious plan, in conference with LaFollette in September, to appoint staff officers and " crews " throughout the country. The concentration of Progressive strength in industrial centers in the East prevented proper attention being given to the smaller towns and suburbs, sections that were often without any CPPA organization whatsoever. Many of the leaders were high-minded idealists whose political experience was woefully lacking. Well-intentioned and more enthusiastic than experienced, they often proved obnoxious to the more pragmatic wing of the CPPA.[4]

Oswald Garrison Villard, in *Fighting Years,* recalls his days as Assistant National Treasurer of the Progressives, when he toured with Vice-Presidential Candidate Wheeler " in many places finding only the merest skeletons of what a fighting political force should be." " In some states," he adds, " we had no organization whatever." [5]

With all its confusion and political inexperience, the organization of the CPPA in 1924 had a refreshing, hopeful enthusiasm about it which contrasted sharply with the cut-and-dried methods of the old parties. The voluntary workers for the Progressives imparted some of their crusading zeal to the whole campaign. Villard noticed this peculiar compensation of the Progressive campaign in a letter to Senator LaFollette.

2 *Ibid.*

3 *Minutes,* Meeting of the Joint Executive Committee, LaFollette-Wheeler Campaign, Chicago, Sept. 26, 1924 (Walsh papers).

4 Mrs. Gilbert Roe recalls this problem vividly, a difficulty especially pronounced in the New York office.

5 Villard, O. G., *Fighting Years,* p. 503.

I have never seen audiences more fascinated, or that listened more closely and attentively. Our audiences were small, the advance work was sometimes not well done, and all along the line we noticed the inexperience in political matters of our workers, which is not only natural, but has its bright side. For I would rather have their inexperience and enthusiasm than the skill of the experienced paid worker of the rotten old parties.[6]

It was indeed commendable of Mr. Villard to despise the methods of the paid workers of the old parties but, after all, they did account for a considerable number of votes on Election Day.

Looking back upon the campaign years later, Mr. Villard recalled the disappointment of travelling about with Mr. Wheeler on his campaign tour, and finding that no preparations had been made by local Progressive organizations. Finding, in town after town, such discouraging evidence of lack of organization disheartened the whole ticket.[7]

There is something pathetic in the account of a *World* reporter of his visit to LaFollette headquarters. The taxi driver, sympathetic towards any visitor to the CPPA, refused to take a tip. Inside the headquarters, nothing seemed organized or efficient. Nobody was at the Information Desk. The woman who had charge of the Speakers' Bureau had had experience only as a reporter.[8]

Arthur Garfield Hays has ably described the conglomeration of inexperienced and sometimes incapable staff workers and speakers:[9]

At the end of the first week of campaigning in New York City, disquieting reports as to what our volunteers were preaching began to drift into local headquarters. Lionel Pop-

6 Letter from O. G. Villard to Sen. R. M. LaFollette, Sept. 13, 1924, (Villard papers).

7 O. G. Villard to the author, Jan. 2, 1941.

8 *New York World,* Oct. 26, 1924.

9 Hays, A. G., *City Lawyer,* pp. 269-270.

kin, chief of our speakers' bureau, made a tour one night to look over the street meetings. He returned to confirm the worst of our fears. The majority of our speakers were paying no more attention to the official platform than was the populace as a whole. On one side of Union Square, Popkin had come upon a LaFollette meeting being harangued by an articulate and alcoholic person who described himself as the man who had exposed the Teapot Dome iniquities. " What the hell did Bob LaFollette have to do with that?" he was asking a puzzled crowd. " I'm the man who showed up the scoundrels. Me! I'm the man." Farther north, in front of the old comfort station called, in those refined days, " The Cottage!" a veteran IWW agitator, wearing as a muffler around his collarless neck the small American flag which we had given him in compliance with police regulations, was shouting, "And when you get into the polling place, yell out, ' Hooray for Bob LaFollette!' and then take an ax and bust up the old ballot box. That's the sort of direct action that will count, fellow workers." At Columbus Circle, an unfrocked priest from the Pacific Coast, speaking under a huge LaFollette sign, was assuring a mob of delighted Irish that the morals of the British upper classes were exactly what his listeners imagined them to be. He intimated that the election of LaFollette and Wheeler would put an end to such doings. At Broadway and and Ninety-sixth Street, the center of bourgeois respectability, our speaker was assuring the crowd that with the election of LaFollette, the workers, following the Russian example, would take over and reside in the apartments that lined West End Avenue and Riverside Drive. All along the line, Marxists, single-taxers, vegetarians, theosophists, radicals of all shades of opinion, gathered under LaFollette emblems to preach their diverse religions. Our emblem was the Liberty Bell, and as Allen McCurdy remarked, " The crack is getting larger every day!"

In the West, conditions were as bad, with the exception of Wisconsin where the LaFollette state machine functioned for the CPPA, and sections of the Northwest like North Dakota and Minnesota where the Non-Partisan organizations could be utilized. In Montana the wholesale desertion of Democrats to LaFollette (some Republicans charged it was a deal between Walsh Democrats and the Progressives) enabled the Progressives to employ the services of experienced political workers.

The scattering of volunteers working for LaFollette must have looked puny compared with the army of challengers, watchers, field workers, wardheelers, and Election Day runners functioning for the Democrats and Republicans.

The problems of a new political party in America, even under the most favorable auspices, are sufficiently complex. Various legal barriers to the formation of a new party have appeared as the states have become more precise in their definition of a political party and more exacting in the procedures of petitioning and filing. State election laws become an almost insuperable obstacle to a new party. Perhaps the chief value of the Socialist Party to the CPPA in 1924 was its already established state machinery in forty-four states — saving the Progressives, in many cases, from the discouraging business of collecting signatures and filing ballot and election fees. This was not entirely satisfactory because it necessitated the Progressives' running on the Socialist ticket, a condition sometimes as unpalatable to the Progressive electors as to those voters who favored LaFollette but hesitated to vote in the Socialist column.

In practically all the states, petitions had to be filed with the Secretary of State or with the State Election Board. The time for filing the nominating petitions varied from 100 to 10 days before election. Each state had its own requirements, often complicated and ambiguous. Recognising the difficulties involved, the Executive Committee of the CPPA, immediately upon LaFollette's decision to run for the Presidency, chose Gilbert Roe, with his wide knowledge of the law, as chairman of a committee to place LaFollette's name on the ballot. It took weeks just to learn what the various state requirements were. With as much truth as flippancy, the New York *Post* remarked that " Senator LaFollette will have more difficulty getting his name on the ballots in the various states than he will in getting votes." [10] Altogether it was estimated that 50,000 voters throughout the nation, in most instance non-primary voters, would have to sign for LaFollette.[11] The wide range of requirements in our election laws reminds one of the bewildering confusion of the state marriage and divorce laws. In some states getting on the ballot was—and is—a mere formality. In states like Georgia and Virginia, LaFollette merely had to file notice of candidacy. In Tennessee, another liberal state as far as filing was concerned, only fifteen signatures were needed.

But it was not so easy to get on the ballot in most states. In Nevada, to get a place on the ballot, the managers of the new ticket had to secure the signatures of ten per cent of the number of voters at the last presidential election. Moreover, the signatures had to be submitted by the first Tuesday in August! In Florida, not less than thirty days before election, a petition signed by at least twenty-five voters in each of the fifty-four counties had to be filed![12]

Inasmuch as the CPPA was looked upon, especially in those sections of the country where the problem of getting on the ballot was most acute, as an organization of left wingers and radicals, the task of obtaining signatures was increased. " Since the names of petitioners are not secret, and since those who sign pledge themselves to support the new party's candidates at the election, thousands of persons are undoubtedly dissuaded from signing such petitions by fear of social ostracism, intimidation, and reprisal."[13]

The total effect of the state election laws upon the candidacy of the Progressives was, first, to force LaFollette to run under

10 *New York Post*, July 11, 1924. After securing a place on the ballot, the Progressives, as newcomers, were often compelled to accept a disadvantageous ballot position.

11 *New York Times*, July 11, 1924.

12 *Ibid.*

13 Odegard, P. and Helms, E., *American Politics*, p. 790.

a variety of party labels, Progressive, Independent, Independent-Progressive, and Socialist, and, second, to divert precious funds and campaign activity from the business of persuading voters to cast their ballots for LaFollette to the less fruitful job of complying with the technical regulations of the conglomerate election laws. Indeed, the state election laws must be considered one of the most effective devices to discourage formation of a new party.

In many states, as in New York, the LaFollette-Wheeler electors appeared in two columns, Progressive or Independent and Socialist.[14] This was done, when possible, to meet the objections of liberals who hesitated to vote the Socialist ticket. In North Carolina, the LaFollette electors did not appear on the ballot except in the nineteen counties using the Australian ballot.[15] In West Virginia, the Progressives failed to place on the ballot because their petition was not filed in time.[16]

The Progressives were most annoyed by legal efforts to impair their election efforts in California, Louisiana and Ohio. In each of these states, the old parties either made use of a legal technicality to ban the Progressives from the ballot, as in California and Louisiana, or, as in the case of Ohio, to interfere seriously with the Progressive attempt to conduct an honest election.

In California, the election law was revised in 1912 at a time when the old party organizations were perturbed by the threat of Roosevelt progressivism. The 1912 law was designed chiefly as a measure of self-preservation for the old parties. By intent or oversight, no provision was included for placing electors on the ballot by petition. Claiming that the failure to provide for placing electors by petition was an oversight, the LaFollette managers appealed to the courts and eventually the State Supreme Court handed down a decision. By a vote of 4-3, the

14 *New York Times*, July 13, 1924.

15 *Christian Science Monitor*, Sept. 30, 1924.

16 *New York Times*, July 17, 1924.

Court denied the petition for a rehearing on the adverse decision in the lower courts.[17] This barred LaFollette as an Independent or Progressive, the only recourse open to his supporters being to vote the Socialist ticket. This was a hard blow to the Progressives who had high hopes of carrying California, with the straw votes showing LaFollette almost tied with Coolidge.

Secretary of State Barley of Louisiana barred the LaFollette-Wheeler electors from the ballot on the grounds that their petition contained largely names of Democratic registrants. According to the Louisiana law, he ruled, only independents, with no party or primary affiliation, could sign.[18] The difficulties this kind of law poses for a new party in the Solid South can be readily appreciated!

The blow to the Progressives in Ohio was of a different nature. Although experiencing no trouble in getting on the ballot in that state, the decision of the Ohio State Supreme Court, on the eve of the election, not to allow the Progressives to have watchers at the polls, left the CPPA little better than helpless on Election Day. On the grounds that the watchers would not be the representatives of a recognized political party, the judges, 4-3, voted against the CPPA. Inasmuch as the action was unexpected, the Progressives were totally unprepared and disorganised by the decision. As a result, there were numerous charges of fraud and intimidation on Election Day in Cleveland where the Progressive strength was feared and where the Chairman of the Election Board was also Chairman of the Cuyahoga County Republican Committee. In the Negro districts, Republicans accompanied voters into the booths; marked ballots were common; and " election judges were expected to go blind for three dollars." [19]

17 *Ibid.*, Sept. 26, 1924. Electors could be nominated only by a bona-fide political party convention, according to the Court's interpretation of the statute.

18 *Ibid.*, Sept. 29, 1924.

19 *Brotherhood of Locomotive Firemen and Enginemen's Magazine*, 77:6, Dec., 1924, p. 422. See also *Nation*, 119:3098, Nov. 19, 1924, p. 546.

In one Cleveland district, the Progressive candidate received no votes officially, although various citizens signed affidavits that they had voted for him. In another precinct, eight members of a family voted for LaFollette where no votes for him were reported.[20]

The extent of fraud encouraged by the unfortunate decision of the Supreme Court moved the conservative *Cleveland Plain Dealer* to call for a thorough investigation. " The public is not satisfied with blanket denials on the part of election officials," the newspaper editorial stated, ". . . two obligations exist, related perhaps but not identical. Investigate the recent election for possible fraud, or for bad management. Then revise the election machinery of Ohio." [21]

The publicity attendant upon all the campaign expenditures in 1924 was as generous as the sums contributed to the Republican party. Charges and countercharges, spectacular " revelations " of slush funds and plots to buy the election were thrown about recklessly. When the campaign was over and the dust of battle had subsided, it was easy to see that once more, as in 1916 and 1920, the Republicans had been able to collect the lion's share of the campaign contributions.

In two respects, the 1924 financing campaign differed from those of 1916 and 1920. First, the disclosures of extravagant expenditures in 1920—the Republicans admitted to spending four million dollars—and the shocking disclosures of the Newberry case in Michigan began to make responsible citizens consider sumptuary curbs upon reckless and unfair use of money in electing candidates for office.[22] The Newberry decision, limiting the jurisdiction of Congress to regulate state elections, emphasized the need for more systematic controls of campaign

20 *Brot. of Loco. Firemen and Enginemen's Magazine*, ibid.

21 *Cleveland Plain Dealer*, Nov. 25, 1924.

22 See Overacker, L., *Money in Elections*, for an excellent consideration of the entire subject of expenditures in American political campaigns.

funds.[23] This unprecedented publicity on election expenditures culminated in the federal corrupt practices act of 1925.

The second unusual feature of financing in the 1924 election campaign was the manner in which the plight of the third party became eloquent testimony for the necessity of having and using ample supplies of money in an American national election. The CPPA was the horrible example of what happens when a party does not have enough money.

On June 7, 1924, before the campaign activities had begun in earnest, the Senate, responding to the public concern over the extravagance of recent elections, approved the LaFollette resolution creating a special committee to investigate and report on the campaign expenditures of candidates for the Presidency and Vice-Presidency.[24] In the absence of any regulatory federal legislation, it was thought that this white light of publicity would serve to restrain the more extravagant uses of money in the campaign. At the end of the campaign, the report of this committee, with Borah of Idaho as chairman, was submitted to the Senate.[25] The expenditures during the campaign had been as follows, the sums referring to the amount of money each national organization had spent: [26]

Republican Party
        Collected $4,360,478.82
        Spent $4,270,469.01
        Returned to states . . . $573,599.20
Democratic Party   ..
        Collected $821,037.05
        Spent $903,908.21
LaFollette-Wheeler National Headquarters
        Collected $221,837.21
        Spent $221,977.58

23 *Newberry vs. U. S.*, 256 U. S. 232.

24 68th. Congress, 1st Session, *Senate Resolution 248.*

25 68th. Congress, 2nd Session, *Senate Report No. 1100,* " *Campaign Expenditures.*"

26 *Ibid.*, p. 2.

Great as the disparity between the sums expended by national organizations appears to be in this formal report, it is not the complete story. Frank Walsh, LaFollette's legal representative before the Borah Committee, classified four types of Republican contributions, only the first of these being included in the report above. These four classifications were: [27]

1. The money that was raised and sent to the Republican National Committee (which was publicly reported, of course, by that committee).

2. Contributions made but never reported.

3. Sums raised by the various state, district, county, and city committees expended in the respective districts to support the entire Coolidge ticket.

4. Propaganda carried on by individuals and organizations benefited by the tariff and other special legislation, through the medium of newspaper ads, circulars, printed pamphlets, and letters to the trade.

Walsh estimated that the Republicans would spend a grand total of $15,700,000 in the campaign, raising $3,000,000 " from postmasters, liquor permittees, federal employees to whom a request is a demand." [28] Walsh also estimated that the Republicans spent $2,000,000 on advertising and propaganda.

Discounting Walsh's personal interest in the LaFollette candidacy and the flimsy, insubstantial nature of the second type of contribution to the Republican fund, described by Walsh, one cannot deny the very real advantage the Republicans possessed in having, already established, local organizations receiving contributions and in turn using those funds to promote, either directly or indirectly, the Coolidge candidacy.

Without doubt, LaFollette's candidacy made the task of Coolidge's campaign managers to raise money easier. The Progressive attacks upon certain aspects of our economic life,

27 Memo, (Walsh papers).

28 *Ibid.*

interpreted by business and financial leaders as a frontal assault upon the profit system, started the money pouring into the Republican coffers. Industrialists, bankers and brokers came to the aid of their party. Walsh stated that 92 per cent of the contributions being made to the Republican party were made by officers or directors of large industrial and banking concerns.[29] Moreover, 71.4 per cent of the contributions were made in sums of $1000 or larger.[30]

Especially fruitful to the Republicans were their endeavors to get business men to answer LaFollette's attack upon existing institutions with a signed check to headquarters. The Walsh memoranda would certainly indicate that the practice of obtaining funds through direct appeals to business men was highly successful. Typical of many approaches was the following, a letter dated September 30, 1924, from Mr. George Murnane, Vice-President of the New York Trust Company, to Mr. James H. Warburg, International Acceptance Bank, New York:[31]

"Attached to this letter there is a list of firms, the task of securing subscriptions from whom I would like to assign to you.

"The general plan is to secure within each company an individual who will be willing to canvass the officers or partners and if possible the employees, using for that purpose the subscription blank of which copy is enclosed. . . . " The appeal, of course, was for funds to support Coolidge and Dawes.

There were the usual charges of the more obvious misuses of money in the campaign, through bribery and fraud, but perhaps not much more than the average, if one considers the amount of money available to the Republicans. Rudolph Spreckels, one of LaFollette's chief backers on the Pacific Coast, charged that the ZR-3 would be christened the *Los Angeles* because, with that understanding in mind, the business

29 *New York Times,* Nov. 2, 1924.
30 *Ibid.*
31 Letter in Walsh Papers.

men of that city had turned over a large sum to the Coolidge-Republican committee.[32] In some districts, the funds were misused in a manner described by a New York State observer:[33]

" They (the Republicans) approached all doubtful voters in each district and offered them $10.00 for their services and influence (?) in getting out the Republican vote on Election Day, saying that if the returns show a gain over last year, they will receive more. . . . "

Regardless of how extensive this misuse of money was in the 1924 campaign, the fact remains that the chief advantage of the Republicans lay in the comparative ease with which, through skillful recourse to methods and issues designed to arouse the apprehensions of business men throughout the nation, their campaign chest could be swollen. The Republicans did not have to go out to find the funds. Industrialists, bankers and business men, perturbed by LaFollette's attacks upon the Supreme Court, unregulated private ownership and the malpractices of business elements, collected the money and brought it to the Republican headquarters.

An analysis of Republican contributions from June 19, 1924, to October 15, 1924, made by Samuel Untermyer, revealed that of total contributions amounting to $2,101,400.80, contributions given in sums of $5000 or over amounted to $682,189.50.[34] Large contributors included William Wrigley, Jr. of Chicago, $25,000; James A. Patten, Evanston, Illinois, $20,000; Payne Whitney, New York, $15,000; Arthur Curtiss James, New York, $15,000; J. B. Duke, New York, $12,500. What has been said about the nature of the Republican contributions applies, in large part, to the Democratic fund. Like the Republicans, the Democrats depended heavily upon large contributors. John D. Ryan of New York gave $55,000. Thomas L. Chadbourne of New York contributed $20,000.

32 Memo, (Walsh papers).
33 Letter from A. D. Lewis, Jordan, N. Y., to Samuel Untermyer, Oct. 24, 1924, (Walsh papers).
34 Memo, (Walsh papers).

Jesse Jones of Houston contributed $25,000. The Republican " scare " campaign that Bryan might be elected in the event of a close election probably hampered the efforts of the Democratic fund-raisers greatly towards the end of the campaign. They had to borrow $120,000 from the New York Trust Company, and Election Day found the Democratic party heavily in debt.[35]

The disappointing results of the CPPA efforts to raise election funds for LaFollette and Wheeler suggest that the leaders of the movement were far too sanguine at the start of the campaign in their expectations of financial aid from the rank and file of labor and agriculture. Apparently the generosity displayed by some of the railroad unions in the early days of the CPPA buoyed up the hopes of the Progressive leaders to the point where they thought a substantial part of the financing could be undertaken by trade union contributions. Perhaps the success of the British Labour Party, with its financial support obtained this way, reinforced this expectation. William H. Johnston, recognising the magnitude of the task, sent out a form letter to all local lodges and divisions of organized labor at the beginning of the campaign, suggesting the appointment of a committee of three in each local lodge, charged with the responsibility of collecting a dollar from each member.[36] On paper such a plan no doubt looked imposing. In view of the membership of the AFL and the Brotherhoods, several million dollars might have been collected for the LaFollette campaign. But one of the greatest disappointments for the CPPA was the lack of financial support from the unions. Instead of several million dollars, perhaps not more than $50,000 was realized from this source. The American Federation of Labor was only able to collect a paltry $25,000 for election purposes! Labor leaders had been more generous with their promises than with

35 Contributions as reported in *Senate Report, No. 1100,* " Campaign Expenditures ".

36 Form letter mailed out from William Johnston's office in Washington, D. C. (On deposit now in private collection of papers).

their purses. The charge made by many Socialists, that the unions pulled out on LaFollette before Election Day, might be somewhat substantiated by the insignificance of their financial support.[37]

The failure of the unions to provide left LaFollette no alternative but a direct appeal for funds, at meetings, rallies, and through the organs friendly to him. The farmers had no organization capable of raising money. How LaFollette could have used someone with Townley's genius for gathering funds among the farmers! But the Non-Partisan League could not give LaFollette much more than a collection of worthless postdated checks.

So the LaFollette managers had recourse to direct methods of money-raising which, even when partly effective, seemed amateurish and pathetically inadequate. Admission was often charged to hear campaign speeches. At Madison Square Garden, one could sit in the first balcony for $.55 or buy a box seating nine for $27.50. The plate was usually passed at LaFollette rallies. " Emancipation Bonds " and the LaFollette-Wheeler *Text Book* were sold. Campaign buttons and plaques were sold at a slight profit. Progressive organs like the *Nation* made urgent appeals to their readers to keep the battle going by sending contributions at once to LaFollette headquarters.

The results were, of course, disappointing. Often the men and women who came to hear LaFollette were not the kind to have much money in their pockets and what little was there had to be budgeted for more urgent requirements. It was discouraging to find so large a proportion of silver on the collection plate. The dollar bills were scarce. When admission was charged for seats at a campaign meeting, there was always the risk of a disappointing turn-out. As early as July, the lack of funds was interfering with the progress of the CPPA campaign.[38] On LaFollette's western tour, no plans could be made

37 Harris, H., *American Labor*, p. 377.

38 Letter from Sen. R. M. LaFollette to O. G. Villard, July 31, 1924, (Villard papers).

in advance because of the lack of cash. The trip, in the words of a *New York Times* reporter, developed into "hand-to-mouth" affair.[39] The campaign managers had paid their last available cent to the Pennsylvania R. R. Co. and the amount could not finance the trip beyond St. Louis and Kansas City.[40] More than any other factor, the lack of funds curtailed the activities of the Progressives in 1924.

The nearest thing to a "party angel" that the Progressives possessed was William T. Rawleigh of Freeport, Illinois, who had accumulated a considerable fortune by selling patent medicines of the variety which appealed to many Americans of a generation ago. Rawleigh was appointed National Treasurer for the campaign and seems to have been most successful in collecting from himself. According to the Borah report, Rawleigh contributed $28,000 to the LaFollette fund, approximately 13 per cent of the total! The men who were associated with Rawleigh in the campaign speak highly of him, explaining his enthusiasm for the Progressive cause in terms of his Wisconsin boyhood and youth when he came to know and to hero-worship Senator LaFollette.[41] Mr. Manly emphasizes the fact that there was no trace of *quid pro quo* about the Rawleigh contributions beyond his ardent desire to promote the political career of his favorite statesman.[42] There were few other large contributors to the Progressive campaign chest. Irene Richter, daughter of Samuel Untermyer, gave $5,000. Willard Straight's widow contributed $2500. The list of those contributing $1000 or more follows:[43]

39 *New York Times*, Oct. 6, 1924.

40 *Ibid.*

41 Rawleigh was the chief financial supporter of the People's Legislative Service. Later he subsidized the Rawleigh Foundation, mainly devoted to attacking high tariff policies.

42 Basil Manly to the author, June 16, 1943.

43 *Senate Report, No. 1100,* "Campaign Expenditures," p. 24.

Chicago Office

W. T. Rawleigh, Freeport, Illinois	$2000.
W. T. Rawleigh, Freeport, Illinois	1000.
C. M. Dow, Madison, Wisconsin	1000.
J. A. Padway, Milwaukee, Wisconsin	1000.
A. C. Dick, Milwaukee, Wisconsin	1005.
H. L. Bromson, (sic), Washington, D. C.	1500.
C. M. Dow, Madison, Wisconsin	1092.10
A. B. Melzner, Washington, D. C.	1500.
Mrs. Dorothy W. Straight, N. Y.	2500.
Walter R. Demmler, Pittsburgh, Pa.	1000.
J. J. Hanman, Cleveland, Ohio	2000.

$5000 or more

W. T. Rawleigh, Freeport, Illinois	10,000.
W. T. Rawleigh, Freeport, Illinois	10,000.
W. T. Rawleigh, Freeport, Illinois	10,000.

Washington Office

| Miss Irene Richter, New York, N. Y. | 5000. |

It was indeed discouraging, this critical need for funds with which to meet campaign expenses. There were especially dark and gloomy days when only a few dollars would trickle into national headquarters.[44] Under the impact of Republican dollars, some of the LaFollette support drifted away. In Omaha, for example, a German paper of large circulation, the *Omaha Tribune,* at first endorsed LaFollette. During the campaign it received more than $10,000 for advertisements from the Republican National Committee. It switched its support from La-Follette to Coolidge.[45] Of course, its changes of policy might have arisen from the most altruistic of motives, but it was difficult for Progressives not to become discouraged by this turn of events.

In the state of Maine, for example, the labor unions, falling far short of their early promises, contributed only $200. In addition to the unions, there were only twenty-eight contribu-

44 Villard, *op. cit.,* p. 503.
45 Memo, (Walsh papers).

tors whose total contribution came to a paltry $114.75! The lack of funds was so acute in Maine that printed material at headquarters could not be delivered.[46] On Election Day, the Progressives had only fifty dollars to spend in New York City![47]

The Progressive strategy, both in attacking the size of the Republican funds and in appealing for contributions for themselves, was ineffectual, if not inept. 1924 was no year for a moral crusade, and the LaFollette-Wheeler charges that business was accumulating a vast "slush fund" for Coolidge and the Republicans made little appeal to the voters. At a time when so many Americans resembled Sinclair Lewis' *Babbitt* and when so many of them extolled the same acquisitive virtues, many voters were inclined to give the Republicans credit for getting as much as they could. It was also unfortunate for the Progressives that their most serious "slush fund" charge turned out to be the result of a hoax, forged telegrams that had contained sensational evidence that the federal reserve banks were instructed to underwrite the Coolidge expenses. LaFollette had shown better political sense than most of his advisors by his reluctance to make them public—he had "grave doubts of their authenticity."[48] Nevertheless, on such flimsy evidence, the Progressives went ahead and made the charge. The resultant exposure of the hoax reflected discredit more upon his campaign advisors than upon LaFollette.

The unhappy state of affairs in the CPPA caused by the continued lack of funds should be a constant reminder to the founders of any third party in America that a major dilemma that cannot be avoided—especially by a liberal group—is the pressing need for money. The problem is manifold; the new

46 Ring, E., "The Progressive Movement of 1912 and the Third Party Movement of 1924 in Maine," *The Univ. of Maine Bulletin*, 35:5, Jan. 1933, p. 51.

47 *New York Herald Tribune*, Nov. 5, 1924. Statement by Arthur Garfield Hays.

48 Telegram from Sen. R. M. LaFollette to Frank Walsh, Oct. 27, 1924, (Walsh papers).

party is in urgent need of funds, yet its very appearance almost automatically (if it is liberal or radical, of course) results in increasing the contributions of its old adversaries. The defects of a plan of depending upon voluntary contributions from individuals overtaken by the spirit of generosity were obvious in 1924. The only possibility of successfully financing a liberal-labor-agrarian third party, it would appear, lies in the assessment policy adopted by the British Labour Party or as practiced, with certain qualifications, by the United Mine Workers in America when they supported Franklin D. Roosevelt in 1936. Without such organization, a third party movement can never hope to compete with the convincing appeals made by the established parties nor with the smoothly-functioning machinery of collection which operates for the old parties.

If, in the midst of political defeat, any grains of comfort can be obtained by a sense of moral victory, then the following figures on the cost per vote in 1924 should help to sustain those who voted for LaFollette. But elections are never won by an analysis of cost per vote.

The cost per vote, all votes, Democrat, Republican, Progressive *et al.* in the 1924 election was fifteen cents. But it only cost the Progressives five cents to produce a vote.[49] Still more comforting to the Progressives must be the fact that, with reference to the expenditures made, the results were considerably better than other recent third party efforts.[50]

Party	Year	Vote Received	Cost per Vote Received
Socialist	1908	95,504	.23
Socialist	1912	71,598	.08
Roosevelt Progressive	1912	665,420	.16
LaFollette Progressive	1924	235,693*	.05

* includes Socialist expenditures

Difficult to disentangle from the general problems occasioned by the lack of organization during the campaign was the handi-

49 Overacker, *op. cit.*, Table XX, p. 79.
50 *Ibid.*, Table XXI, p. 80.

cap due to the fact that, with the exception of incomplete slates of Socialist or Progressive candidates here and there, LaFollette and Wheeler had no supporting ticket. The movement, concentrating on capturing national office, overlooked a condition of American politics obvious to the most casual observer, namely, that the great national political machines are established upon sound, substantial local structures.

The failure of the Progressives to provide a local supporting ticket—almost inevitable when the choice to endorse LaFollette instead of immediately organising a new party was made—left the Progressive candidates standing on a shaky foundation, with the local organizations in the hands of indifferent politicians or inexperienced idealists. If there had been local tickets, unquestionably the candidates on those tickets would have taken a lively interest in promoting an efficient LaFollette organization and in getting the vote out on Election Day. Their interest in the success of the Progressives would have been far more personal.

Moreover, candidates for local office who might have been inclined to support the CPPA had to keep quiet in order to insure their own success or, in most cases, renew their allegiance to the old parties. An organiser for LaFollette received the following answer from a candidate for office in New England: [51]

> How can I openly support LaFollette? I am a candidate on the——————— ticket. If I declare for LaFollette, I cut myself off from my own party and I cannot join the LaFollette party because you have not got any. I am in sympathy with the LaFollette movement but I cannot run as your candidate because the LaFollette group has no local candidates. Both I, personally, and organized labor, for whose measures I have always worked, have everything to lose and nothing to gain by my doing so.

51 *Socialist World*, Nov. 1924, p. 7.

The failure of several distinguished liberal leaders to support LaFollette's candidacy disappointed many Progressives and undoubtedly dampened the enthusiasm for the cause. Although LaFollette was endorsed by such prominent state and local leaders as Senator Brookhart of Iowa, Senator Johnson of California, and Representative LaGuardia of New York, neither Senator Borah of Idaho nor Senator Norris of Nebraska gave the progressive movement unqualified assistance. Borah, in fact, stayed with the Republicans, speaking out in support of Coolidge's election. His biographer gives three reasons for Borah's loyalty to his party in 1924: first, the court issue; second, Borah's faith in Coolidge's personal integrity; and finally, his conviction that a third party was futile.[52] Borah's apprehensions over the court issue appear inconsistent with his earlier suggestions for restricting the Supreme Court. It is possible that the astute Borah recognised the risks involved in breaking his ties with the Republican organization. Perhaps he was receptive to Republican suggestions that regularity in 1924 might enable him to assume leadership of the party in 1928.

Norris' case was different. The Senator from Nebraska made no attempt to help the Republican candidates or to remain within the party framework. He did nothing to conceal the obvious fact that LaFollette was his choice for the Presidency.[53] But Norris took no active part in the progressive movement, restricting his speech-making to his own campaign in Nebraska for re-election. Norris' whole attitude toward a third party movement was revealed by his behaviour in 1924:

> If there is any inconsistency in George W. Norris' long career, it is the fact that in 1924 he was not an active adherent of his friend and mentor, Robert M. LaFollette. Back of this seeming incongruity are a number of factors which have been forgotten with the passing years. In the first place,

52 Johnson, C., *Borah of Idaho*, p. 303 ff.

53 Neuberger, R. L., and Kahn, S. B., *Integrity, the Life of George W. Norris*, p. 155, by permission of the Vanguard Press, publishers.

Norris had confidence in no political party. He thought the very nature of a political organization, regardless of how progressive the party's principles might be, tended to make men place loyalty to it above the general welfare of the country. When demands were coming from the hinterlands that La-Follette organize a third party, founded on liberal principles, Norris said, " I have small faith in a new party. There is too much belief in parties in this country. Unless its leaders were Christlike men—in which case they would not be political leaders———its candidates would be dictated by a few bosses conferring in private just as in the old parties." [54]

To many Socialists, disappointed by the Progressives' reluctance to strike out boldly in the formation of a new party, this lack of a supporting ticket was the major mistake of the campaign. One of their writers was calling it " the weak spot of the LaFollette campaign. . . . the lack of local candidates for Congress, the state legislatures, and the smaller officers, and the lack of an organized party instead of a mere presidential movement." [55] Lindsay Rogers had the same weakness in mind when he commented that " third parties . . . have usually attempted to secure the presidency. They have concentrated on that and when they failed they extinguished themselves as factors in the government." [56]

Without doubt, more attention to placing state and local candidates in the field would have enhanced both the short-run and long-run opportunities of the CPPA. In the short run, it would have provided the Progressives with a host of local campaigners whose concern for personal success would have been a guarantee of earnest endeavor. In the long run, to the extent that its candidates were successful, the CPPA would have had the beginnings of a permanent political organization on the day after election instead of the memory of a whirlwind campaign for the Presidency.

54 *Ibid.* By permission of the Vanguard Press, publishers.
55 *Socialist World,* Nov. 1924, p. 7, Comment by Alfred Baker Lewis. The same opinion was expressed to the author by Bertha Hale White, who was Executive Secretary of the Socialist Party in 1924.
56 Jenks, L. H. (ed.), *Future of Party Government,* p. 82.

CHAPTER X
DISAPPOINTMENTS EAST AND WEST

THE marriage of convenience between the Socialists and the trade unions was neither happy nor of long duration. The basic issue over which the friction between these wings of the CPPA developed was the proposed immediate formation of a third party.

When Theodore Parker was thundering against slavery in Boston, some wise friend placidly assured him that slavery would disappear in God's good time. " The trouble is," Parker is suposed to have replied, " that God isn't in a hurry and I am! "

The third party advocates in 1924, like Parker, were in a hurry. They were impatient to get on with the task of constructing the organization and formulating the policies of a new political party. This cleavage within the ranks of the CPPA became more and more apparent. The trade union and Railroad Brotherhood wing, inclined to be conservative and cautious, was reluctant to sever its ties with the major parties.

The Socialists, long used to defeat and disappointment at the polls, wanted to concentrate on the problem of establishing a sound, enduring third party composed of liberals and progressives who would subscribe, more or less, to a program of Marxian reforms. The trade unionists, in particular the Brotherhoods and the A.F.L., were not ready to take the plunge. At the July 4 convention the latter's wishes prevailed and the Socialists, resignedly, agreed to endorse the CPPA in the expectation that, in return for the favor, the Progressives accede to the Socialist desires immediately after election.

The Socialists were not alone in their visions of a new party. In general, the so-called " intellectual " element of the CPPA, like the Committee of Forty-Eight and the editors of the *Nation* and the *New Republic*, favored taking this decisive step. Although disappointed by the attitude of the labor leaders

197

whom they met at Cleveland, and perhaps equally disappointed by LaFollette's decision to run as an independent rather than as leader of a new party, the Socialists concealed their feelings and threw themselves enthusiastically into the campaign to elect LaFollette.

A general tendency, on the part of the labor leaders, to take the Socialists' support for granted and to look disparagingly upon their efforts must have had much to do with the growth of the friction which culminated in the strained feelings of the last CPPA conference in February, 1925.

At the Cleveland convention, the Socialists began to have the feeling that they were not full and equal members of the council table at the inner sanctum of CPPA headquarters. Hillquit remembered that " the idea (non-partisan strategy) was quietly spread among the principal railway unions, much to the dismay of the Socialists and other third-party advocates. I do not know to this day whether the strange notion originated with the Senator and was acquiesced in by the Brotherhood chiefs or, what seems to me more likely, the reverse was the fact. In either event, it struck me as a case of deliberate sabotage or monumental folly." [1] A Socialist delegate to the Cleveland convention complained that until the CPPA gathering had actually convened, the Socialist Party caucus had no authentic information of what had transpired in the CPPA National Committee.[2]

The Socialists were not ready to buy a pig in a poke. To change the metaphor, the Socialists were willing to give away the bride at this marriage of progressive forces, but they wanted a look at the bridegroom first. Some were afraid, at the party convention which met immediately after the CPPA endorsement of LaFollette, that the party was surrendering to forces which might wipe out the identity of American Socialism. A minority report, objecting to the alliance with the

1 Hillquit, M., *Loose Leaves from a Busy Life*, p. 316.

2 *Socialist World*, Jan. 1925, p. 10.

CPPA, spoke of the latter's "delightfully vague" platform, a "platform so meaningless it might have been written by W. J. Bryan thirty years ago." [3]

But once committed to the CPPA, the Socialists never hesitated. Young Bob LaFollette has spoken of "their yeoman service" to the progressive movement, and of their accepting CPPA decisions "manfully" in spite of their own desires and plans.[4]

No such ardor burned in the hearts of the labor men. Having fashioned the CPPA policy to suit its needs, the leaders of Organized Labor, in most instances, endorsed the movement with varying degress of mild enthusiasm. The support of the American Federation of Labor, which even at the start of the campaign had been an endorsement of LaFollette and Wheeler and not allegiance to a third party movement, dwindled both morally and financially as Election Day approached. Some unions refused to back LaFollette. The Pressmen, led by George Berry, supported John W. Davis. The Carpenters, with their leader, William Hutcheson, and the United Mine Workers, under John L. Lewis, endorsed Coolidge.[5] The Trainmen did not go along with the other railroad unions in supporting LaFollette; W. G. Lee, President of the Trainmen, announced early in the campaign that the constitution of the union did not permit the organization to endorse any candidate.[6] Labor's interest in the LaFollette candidacy seems to have been in proportion to LaFollette's chances of winning. Conditioned to a campaign strategy by which success was measured by the immediate standard of victory or defeat at the polls, the labor leaders began to fear, before the campaign was completed, that their bargaining power within the old parties would be seriously impaired. Lost causes held no special attrac-

3 *Socialist World*, July 1924, p. 12.

4 R. M. LaFollette, Jr., to the author, June 17, 1943.

5 Harris, H., *American Labor*, p. 377.

6 *American Labor Year Book*, 1925, p. 129.

tion for men whose policy had been to reward their friends and punish their enemies on Election Day.

The funds which labor had promised failed to materialize; the organizations they had planned were never completed and, before Election Day, scores of labor leaders—impossible to estimate—had abandoned ship. American Federation leaders were forced into the ludicrous position of reiterating throughout the campaign that they really meant what they were saying when they endorsed LaFollette. The opportunistic policies of American labor dictated a hasty retreat from such an ill-starred venture. The retreat was not official until after Election, when the AFL returned to its traditional voluntarism and the Brotherhoods withdrew from the CPPA. But the labor leaders sensed defeat before the polls opened. They were already making their peace. The most obvious of the labor retreats came in New York City where the Executive Council of the Central Trades and Labor Council withdrew its earlier endorsement of La-Follette and endorsed Davis just five days before election.[7] The actions of the New York labor leaders were probably a more reliable portent of the election than any of the numerous straw ballots.

Familiarity breeds contempt, especially in an organization as conglomerate as the CPPA. Before the campaign was over, the labor men were weary of their colleagues. Without doubt, contemptuous terms like " starry-eyed idealists " and " visionaries " and " impractical dreamers " were used countless times as trade unionists described, among themselves, the shortcomings of their strange political bedfellows.

In like manner, marked feeling of distrust and disappointment in their labor associates crystallized among the intellectuals and Socialists, a reaction destined to become more intense after the election. The Socialists were unable to appreciate the " short-run " view held by the unions. The unions were thinking in terms of Election Day; the " third-party boys " had

7 *New York Times,* Oct. 30, 1924.

their eyes focused on the political horizon. To the Socialists, the labor leaders were showing traits of timidity and even cowardice.

One observer, close to the Socialist movement in 1924 and both a participant in and historian of Socialist campaigns, has summed up the defects of the labor leaders under the following five headings: [8]

1. The trade unions were novices in politics. They played into the strategy of the old parties, especially the Republican party.

2. They were tangled up in their own demands and obligations. Politics within their own organizations prevented any long-term view.

3. They lacked self-sacrifice. They were all accustomed to getting paid for their services.

4. The veteran labor leaders, grown tired and cynical, were thinking merely of what they could get.

5. The unions were beset with all kinds of organizational difficulties.

Whether or not such a sharp indictment of the role played by the labor unions is justified, Mr. Fine's remarks reflect the widespread opinion among the Socialists that the unions backed out of the campaign. Socialists were convinced that the dead hand of craft unionism had weighted down the campaign. Norman Thomas, recollecting the 1924 days when he ran on the ticket with LaFollette in New York as Socialist candidate for Governor, has little praise for the part the unions played: [9]

> I personally and the Socialist Party ticket in New York State in 1924 got very little support from the A.F. of L. We got some support from unions affiliated with the A.F. of L. which at that time were close to the Socialist Party; for instance, the International Ladies Garment Workers. As a mat-

8 Nathan Fine to the author, June 21, 1943.
9 Norman Thomas to the author, May 21, 1943.

ter of fact, the LaFollette ticket nationally got less support as the campaign wore on from the A.F. of L. than was expected and, as I remember it, the executive council rather backed down on its endorsement toward the end of the campaign.

Ben Marsh, who had been a diligent worker for a third party since 1922, and a member of the original Executive Committee of the CPPA, is even more outspoken in his expression of disappointment in labor's contribution. He feels that many labor leaders were not interested in anything " basic " in 1924 but merely wanted a " larger cut of the capitalist swag." [10]

As the breach widened, the fundamental differences in approach became more apparent. The Socialists were seeking to establish, not in months but over a period of years perhaps, a party devoted to the elimination of the evils of the profit system. The conservative—or moderate—wing of the CPPA wanted to elect LaFollette and effect certain immediate revisions in governmental policy. The former stood upon their party principles, the latter were willing—even anxious—to make concessions and gain votes. It is futile to sit in judgment upon the two methods. Certainly, in terms of fundamental reform, the Socialist program held more promise. But since successful American political parties have always been a collection of disparate pressure groups of rich variety, held together by a dubious and often temporary affinity for holding office, the labor leaders were simply taking their cue from the methods employed by the old parties to gain and maintain political power.

Some of the more conservative—or pragmatic—CPPA supporters went so far as to suggest that the Progressives break away from their Socialist brethren. The following letter is probably typical of the reaction of many moderates to the Socialist side of the ticket: [11]

10 Benjamin Marsh to the author, Nov. 22, 1943.

11 Letter, Bruce Rogers, General Editor of Interport Feature Service, to Frank Walsh (date not given), (Walsh papers).

I can't see the state end of the Independent ticket. It is some more Socialist romanticism.

Thomas is running like a flat tire and it's a pity to slow down Bob's speed that way. What a fine strategic gesture it would be to withdraw state ticket but, of course, Hillquit, Thomas and Co. are too romantic for that.

How about a LaFollette-Smith Non-Partisan League, for information of split voters, and circulation of advisory ballots, etc? . . . . . .

The coolness between the labor leaders and the Socialists was especially noticeable in New York State where the Socialists, with a strong organization and brilliant leaders like Hillquit and Thomas, were in a position to stand up for their demands. In addition, the fact that Governor Smith, to whom many labor leaders were very friendly, was running for re-election, disturbed unionists who feared that a large Thomas vote would enable Theodore Roosevelt, the Republican nominee, to win. Algernon Lee, one of the Socialist leaders, drew attention to this divided loyalty of many Progressives early in the campaign.[12] The lack of enthusiasm among labor leaders for Norman Thomas at the New York State CPPA convention was apparent to the newspapermen.[13]

Of course, a large part of the bad feeling and misunderstandings among the CPPA supporters can be traced back to the absence of a supporting ticket. There was something absurd in the spectacle of the candidates of the progressive movement denouncing the two capitalist parties as alike while a large section of the same progressive group worked for the election of many candidates of the old parties. It is difficult to see how any national coalition, continuing such an anomaly, could have avoided disruptive disputes fatal to its success. When the Socialists perceived the anomaly, it reinforced their faith in a third party and convinced them that LaFollette's fatal error

12 *New York Herald Tribune*, Aug. 16, 1924.
13 *New York Herald Tribune*, Aug. 17, 1924.

had been in his refusal to run as the candidate of a new party.[14] Perhaps, from the point of view of a Progressive, the tragic irony of the 1924 campaign and elections is that the rigors and experience of trial by battle merely widened the breach between the wings of the party. The third-party advocates thought the election proved the need for a new party with a ticket to support the national candidates. The advocates of non-partisan political action within the labor unions were equally convinced that the 1924 experience proved the futility of forming a new party. Both groups were not only back where they started, but farther apart.

The behaviour of the labor unions during the campaign and the friction and disagreements within the CPPA lead one to draw some general conclusions about the role that labor played. First of all, it is obvious that labor defaulted, in large part, its leadership of the third party movement, a leadership so apparent at the time that the CPPA was founded by direction of the railroad unions. A second salient fact that the campaign revealed is that labor has commitments, and obligations, *quid pro quo*, with politicians within the old parties which it is reluctant to jeopardize by a forthright espousal of a new political movement.[15] No matter what kind of action the executive councils of American labor take, these local relationships remain. Professor Orton has called them " the vested interests " of labor. To Professor Orton, the matter of co-operation between third-party advocates and labor unions resolves itself into the question of " whether, or how far, the intellectuals can afford to recognize the vested interests of the labor movement." [16]

14 See editorial by James Oneal in *The New Leader,* Nov. 20, 1924, p. 12.

15 A provocative discussion of this condition, and its consequences, as they affect labor abroad, appears in Strumthal's *The Tragedy of European Labor.*

16 See Orton, W., "American and British Progressivism," *New Republic,* 42:536, Mar. 11, 1925, pp. 59-62.

In the East, the general reluctance of labor to make a clean break with the old parties and enthusiastically and unreservedly support LaFollette was a keen disappointment to the Progressives. But only slightly less discouraging was the readiness of the American farmer to return to the Republican fold when farm prices started to rise in 1924. The behaviour of farm prices was indeed providential for the Republican party. Most political observers, traveling through the Northwest country during the campaign months, were inclined to consider the advance in the price of farm commodities as the principal reason why that section would vote for Coolidge. A veteran political correspondent for the *Chicago Tribune,* whose prediction of the outcome of the election was almost identical with the result, stated that it meant the difference between victory and defeat for Coolidge.[17]

In 1924 America was recovering from the primary post-war depression and the upturn of the cycle was beginning to be felt on the farmers of the Middle West. Coupled with the increased demand for farm commodities at home was a disappointing harvest abroad, in Canada and on the continent. In October, 1924, hog prices had moved above eleven dollars, four dollars more than in the first week of July and the highest quoted price in two years![18] In Minneapolis wheat reached $1.50 on the second of October, the highest price since 1921. The prices of rye and flax rose accordingly in response to a heavy export demand. The European buyers, indirectly assisted by the extensive credits provided as a result of the Dawes Plan settlement, were able to make purchases in America. The rise in grain prices was general throughout the Mid-West. In Duluth grain prices rose as an average from .97 to 1.40 in the twelve months preceding election.[19] In Chicago the corresponding rise

17 *Chicago Tribune,* Oct. 11, 1924. Article by R. Henning. See also Chart 9, " Prices of Farm Products," *Recent Economic Changes,* Vol. II, p. 620.

18 *Minneapolis Journal,* Oct. 10, 1924.

19 *Chicago Tribune,* Nov. 1, 1924.

was from 1.07 to 1.43.[20] In early October the indications of prosperity were visible throughout the whole section where once the angry farmers had flocked to join the Non-Partisan League and where LaFollette's greatest hope of victory lay. For the first time in three years, the daily bank clearings in Minneapolis passed $20,000,000.[21] Of course, the Republican press lost no time in featuring these stories of the return of good times. Having for so long known only the lean years, the farmers of the Northwest were hardly in a mood to risk the fat years in political experimentation. The farmer was no longer embattled. The Non-Partisan League had disappeared as a national organization. Bankrupt and—in some circles—discredited, the state units were struggling against defeat and loss of membership. The last issue of the National Non-Partisan *Leader* had appeared in July, 1923. Perhaps impressed by the evidences of prosperity in the East, the farmers were willing to give Coolidge, Mellon and the Republican Administration a chance to bring it to them.

The rise in farm prices was not alone responsible for the alienation of LaFollette support in the West. The Supreme Court issue hurt LaFollette among property-conscious farmers who had a healthy respect for law and order. The bogey of a deadlocked election probably induced many farmers to vote for Coolidge. The *Minneapolis Journal,* violently opposed to LaFollette, featured an article that Villard had written for the *Nation* suggesting the likelihood of the election being thrown into the House.[22] The intent was clearly to frighten its readers with the prospect of an indecisive election.

The traditional reluctance of the American farmer to consider himself as an exploited peasant with interests and aims in common with the landless proletariat of the cities most certainly cooled the ardor of the agrarian wing of the CPPA.

20 *Ibid.*

21 *Minneapolis Journal,* Oct. 3, 1924.

22 *Ibid.,* Oct. 30, 1924.

The American farmer will have to undergo a fundamental change in his attitude toward labor before an effective, permanent farmer-labor alliance is possible in this country.[23] With the exception of the large cities where they had organized industrial workers, the Socialists were useless to the CPPA in the West. The intellectuals, perhaps as much so as the Socialists, misunderstood the temper and voting behaviour of the American farmer. Arthur Garfield Hays recalls how the learned speeches of third-party men would be interrupted by farmers who would ask " What's all that got to do with the price of hogs? "[24] The provincial farmers of the West resented the terminology of the Marxian. The indigenous stock of the central states looked distrustfully upon the so-called " New York Socialists," bearing strange and unfamiliar names. The newspapers opposed to LaFollette often capitalized upon this opportunity to widen the breach between the agrarian and industrial wings of the CPPA by caricaturing the progressive movement as a small, dark-complexioned and bespectacled " long hair," obviously of foreign extraction.[25] At the same time, Eastern periodicals were picturing the LaFollette supporters as a confused crowd of guileless hay-seeds, outlandishly bucolic!

In the West not only the great majority of the newspapers but also the larger part of the farm periodicals opposed La-Follette. The characteristic attitude of the influential farmer journals was to support Coolidge in an unobtrusive manner, perhaps to retain their advertising without alienating too many progressives. The most important group of farm periodicals—those joined together in the Standard Farm Paper Editorial Service—supported Coolidge. Included among these papers were *Wallace's Farmer* of Des Moines, the *Prairies Farmer*

23 See Tugwell, R. G., " Is a Farmer-Labor Alliance Possible? ", *Harper's Magazine*, 174:1044, May 1937, pp. 651-661.

24 Hays, A. G., *City Lawyer*, p. 270.

25 See, for example, McCutcheon's cartoons in the *Chicago Tribune* during the campaign.

of St. Paul, the *Progressive Farmer* of Birmingham, Alabama, the *Pacific Rural Press* of San Francisco, and the *Wisconsin Agriculturist* of Racine, Wisconsin. Altogether there were ten periodicals belong to this group. The strong *Breeder's Gazette,* a member of the S.F.P.E.S., announced its support for Coolidge when farm prices continued to rise despite some indication that it might have supported LaFollette.

LaFollette's chief farm periodical support came from the several Pierce publications, of which the *Wisconsin Farmer* and *Iowa Homestead* were the most influential and widely circulated. With a circulation of more than 100,000 weekly, the *Wisconsin Farmer*—through its energetic editorials and stimulating political articles—probably influenced voters as much as any farm publication in the country. Senator LaFollette wrote for Pierce during the campaign.[26] Actively engaged in getting women to vote for LaFollette, the *Wisconsin Farmer* emphasized the support the Progressives were getting from such outstanding women as Helen Keller, Jane Addams and Zona Gale. It is interesting to conjecture upon the effect this campaign directed toward the women had upon LaFollette's victory in Wisconsin. One of the Progressive campaign managers looked upon the support that Pierce's *Iowa Homestead* provided as LaFollette's chief source of strength in that state.[27] One of the severest setbacks to Progressives hopes of informing the electorate in the farm sections was the deterioration of the Non-Partisan League. By 1923, the national *Non-Partisan Leader,* with its powerful editorials, made even more graphic by John Baer's vivid cartoons, had discontinued publication. Only haphazardly did the state Non-Partisan organizations carry on a program of publicity.

The great majority of the newspapers of the country, of course, supported Coolidge. As was to be expected, the attitude

26 *The Wisconsin Farmer,* Oct. 9, 1924.

27 Villard, O. G., " Summing Up the Campaign," *Nation,* 119:3095, Oct. 29, 1924, p. 467.

of the conservative press toward the LaFollette candidacy ranged all the way from the precise correctness of the *New York Times* to the flagrant distortions in violently anti-LaFollette journals. Some of the most evident examples of journalistic unfriendliness to LaFollette came from the West, where— for many years—the Wisconsin Senator had been an issue all by himself. The *Chicago Tribune* did not conceal its dislike for LaFollette. In the Northwest, the *St. Paul Pioneer Press* headlined its front-page story on LaFollette's speech to the CPPA convention as: [28]

VITRIOLIC OUTBURSTS FROM BOB'S STATEMENT.

The *New York Times* earned the expressed thanks of *The Nation* magazine when the campaign was over for its fair and reasonably complete coverage of the third party campaign.[29] The Hearst papers exhibited a kind of indecisive neutrality throughout most of the campaign, finally declaring for Coolidge during the latter part of the campaign. Hearst had supported the idea of a third party with LaFollette in 1920 and was expected by many to support LaFollette again in spite of some of the liberal planks in the Progressive platform. It was, no doubt, LaFollette's record of isolationism that maintained the strange and illogical friendship—or at least, friendly neutrality —of the Hearst chain.

The Scripps newspapers represented LaFollette's chief source of journalistic strength in 1924. E. W. Scripps—" the Old Man "—had a fine record of liberalism behind him, vigorously supporting Cox in 1920; but he was growing old and tired. " By the time 1924 rolled around, Scripps was not interested enough in politics to take charge himself but he watched with interest the campaign for LaFollette directed by Robert P. Scripps." [30] There were, by 1924, twenty-five newspapers in

28 *St. Paul Pioneer-Press*, July 5, 1924.

29 *Nation*, 119:3098, Nov. 19, 1924, p. 531.

30 Cochran, N., *E. W. Scripps*, p. 186.

the Scripps chain, a majority of them in the Mid-West. First and foremost of them was still the *Cleveland Press,* whose vigorous editorial support helped no little in carrying that city for LaFollette. Scripps had secured brilliant editors for his papers—like Briggs of the *Cleveland Press* and Cochrane of the *Toledo News-Bee.*[31] Progressive managers still recall with gratitude the role they played—sometimes against the advice of the business office. But Scripps' policy of allowing his editors considerable latitude in formulating editorial policy sometimes hurt the progressive movement. Editors more cautious than Briggs or Cochrane moderated the Scripps support for La-Follette. Hence the attitude of the different Scripps papers varied, from city to city, from editor to editor.

The chief support for the CPPA, outside the Scripps newspapers, came from the liberal weeklies, the *Nation* and the *New Republic,* and the official organs of the labor unions, like the Amalgamated Clothing Workers' *Advance,* the *Journal* of the Locomotive Engineers, and, in particular, *Labor,* the official newspaper of the Railroad Brotherhoods. Of necessity, the circulation of these publications was limited. The combined circulation figure for the two liberal weeklies was probably not in excess of 75,000, confined mostly to the metropolitan area. With the exception of *Labor,* the union journals were little read outside of trade circles. Socialist organs like the *World* of Chicago and the *New Leader* of New York supported LaFollette. Of these union journals, *Labor* was the most widely circulated and undoubtedly the most influential. The weekly edition of approximately 500,000 copies was avidly read by Brotherhood members both fraternally loyal and politically conscious. Ably directed by Edward Keating, former Congressman from Colorado, whose devotion to the Railroad Brotherhoods gave the periodical an unconfused singleness of purpose, *Labor* had already tasted the fruits of victory in its novel program of political action; in 1922 it was credited with a large

31 Basil Manly to the author, June 16, 1943.

role in the surprising election of Wheeler and Dill to the United States Senate. In addition to its vigorous and wholehearted support for the LaFollette ticket, *Labor* issued special campaign editions designed to aid senatorial candidates endorsed by the railroad unions. Such special issues—sufficient to reach every voter in the states affected—were sent into Massachusetts to assist David I. Walsh, who defeated Coolidge's friend, Senator Butler; into Iowa to aid Brookhart; into North Dakota, for Nye; and into Pennsylvania—vainly—on behalf of William B. Wilson, former Democratic Secretary of Labor. With the assistance of such a special edition, Alben Barkley, who had endeared himself to the railroad workers by supporting their bill to abolish the Railroad Labor Board, won a handsome victory over Senator Ernst. To offset the effects of *Labor,* the supporters of Senator Ernst circulated a newspaper resembling *Labor* and bearing a Washington date-line.[32] The roorback failed, however.

The press of the nation appears to have committed two sins against the Progressives of 1924; one, a sin of omission—lack of coverage, and the other a sin of commission, the distorted reporting of Progressive issues and activities, sometimes accidental, sometimes intentional. The importance of the newspapers in the campaign led Upton Sinclair—one of the Progressive leaders in California—to suggest that a national organ for liberal political action be established before another campaign. Bitterly he commented upon this disadvantage of the Progressives: [33]

> In this campaign the capitalist newspapers could tell the public any lies they pleased, and we were helpless. For example, there was the lie that the LaFollette people had distributed minature champagne bottles, ' made in Germany ', to the audience at their rally at the Pasadena High School. The *Los*

32 *Baltimore Evening Sun,* Nov. 10, 1924.

33 Letter to the Editor from Upton Sinclair, *Locomotive Engineers Journal,* 78:1, Jan. 1925, p. 43.

Angeles Times featured that lie and refused to correct it. The writer took the trouble to telegraph to the LaFollette national headquarters for an authoritative statement of LaFollette's attitude on Prohibition. He got this statement, and sent it to the editors of our two local newspapers; one paid no attention to it, while the other destroyed it.

Unusual interest in the election was shown by the foreign language press. The foreign born, as a rule, accepted the multiple party system and, in addition, were disposed to support the LaFollette-Wheeler ticket as a means of disciplining the old parties. To many immigrants who had brought their European brand of Socialism with them, the third party movement provided an opportunity to renew their loyality to their principles. LaFollette's pronounced views on the war, the advanced views of the Progressives on government ownership, and the Socialist-Progressive alliance served to kindle an interest in the new political movement. In the compact and crowded urban areas where, for example, the clothing workers lived, Progressivism assumed a class-consciousness that perhaps only Socialist leaders like Hillquit appreciated. *Vorwärts* of Berlin hailed the formation of the CPPA as the beginning of successful Socialism in America.[34]

Of course, the considerable number of Communist-dominated foreign language periodicals were unalterably opposed to LaFollette. Vitriolic attacks, branding the Progressives as shams and LaFollette as a would-be dictator, came from such Workers' Party organs as *Laisve* (Lithuanian) and *Uj Elore* (Hungarian) in the metropolitan area.[35]

For the first time, in a presidential campaign, the radio was employed, though still on a small sale. The radio broadcasts of the Democratic convention at Madison Square Garden during the summer had underscored the importance of the radio

34 *New York Times,* July 5, 1924.

35 *Editorial Digest* (Foreign Language Information Service), Aug. 20, 1924, p. 6.

as a vehicle for distributing campaign material. It was an entertaining novelty for the American people to "listen in" upon the doings of a national convention. However, most of the receiving sets were in the urban centers of the North. Their comparative scarcity in the rural areas limited radio's usefulness. The first political speech delivered on a nation-wide hook-up—Senator LaFollette's Labor Day address—was considered a failure in terms of the cost-per-listener.[36] By 1928 raido was to make great strides. In 1924 the Democrats spent $40,000 on radio time. Four years later $600,000 was spent on the same item. By 1928 the major parties were spending ten times as much on radio as they did in newspaper advertising.[37]

The Progressives were handicapped a number of ways in employing this new political instrument. First of all, it was expensive and the Progressives did not have the money to spend. It was estimated that the Republicans bought ten times as much radio time as the Progressives.[38] Second, the families who possessed radio receiving sets in 1924 were largely middle-class, prosperous and comfortable, and usually impervious to calls from the Left. Neither the proletarian nor the agrarian had purchased his radio set yet. A third drawback to the radio, as far as the Progressives were concerned, was the comparative advantage it gave Coolidge and Davis over LaFollette. The latter, a veteran campaigner, thrived on the pageantry and rapport of the great public meeting. His vigorous personality, his facial gestures, his eloquent mannerisms had to be seen to be fully appreciated. Over the radio, much of that was lost. Moreover, Senator LaFollette never quite acclimated himself to the "radio technique." [39] He was too restless, too much the old-fashioned orator, to stand patiently behind a microphone. His voice would fade out as he moved across the stage; it would

36 See p. 156.

37 Odegard, P. and Helms, E., *American Politics,* p. 634.

38 *New Republic,* 40:520, Nov. 19, 1924, p. 284.

39 Verified by members of the LaFollette family.

come through the receiving sets too forcefully as he raised his voice. Most serious of all, the Senator could not discipline himself to the split-second timing so necessary on a radio schedule. Young Bob, in accompanying his father on his campaign tours, had to keep reminding the Senator not to depart from the prepared manuscript. The radio suited the talents of the introverted Coolidge much better than those of a consummate and experienced orator like LaFollette. The largest network ever assembled—twenty-three stations—was "hooked up" for a speech by Coolidge near the end of the campaign.[40]

Religious and racial issues were probably more spectacular than effective in the 1924 campaign. Both issues were double-edged swords whose cutting was done in either direction. It is unlikely that the outcome of the election was affected materially by these irrelevant issues, despite the disproportionate space accorded to them during the heat of the campaign.

The meteoric rise of the Ku Klux Klan—just about at the crest of its power in 1924 and claiming a membership that ran into the millions—had once again injected the issues of nativism and Roman Catholicism into American politics. As already noted, the Democratic National Convention had almost broken in two over this electric issue.[41] Politicians, as the campaign began, trod warily lest they alienate either Klan votes or the support of the Catholics, Jews and Negroes. LaFollette, in his letter of August 8, 1924 to E. W. Scripps, had been the first candidate for the Presidency to denounce the Klan by name. A week later John W. Davis did the same. Calvin Coolidge, throughout the campaign, maintained an unbroken silence on the Klan despite the ardent Democratic and Progressive efforts to smoke him out.

It was not strange that the Klan should dislike LaFollette. The Klan hated LaFollette because it knew that his words of denunciation of the Klan and its principles were not the weasel

40 *New York World*, Oct. 24, 1924.

41 See pp. 99-105.

words of a politician but the clear, ringing language of a man to whom narrow-mindedness and intolerance were evidence of petty and contemptible character. The Klan could not hate LaFollette for the color of his skin, or because he was Jewish or Catholic; it hated him for what it termed his " hyphenism," his pacifism, and for his liberal associations whence came the bravest words of indictment of the Klan.

The great minds of the Klan lost no time in attacking La-Follette and the Progressives. As early as August, the Imperial Wizard, Hiram Evans of Georgia, was explaining the progressive movement to his loyal and faithful followers. " The most pernicious thing in the political life of America," the Wizard pointed out, " is the appeal being made by a group of dissatisfied political leaders led by Senator LaFollette to destroy the people's confidence in this, the soundest, the greatest and the best government on earth." [42] Several weeks later, as if to maintain a correct neutrality between the two parties devoted to maintaining the soundest, greatest and best government on earth, Mr. Evans magnanimously announced that conscientious Klansmen could vote for either the Republican or Democratic candidates.[43]

There are two reasons why the importance of the Klan in the campaign should not be over-estimated. First, it is highly probable that the Klansmen who voted against LaFollette would have done the same had there been no Klan. The average Ku Kluxer was a conservative, fearful of encroachments upon his property, suspicious of strange people and new ideas. It did not take membership in the Klan to send his blood pressure up at the thought of government ownership or collective bargaining. Moreover, it is likely that many Western Klansmen, placing their personal economic interests ahead of allegiance to the Imperial Wizard, voted for LaFollette. A member of

42 *New York Times,* Aug. 11, 1924.

43 *Ibid.,* Sept. 2, 1924.

the CPPA executive committee believes this to have been the case in many instances.[44]

The charge that LaFollette had been pro-German during the World War has already been considered with reference to its use as a device with which the old parties sought to discredit his campaign in 1924.[45] Like almost all personal issues of this sort, it sometimes boomeranged. His critical attitude toward participation in the War endeared LaFollette to many persons of German descent, both within and outside Wisconsin. The Steuben Society of America officially endorsed LaFollette and Wheeler.[46] Grateful as they were for his wartime attitude and his stand in foreign affairs, the members of the Steuben Society were not judicious in their display of enthusiasm for LaFollette. Shrewdly presented to the American people by the campaign strategists of the old parties as another evidence of his hyphenated Americanism, the Steuben endorsement probably lost more votes for LaFollette than it gained.

The ubiquitous Irish question appeared as a minor issue in the 1924 campaign. The CPPA convention had gone on record in favor of Irish independence.[47] On July 20th, LaFollette received the endorsement of the impressive-sounding American Association for the Recognition of the Irish Republic. In view of LaFollette's wartime remarks about British imperialism and the expressed sympathies of many CPPA leaders for Irish freedom, the endorsement was not unexpected. Austin Ford's *Irish World* vigorously supported LaFollette. Indeed it is possible that Mr. Ford was influential in LaFollette's decision to take a strong stand against the KKK. Several days before LaFollette sent his letter denouncing the Klan to Scripps, the *Irish World* had urged him to come out as unequivocally as

44 Benjamin Marsh to the author, June 4, 1943.

45 See pp. 162-164.

46 *New York Herald Tribune*, July 21, 1924.

47 *Proceedings*, CPA Convention, July 4-5, 1924, Vol. II, p. 228 (M. G. Johnson papers).

Levi Morton had done against the APA when running for governor of New York.[48] The prominence of the article in the Walsh papers suggests that Mr. Walsh, active in Irish-American circles, might have brought it to the attention of his close friend, Senator LaFollette.

As the campaign progressed and Republican emphasis upon the threat to the Supreme Court took effect, some of LaFollette's initial advantage among the Germans and the Irish was lost. At a time when the Constitution and the courts seemed to be their only bulwark against Klan-controlled legislatures determined to strike against their parochial schools, the Catholics and Lutherans became apprehensive over the suggestions of the Progressives that the power of the Supreme Court be curbed.[49] Germans, both Protestant and Catholic, remembering the emotional excesses of 1917-1918 and recalling that occasionally the courts protected their rights, were reluctant to vote into the discard—as the old party chieftains told them they would be doing—the indomitable and vigilant protector of their liberties. Charles G. Ross, the veteran political correspondent for the *St. Louis Post-Dispatch,* ascribed the disappointingly small vote for LaFollette in Missouri to the vivid impression the Court issue made upon the German-Americans of that state.[50]

When the campaign began there were high hopes in Progressive circles that the Negroes would rally to the cause. The intellectual wing of the CPPA was most hopeful. Others, more pragmatic or more cynical, did not bank so heavily upon support from that quarter. At the July 4th convention, William Pickens, brilliant graduate of Yale, appeared as a delegate from New York. He brought with him a message from the National Association for the Advancement of Colored People.[51] Oswald

---

48 *The Irish World* (New York), July 26, 1924.

49 See letter of Chester C. Platt, Secretary, Wisconsin Non-Partisan League, *Nation*, 119:3099, Nov. 26, 1924, p. 573.

50 *St. Louis Post Dispatch*, Nov. 5, 1924.

51 See p. 115.

Garrison Villard was most sanguine about the prospects of Negro support and urged LaFollette throughout the campaign to give more attention to this source of strength. The following excerpt from a letter written by Mr. Villard to Senator LaFollette not only indicates what action the Negroes were taking, but also the efforts Villard made—without much success—to bring this important minority group within the CPPA:[52]

> . . . Probably you have not heard that the National Association for Colored People (*sic*), of which I was one of the founders, now the most important organization working on behalf of colored people with a membership of some 70,000, at its Philadelphia Convention came out in favor of a third party. It was, of course, an unprecedented course for a negro organization to take. They were correspondingly disappointed that there was no mention of their course in the Cleveland platform, although Haiti and Santo Domingo were touched upon, and other matters. A ringing letter or a giving of part of one of your speeches to this subject, would have a tremendous effect upon the colored people . . . .

There is no indication that any substantial effort was made, on behalf of the progressive movement, to organize the Negroes or that the Negroes as a group supported LaFollette on Election Day. Negro leaders, like William Pickens—a LaFollette elector in the State of New York—W. E. Burghart DuBois, and James Weldon Johnson, wholeheartedly and actively supported LaFollette. Bishop Hurst of the African M. E. Church, urged Negroes to vote for LaFollette.[53] But the great bulk of the colored vote reacted on Election Day like the great bulk of the white vote—to machine politics, local considerations and pressure group interests. Most certainly the Negro vote was not identifiable in the 1924 election.

52 Letter, O. G. Villard to R. M. LaFollette, July 11, 1924, (Villard papers).

53 *New York World*, Oct. 7, 1924.

CHAPTER XI
DEFEAT AND DESERTION

ALL the forebodings of the Progressives were confirmed on Election Day. The resounding ratification of Administration policy and endorsement of the *status quo* probably even exceeded Republican expectations. The peculiarities of the American electoral system, which translate a decided trend towards one candidate into a " landslide triumph " were again, as in 1920, functioning. Sooner than ever before, the American people knew the outcome as the radio broadcast news of the Coolidge lead mounting higher and higher. The following table gives the total national results: [1]

	Popular	Electoral	No. of States
Total no. of votes cast	28,647,709	....	....
Coolidge	15,275,003	382	35
Davis	8,385,586	136	12
LaFollette	4,826,471	13	1
Others	160,649	....	....

Before analysing the totals for the various candidates, it would be well to consider the significance of the light vote cast. It is estimated that 56,925,000 persons were eligible to vote in the 1924 election. Only slightly more than fifty percent of the electorate availed itself of its civic privilege and duty. Approximately twenty-eight million Americans, who had the right to vote, were insufficiently aroused, despite the third party movement, and all the determined activities—of both partisan and non-partisan groups—to make an effort to get to the polls on a day warm and sunny throughout most of the nation.[2]

An historian of the 'Twenties has made a pertinent comment on the apathetic attitude of the American people toward political issues:

1 From Cousens, T., *Politics and Political Organization*, Table 43. Unless otherwise noted, figures on the election of 1924 are taken from official sources.

2 A *Natonal Get-Out-the-Vote League* was enthusiastically supported in 1924 by the women's clubs, service organizations, etc.

So engrossing was the complex life of business, and so exacting the obligations of a life of pleasure, that politics was no longer needed as a popular amusement or topic of conversation. The decline of politics is curiously parallel to the contemporary decline of the pulpit and in both cases the fundamental cause seems to have been simply that people in general preferred the automobile to the affairs of church or state.[3]

Neither the peril of the Supreme Court, so clearly discernible to Mr. Dawes, nor the predatory plots of the monopolists whom Mr. LaFollette would so willingly destroy, were able to compete in public interest and attention with the lure of a drive in the country or another round of golf.

The LaFollette vote reached a total of 4,826,471 of which 3,797,974 were cast as Progressive votes, 858,264 as Socialist, and 170,233 as Farm-Labor votes. LaFollette electors, under some party designation, appeared on all state ballots except that of Louisiana where it was necessary to write in the names of the LaFollette supporters. 4063 such votes were cast in Louisiana. In five states, Connecticut, New York, Pennsylvania, Missouri and Oklahoma, LaFollette electors appeared separately under both Independent (or Progressive) and Socialist designations.

The minor parties (except the Progressive) played an insignificant role in the 1924 election. Herman P. Faris, the Prohibition candidate, polled 57,551 votes, more than half of them from the two states, California and Pennsylvania. Frank T. Johns and the Socialist-Labor ticket secured 39,400 votes. Gilbert O. Nations, depending upon the anti-Catholic elements in his American Party, received 24,430. The Communists turned out 36,386 votes for W. Z. Foster, at the head of the Workers' Party ticket. The old Single Taxers, now called the Commonwealth Land Party, were able to get only 2,882 votes

3 Slosson, W. P., *The Great Crusade and After*, p. 92 (American Life Series, ed. by Schlesinger and Fox). This political indifference lends weight to H. M. Robinson's indictment of the " Twenties " in his *Fantastic Interim.*

for William J. Wallace. Many Single Taxers, no doubt, cast their ballots for LaFollette.

Where did the LaFollette vote come from? What was the composition of the Progressive vote? What conclusions can we draw about the five million votes cast for LaFollette and Wheeler? How much support did the Socialists provide? In 1920 Eugene Debs, as Socialist candidate for the presidency, received 919,799 votes. Allowing for the increase in the whole vote in 1924, we can credit LaFollette with one million Socialist votes in 1924. This would include about 150,000 votes in addition to those cast for LaFollette in the Socialist column. It is reasonable to assume that a considerable number of Socialists, through necessity or preference, voted for LaFollette in the Independent or Progressive column. How many votes did LaFollette receive from the farmers or "agrarians"? The Progressive vote in the Granger states and on the Pacific Coast was 2,957,570. Deducting from this an estimated Socialist vote of 425,000 (slightly larger than the Debs vote of 1920) we arrive at a LaFollette farm vote of 2,530,000. Add to this the vote—compact and organized as it was—of the Railroad Broth-1,100,000 votes to be credited to various liberal and protest groups like the American Federation of Labor, the Committee of Forty Eight, and the independent voters.[4] It is likely that Railroad Brotherhood support accounted for more than 200,000 LaFollette votes inasmuch as the influence of the railroad unions extended into the ranks of labor beyond their own affiliates.

What effect did the Progressive vote have upon the major parties? From which of the old parties did LaFollette draw more heavily? In 1920 the distribution was as follows:

4 See the analysis of this election in Keenleyside, H., "The American Political Revolution of 1924," *Current History Magazine*, 21:6, Mar. 1925, pp. 833-840.

Candidate	% of Total Vote
Harding	60.2
Cox	34.4
Others (inc. Debs)	5.4

In 1924 the results were:

Candidate	% of Total Vote
Coolidge	54.0
Davis	28.8
LaFollette	16.5
Others	.7

Thus it would appear that the injection of the Progressive movement resulted in the following decreases:

	Decrease in % of Total Vote
Republican	6.2
Democratic	5.6
Others	4.7

These over-all figures on the whole country are apt to be misleading. If one breaks these results down into sectional percentages, distinct regional characteristics in the election become obvious. To observe this, note first the 1920 figures for the various sections of the country.

Region	Republican	Democratic	Others
Pacific Coast	63.3	25.2	11.2
Mountain	61.4	35.1	3.5
New England	66.1	29.1	4.8
Middle Western	65.1	29.2	5.7
Middle Atlantic	60.5	33.6	5.9
Southern	40.3	55.3	4.4

In 1924, the results were:

Region	Republican	Democratic	Others	Progressive
Pacific Coast	55.2	10.8	1.5	32.5
Mountain	50.4	21.4	..	28.2
New England	63.2	26.4	.6	9.8
Middle Western	55.6	23.2	.6	20.6
Middle Atlantic	56.9	29.2	.7	13.2
Southern	34.4	59.1	1.0	5.5

Two conclusions can be drawn from a comparison of these tables. First, the Republicans suffered most, as a result of the Progressive campaign, in the Mid-West, the South and New England. Second, the Democrats were hurt most on the Pacific Coast and in the Mountain and Middle Atlantic sections. If one considers these losses in terms of electoral vote potential, it becomes apparent that, for the greater part, the Republicans suffered in those sections where the result was already a foregone conclusion, as in the South. The Democrats, on the other hand, lost valuable " pivotal " votes to the Progressives in those parts of the country where (like New York and California) it is imperative that the Democrats score the victories that mean the difference between winning and losing the national election.

It is interesting to conjecture whether Davis' electoral vote would have been larger if LaFollette had not made the race. There seems little doubt that the Democratic candidate would have been able to obtain more electors but still a number woefully insufficient to carry the election. President Coolidge won thirteen states by a plurality rather than by a straight majority. These states were Arizona, Idaho, Kentucky, Maryland, Missouri, Montana, Nebraska, Nevada, New Mexico, North Dakota, South Dakota, Utah and West Virginia. Without question, if the battle lines had been strictly bi-partisan in these states, some would have chosen Democratic electors.

When the LaFollette candidacy had been announced, in July, 1924, Davis and other Democratic leaders were of the convinced opinion that the third party movement would adversely affect the Republicans far more than it would affect the Democratic party. After the election, Davis was sure that the LaFollette candidacy had produced exactly the opposite effect and that it had considerably helped the Republicans.[5] The election results confirm Davis' conclusions. Unlike Coolidge, the Democratic candidate was a minority victor in only one state, Oklahoma.

5 John W. Davis to the author, May 24, 1943.

In his home state of Wisconsin, Senator LaFollette won easily, with votes comfortably ahead of the combined totals of his opponents. LaFollette secured more votes than Davis in eleven other states: California, Idaho, Iowa, Minnesota, Montana, Nevada, North Dakota, Oregon, South Dakota, Washington and Wyoming. In each of these states, Coolidge ran first. In thirty-six states LaFollette came in third. The twelve states in which LaFollette ran better than third accounted for 19.1% of the presidential vote of the entire country. But these dozen states gave LaFollette 42% of his total.[6] In these same states, LaFollette's vote was 36.4% of the vote for all the candidates. In these states the LaFollette popular total was 2,208,655. The popular vote in the same area for Davis was 508,064 or 25% of the LaFollette figure! Certainly one of the salient facts of the 1924 election was this wholesale desertion of the Democratic party by the Mid-West and Trans-Mississippi section. Obviously Westerners who had voted Democratic in previous elections were attracted by the campaigning of the Progressives. The voting behaviour of these Western voters in 1924 suggests that the Democratic party members in the West are not nearly so anchored to their moorings as the Democrats of South and East. Westerners have utilized the Democratic party as a vehicle through which to register their protest. When a more forceful instrument of protest is available, they have no hesitancy in deserting the party. The essential negativism of a third party which merely transfers the protest vote from an old party to a new one, without submitting a program of common action upon which the dissident elements within the new party can agree, is likely to afflict any reform movement with a fatal paralysis.

The extent of this shift from the Democrats to the new political grouping provides the key to the election in the West.

6 Basil Manly, Eastern Campaign Manager for the Progressives, recalls Senator LaFollette, early in the campaign, drawing a line on a map to include Wisconsn, the Northwest and California and remarking that in that area was his political strength. Basil Manly to the author, June 16, 1943.

In highly important California, the Progressives polled 424,649 to an insignificant 105,514 for the Democrats. Washington gave LaFollette 150,727 to 42,842 for Davis. The alacrity with which the West supported liberal Democrats in the 1930's was matched by its reluctance to support a conservative in 1924. Ewing's comment on the poor showing of the Democratic national ticket in the West is especially pertinent: [7]

> One cannot say that the West was particularly concerned over the deadlock at Madison Square Garden between Mc-Adoo and Smith forces. But there is one thing sure—the western democrats wanted a liberal candidate. When John W. Davis emerged as the eleventh-hour choice of the convention, the West was definitely lost to the party. He wore none of the West's liberal colors and they treated him as they had treated Parker and even Grover Cleveland.

The analysis made of the distribution of the vote in terms of county areas by Professor Macmahon discloses the ecological and geographical factors which play so important a role in sectional politics.[8] With the exception of the Wisconsin counties, LaFollette carried only one county (Clinton, in southeastern Illinois) east of the Mississippi. But the Progressives ran second in 25 Illinois counties, in 20 in Michigan, in 10 in Ohio, in 9 in Pennsylvania, in 2 in New York and in 1 in New Jersey. The location of these counties in highly urbanized and industrialised sections is, of course, more than coincidental. In the industrialised north of Illinois and the urban fringe of Lake Erie, from Michigan to New York, clustered the bulk of the LaFollette counties. In Alleghany County, in Pennsylvania, containing the tremendous industries of Pittsburgh, LaFollette ran close behind the Republican candidate, with four times as many votes as the Democrat.[9] In Monroe County, New York,

7 Ewing, C., *Presidential Elections*, p. 99.

8 Macmahon, A., " Political Parties and Elections," Special Supplement to *Political Science Quarterly*, Vol. XL, 1925, p. 51.

9 Robinson, E. E., *The Presidential Vote*, 1896-1932, p. 308.

the great city of Rochester scored heavily for LaFollette. In New Jersey, the textile centers of Paterson and Passaic were the source of LaFollette's chief strength. Professor Macmahon remarks cogently upon the gratifying results for the Progressives in these sections.

> In nearly every one of these areas some influence had been at work in advance of the campaign, preparing at least the raw materials of organization, like the longstanding movements of social reform and labor leadership in Cleveland, the constant efforts at organization on the part of the Farmer Labor Party in northern Illinois for over five years, the unusually strong interest of the Pennsylvania State Federation of Labor, under Mr. Maurer, in politics and in Rochester, the movement which at the same election returned Mr. Jacobstein to Congress with combined Democratic and Socialist endorsement. The spotty character of the LaFollette vote in the East was not accidental.[10]

The election confirmed the apprehensions of those who began to fear, as the campaign progressed, that organization is of such primary importance to the success of an American political party that the improvised machinery of the Progressives would prove woefully inadequate on Election Day. In those sections of the country where established reform groups like the Socialists were functioning on behalf of the LaFollette ticket, the results of the election were not too disappointing. Where it had been necessary for the Progressives to organize themselves, the election totals usually reflected the hasty, ill-conceived or defective methods of local organization.

A comparison of the election results of 1912 and 1924 discloses, of course, how much more successful Teddy Roosevelt was in accumulating votes, especially electoral votes, than was Senator LaFollette.[11] Roosevelt's 88 electoral votes, from the

10 Macmahon, A., *op. cit.*, p. 56.

11 See Parzen, H., *A Comparative Study of the Progressive Presidential Campaigns of 1912 and 1924,* Unpublished Thesis, Columbia Univ., 1926.

states of California, Michigan, Minnesota, Pennsylvania, South Dakota and Washington, may have disappointed his Bull Moose followers, but they provided a better showing than LaFollette's meagre thirteen electors, the Wisconsin total. In popular votes both Roosevelt and LaFollette ran better than the count in the Electoral College indicates. In 1912, Roosevelt obtained 4,126,020 votes out of a total of 15,031,169 or approximately 27% of the whole vote. In 1924, LaFollette's vote was 4,826,471 out of a total of 28,647,709 or approximately 17%. The Progressives of 1924 fared much worse than the Bull Moosers in the East and South. The following comparisons of the third party percentage of the total vote indicate this: [12]

	1912	1924
Maine	39.	5.9
Rhode Island	21.6	3.2
New Jersey	37.	10.
Virginia	16.	4.6
North Carolina	28.5	1.
Tennessee	22.	3.5

What happened in these states was representative of the whole East and South. The story was different on the other side of the Mississippi. In six states, all of them in the West, the 1924 Progressives obtained a bigger chunk of the state totals than had the Bull Moosers. These states were Idaho, Iowa, Minnesota, North Dakota, Wisconsin and Wyoming.

The relative showings of Roosevelt and LaFollette again emphasize the importance of organization in American politics. When Roosevelt broke with the G.O.P., he took scores of local

---

An enlightening comparison of the Bull Moose and 1924 Progressive movements in Maine is offered in Elizabeth Ring's "The Progressive Movement of 1912 and the Third Party Movement of 1924 in Maine," University of Maine Studies, Series II, No. 26 *Univ. of Maine Bulletin*, Jan. 1933, p. 53. Miss Ring points out that Maine farmers, frightened by the threat of competition with Canadian lumbermen and potato farmers, strongly supported Coolidge.

12 Parzan, H., *op. cit.*

bosses and state machines along with him. They paid off in Election Day dividends. Roosevelt's was not so much a third party movement as it was a national schism within one of the old parties, neither more permanent nor enduring than Teddy Roosevelt's high resolve to fight the bosses of the Republican Party. Roosevelt's Progressives had other advantages: the almost limitless financial resources of such ardent supporters as Perkins and Munsey, the sometimes fanatical devotion and support of prominent Republicans and Republican newspapers.

One of the numerous faults of our anachronistic Electoral College system is the readiness with which it conveys the false impression of a political landslide. The Congressional results in the 1924 election did not sustain the appearance of an overwhelming Republican endorsement, so vividly suggested by the electoral totals. The Democrats, in Congress, incurred a net loss of two Senators and twenty-four Representatives. The regular Republicans gained three Senators and fifteen members in the lower house. The " Progressive Bloc " lost a Senator— Magnus Johnson losing to Congressman Schall in Minnesota —but gained two members in the House, one of whom was Fiorello H. LaGuardia, who had, by this time, definitely repudiated the Republicans and publicly joined the Progressives as a self-labeled " Independent." No one, in the New York area, had more actively and unequivocally supported the La-Follette-Wheeler ticket.

So the election had effected a shrinkage in the ranks of the Democrats and anti-Administration forces, but certainly no indiscriminate sweep from office such as accompanied, for example, the Franklin Roosevelt victory in 1932.

A perusal of a map showing the election results in 1924 will quickly disclose the sectional nature of the LaFollette strength.[13] Of course, an analysis in terms of states, such as Table I, will always overlook important but elusive patterns of local political behaviour.[14] Nevertheless, for our purposes,

13 See Appendix #6, Maps I and II.
14 See Appendix #5.

the state lists are a fairly trustworthy guide to the 1924 election. When the votes were counted, it was the West and Midwest which had evinced more than a passing interest in the Progressive campaign. Several general conclusions may be drawn from this. First, it is evident that the old spirit of Populism and political rebellion was not dead. The 1924 vote of the West can be taken as substantially a " protest " vote against Coolidge, rather than as any commitment to a doctrinaire third party. The second conclusion is that the urban centers of " labor politics " in 1924, like Cleveland and Rochester, represented little more than precarious political islands, isolated by a sea of Republicanism. So long as the Electoral College is retained, these small dots of liberal-labor revolt may be safely overwhelmed by the Republican votes of their middle-class neighbors in the suburbs and country districts. The alternative to defeat, for these groups, is to effect a pragmatic alliance with the state and city bosses of the Democratic party, with the long view in mind, perhaps, of eventual control as labor refines its techniques of political action.

The major concession to the third party advocates at the Cleveland convention had been a promise for a conference— after the elections—to consider the advisability of forming a new party. It was thought that the propitious time to launch the party would be after the diverse elements within the progressive movement had been welded together by the unifying force of campaign work and battle.

The following resolution had been adopted by the Cleveland delegates: [15]

> On the 29th day of November, 1924, the National Committee shall meet and issue a call for a special National Convention, to be held in the latter part of January 1925 at such place and such definite date as the Committee may decide.
>
> The object of the Convention shall be to consider and pass upon the question of forming a permanent independent po-

15 *Proceedings,* CPPA Convention, July 4-5, 1924, Vol. II, p. 265.

litical party for National and local elections, upon the basis of the general principles laid down in the platform adopted by this Convention.

Although delayed several weeks, the Convention met in Chicago on February 21-22, 1925, at the Lexington Hotel. About three hundred delegates arrived representing the various organizations and groups of labor, farmer, political and non-partisan movements within the CPPA. The roll-call voting strength of each of the organizations was based on the number of members within the particular group represented. As on previous occasions, the convention was presided over by William H. Johnston, Chairman of the National Executive Committee.[16]

This convention was to be very different—in temper and mood—from that of Cleveland. This time—as Morris Hillquit pointed out—" the delegates had come to bury Caesar, not to praise him." [17] The two opposing groups within the progressive movement had come to a very definite parting of the ways. The railroad men had made up their minds. They had abandoned the third party experiments, immediately after election.[18] The American Federation of Labor had gone on record at its El Paso national convention against further support for a third party. The Executive Council of the AFL National Non-Partisan Political Campaign Committee had applied the *coup de grace* when it reported

the launching of third party movements has been proved wasted effort and injurious to the desire to elect candidates with favorable records. The 1922 and 1924 political campaigns definitely determined this fact. Experience therefore has taught labor that to be successful politically, it must continue

16 *Report*, National Progressive Convention, Chicago, Feb. 21-22, 1925, National Progressive Hdqtrs., Washington, D. C.

17 Hillquit, M., *Loose Leaves from a Busy Life*, p. 321.

18 *Labor*, (Washington, D. C.), Nov. 15, 1924.

in the future, as in the past, to follow its non-partisan
policy.[19]

The American Federation of Labor had lost no time in saying
good-by to its friends of the campaign. Moreover, the American
Federation was publicly stating that it had made a mistake!

The union men who had come to Chicago still hopeful that
a third party would be created realised full well that any action
they took would have to be taken as individuals, not as union
representatives. The attitude of these unionists still loyal to the
third party idea was well expressed by William Johnston. " As
president of one of the labor unions, and as one who believes
in a new alignment, I could not speak for my organization as
such. When the Machinists joined the union with which I
happen to be connected as president, they did not concede to
me the authority to come into a meeting of this kind and
commit them to any party. Personally, I favor a new political
alignment. I see no hope in the old parties." [20] If Mr. Johnston
could see no hope in the old parties, neither could he nor any
other delegate to the Chicago conference see much hope of
starting a new one. The shades of night were falling fast over
the CPPA; and as the delegates arrived, it became more
apparent that this special convention called to form a " permanent political party for national and local elections," this convention called to preside at the birth of a new party, was, in
greater likelihood, to officiate at the interment services of the
expiring LaFollette progressive movement.

The Chicago convention turned out to be an amicable agreement to disagree. The Socialists wanted to form a proletarian
party. The unions were tired and already committed to returning to the fold of the old parties. The Western agrarians were
preoccupied with local politics or entranced by the rising price
of wheat. The net result was the dissolution of the tempor-

19 *American Federationist*, 32:1, Jan. 1925, p. 55.

20 *Report*, Nat. Prog. Convention, p. 3.

ary coalition which had been created in 1922 and had continued to exist, amorphously and haphazardly, through the presidential election of 1924.

There were three distinct groupings at the Chicago meeting: the Socialists, strong for a dynamic program of political action; the unionists, who felt that their fingers had been burned in the 1924 campaign and were now anxious to return to the traditional Gompers' policy of non-partisan behaviour; and finally, the Northwesterners, agrarian and LaFollette supporters. The latter were almost as enthusiastic as the Socialists over the prospect of organising a new party but they were suspicious of the Socialist plans to organise the new movement along economic, rather than geographic, lines. The agrarians and LaFollette people already had their organizations and they had no intention of scrapping them. " Vocational " and " functional " representation within the party sounded too much like the new-fangled and slightly alien nomenclature used by the Eastern intelligentsia, impractical visionaries from Greenwich Village or the editorial office of a left-wing weekly.

It was a foregone conclusion, when this final session of the CPPA convened, that the union men would not co-operate. The AFL report, the expressions of opinion in the labor press, the statements of labor leaders, all left little doubt. When the editor of *Labor,* the official newspaper of the Railroad Brotherhoods arrived in Chicago, he hastened to tell the reporters that " formation of a new party at this time would be futile." [21] Some of the leaders of the Brotherhoods were even opposed to attending this convention which they had, a year before, so specifically and earnestly promised the third party advocates.[22] Arriving in town the day before the opening of the CPPA conference, the Brotherhood leaders, after a lengthy executive meeting, decided by a vote of 9-6 to take part in the conven-

21 *New York Herald Tribune,* Feb. 22, 1925.

22 Edward Keating to the author, Nov. 15, 1943.

tion.[23] There was no question of participation; merely whether to pay the CPPA the courtesy of attendance. Truly the unions had drifted far away from the third party idea! Johnston, of the Machinists, was the only trade union leader to stand by the idea of independent political action at the Chicago meeting. And so a mainstay of the progressive movement was gone; the brotherhoods were attending the meeting merely to wish their comrades of 1924 a fond and friendly farewell. The Progressives were losing their most compact element. The *New York World* headlined its story on the proceedings of the convention, " Debs and Hillquit Inherit Wreck of LaFollette Party." [24]

There was no rancor, no recrimination, as the labor men departed—just a certain sense of poignant sadness. The men who had, together, fought the good fight had come to the parting of the ways. The " practical " men, the " hard-headed " men, were leaving. The " starry-eyed idealists " remained behind to carry the torch. And, to more than one spectator, the drama of the moment did not go unnoticed. Debs, the old crusader, feebler for having arisen from a sick bed, made one last desperate attempt to avert dissolution of the progressive coalition.[25] Years later, Morris Hillquit still vividly recollected the scene when the veteran Socialist leader pleaded with the labor men to stay.

> It was a particularly moving moment when the aged Eugene V. Debs rose to address the gathering. He had taken a leading part in the organization of the railroad workers during the early period of their struggle. He had worked for them unselfishly and untiringly in the days of their weakness and poverty and had suffered persecution and imprisonment in their behalf. And now, as he stood there, tall, gaunt, earnest and ascetic, before the well-groomed and comfortably

23 *New York World*, Feb. 21, 1925.

24 *Ibid.*

25 *Proceedings*, CPPA, Feb. 21-22, 1925, Part I, p. 105ff.

situated leaders of a new generation, he seemed like a ghost of reproach from their past and calling them back to the glorious days of struggle and idealism.[26]

This was Eugene Debs' only appearance before a CPPA gathering. Little realising how numbered were the days of the old Socialist leader, the assembled delegates were nevertheless a hushed and attentive group as Debs began his speech. Almost as though he were aware himself that here was one last opportunity to reaffirm his faith in the Cause for which he had devoted his whole life, Debs revealed the creed by which he had lived: [27]

> ———. Do you know that all the progress in the whole world's history has been made by minorities? I have somehow been fortunately all of my life in the minority. I have thought again and again that if I ever find myself in the majority I will know that I have outlived myself. There is something magnificent about having the courage to stand with a few with and for a principle and to fight for it without fear or favor, developing all of your latent powers, expanding to the proportionable end, rising to your true stature, no matter whose respect you may forfeit, as long as you keep your own. — If a labor party is organized, it must expect from the beginning to be misrepresented and ridiculed and traduced in every possible way, but if it consists of those who are the living representatives of its principles, it will make progress in spite of that, and in due course of time, it will sweep into triumph. So I have learned to be patient and to bide the time, —

Other Socialists joined Debs in his futile attempt to enjoin the labor leaders. In what Lewis Gannett called " one of the finest speeches I have ever heard," Morris Hillquit called upon the unionists to carry on and to organise with the Socialists in

26 Hillquit, M., *op. cit.*, p. 322.
27 *Proceedings*, Part I, p. 105.

a third party.[28] Sometimes scornfully, sometimes emotionally, Hillquit scored the attitude of the labor men. " If five million voters were not enough, will you wait until we have swept the country? ... Did you start your trade unions on that practice? Did you wait until the workers in the different industries clamored to be organised? " [29]

All that remained to be done was to pronounce the CPPA officially dead. After a lengthy and inconclusive discussion of the general question, " Shall there be formed a Progressive party? ", the business of the first day culminated in the motion made by Mr. Shepherd, of the Conductors' Union, " that this Committee (*sic*) on Progressive Political Action adjourn and that those who desire to organise a new or third party, whatever they may term it, may assemble in this room at eight-thirty tonight." [30]

The action suggested by the motion offered the only practical procedure under the circumstances. Formal adjournment of the CPPA would preserve appearances and avoid embarrassments. The union men were saved the ordeal of getting up and leaving the meeting. Individual delegates, who could not have divested themselves of their representative capacity in the non-partisan CPPA, were free to accept the invitation to convene later in the evening in the " new " conference.

Upon unanimous adoption of Mr. Shepherd's motion, the CPPA expired at seven p.m. on Saturday, February 21, 1925. With the exception of the officer-delegates of the railroad unions, nearly all the delegates reassembled at eight-thirty to consider the formation of a new party. Appropriate motions were passed transforming the gathering thus assembled into a Progressive convention. A motion by Mr. Arthur Garfield

28 Gannett, Lewis, " A Party Struggles to be Born," *Nation*, 120:3113, Mar. 4, 1925, p. 240.

29 *Ibid.*

30 *Proceedings*, Part I, p. 108.

Hays, " be it resolved that this convention declare itself a convention of delegates to a new independent political party," was unanimously adopted.[31] William Johnston continued to preside over the new gathering, just as he had in the CPPA meetings, after making it clear that he had no mandate to represent his union in the formation of a third party.

On the grounds that the rank and file of the electorate should be given an opportunity to participate in the formation of a new political party, the convention deferred action on either creating a new party immediately or upon naming it. These tasks, presumably, were to be the responsibility of the delegates to a convention to be called sometime in the autumn by action of an executive committee. This committee was to be headed by William Johnston, the chairman, who was empowered to choose four members to serve with him on the committee. The four chosen by Mr. Johnson were Mrs. Basil Manly, Washington, who was also to serve as Secretary, Dr. Mercer G. Johnston of Baltimore, Mrs. Mabel Costigan and Hartwell Brunson, both of Washington.[32] The chairman had purposely chosen Progressives residing in or near Washington in order to meet more frequently.

Even with the Brotherhood delegates departed, there was still disagreement among the Progressives. No sooner had the supporters of a new party reassembled at eight-thirty on the evening of February 21 than a new cleavage appeared—this time between the Socialists and agrarians, Getting the cart somewhat ahead of the horse, the delegates sharply divided on the issue of representation in the forthcoming autumn convention of a party not yet born or christened! The new clash was precipitated by Hillquit's motion to allow party organization along economic, or vocational, lines, as well as on a geograph-

31 *Proceedings*, Part II, p. 24.

32 *Locomotive Engineers Journal*, Vol. 58, No. 8, Aug. 1924, p. 8.

ical basis.[33] This motion squarely presented the question of group representation versus state autonomy in the formation of the new party. The matter was referred to a committee appointed by the Chairman, in effect postponing the battle over economic or geographic representation until the second and last day of the conference. On Sunday the action of the committee in upholding geographic representation was endorsed by a roll call of the delegates, 93-64, and the Socialists had lost again.[34]

The breach between the Socialists and the agrarians over party structure revealed again a basic difference between the Socialist and Western elements within the progressive movement. The Socialists, anxious to emulate the successful British Labour Party, found support for the idea of functional representation among the radical needle-trades workers.[35] It is interesting to conjecture how much of the Western opposition to the Socialist proposal derived from the realization that— now that the railroad unions had left—the radical clothing workers were the only unionists in the movement. The Westerners wanted a Progressive, not a Labor, party. They became suspicious of the motives of the left-wingers. The Socialists were tactless to suggest that the new party call itself " The American Labor Party." It was at least fruitless for the Socialists to lay so much stress, in their speeches, upon nomenclature misunderstood by the West. Eastern radical leaders have never fully comprehended the reaction of the Western farmer to Marxian terminology and methodology. Nothing could be more exquisitely designed to chill the enthusiasms of the average Western delegate to a political convention that the lexicon of Marxism. An observer at the Chicago gathering noticed their

33 *Proceedings,* Part II, p. 28.

34 *Proceedings,* Part II, p. 100. The Hillquit motion had taken the form of a minority report of the committee, tabled by 93-64.

35 *The Advance* (official organ of the Amalgamated Clothing Workers) (New York), Feb. 27, 1925, p. 6.

antipathy to Socialist orators whose accents betrayed foreign birth.[36]

Having deferred any action on the actual formation of a new party until autumn and having placed its precarious future in the hands of an executive committee, this assemblage of Progressives adjourned on Sunday, February 22. Actually, with the CPPA dissolved, the prospects of a new party seemed more remote than ever. The task of Johnston's executive committee was almost hopeless.

The organization established by the Progressives in February, 1925, provided a graceful means of slipping into oblivion. Although Mr. Johnston's inexhaustible store of energy and optimism had not deserted him, there was a hollow ring to the clarion call sent out by the " National Progressive Headquarters of the New Political Party " on March 6 of that year. Progressives everywhere were called upon to " prepare for 1926" and "be ready for 1928." [37] In reporting the "accomplishments " of the Chicago meeting at which the CPPA had been dissolved and the framework of a new Progressive Party created, William Johnston, as Chairman of the new party's Executive Committee, needed eloquence and faith to revive the flagging spirits of the men who had followed LaFollette.

Sporadically holding meetings of the national committee and vainly attempting, in the face of insuperable financial obstacles and the growing prosperity of the Coolidge Era, to organise a convention of America's liberals, the small band of Progressives carried on until the end of 1927. In this, its last stage, the leadership of the progressive movement reverted to the middle-class reformers and intellectuals who had, as members of the Committee of Forty Eight, been so instrumental in laying the groundwork for the CPPA. William Johnston, seriously ill,

36 Gannett, L., *op. cit.*, p. 240.

37 See " Greetings to Progressives Everywhere," letter distributed from National Progressive Hdqtrs., Washington, D. C., Mar. 15, 1925 (Marsh papers).

yielded the chairmanship of the new organization to Mercer Green Johnston (not related), a Baltimore neighbor of J. A. H. Hopkins, and himself one of the most forceful and crusading figures within the Committee of Forty Eight.[38] An Episcopalian minister by profession, Dr. Johnston, devoted by conviction to lofty ideals and high standards of conduct, was about as far removed from the utilitarian opportunism of the average political party chairman as one could imagine. The names of other officers and members of the National Progressive Headquarters—Peter Witt of Cleveland and Mrs. Gordon Norrie of New York, Vice-Presidents; Dr. Donald Hooker of Baltimore, Mrs. Mabel Costigan of Washington; Mr. Arthur Garfield Hays and Mr. Oswald G. Villard, both of New York— reflect the sectional character of the group. The progressive movement had declined into a small nucleus of earnest, literate reformers, with both the " practical politicians " and the Marxians absent.

National Progressive Headquarters had been charged, at the February meeting, with the responsibility of calling a convention at which the new party would be officially christened and a nationwide organizational framework constructed. It became Dr. Mercer Johnston's difficult task to prepare the " call " for this convention. Much more cognizant of the financial and organizational problems involved in calling a national convention than some of his colleagues, Dr. Johnston, with the approval of the national committee, sounded out state units and liberal groups on the advisability of holding such a convention and on the extent to which they would be willing to contribute towards its expense. As Dr. Johnston feared, state correspondents were not nearly so enthusiastic for a national meeting involving work and money. Representatives of only seven states endorsed the convention idea and agreed to contribute it it.[39] Disappointed by the meagre response, the

38 *Minutes*, Meeting of Executive Committee, National Progressive Hdqtrs., held at Baltimore, Md., Jan. 16, 1926, (M. G. Johnston papers).

39 *Minutes*, Meeting of Exec. Comm., Nat. Prog. Hdqtrs., Baltimore, Md., Apr. 10, 1926, (M. G. Johnston papers).

committee decided to postpone the call to convene.[40] The Declaration of Progressive Faith, composed for the National Committee by Oswald Garrison Villard and Peter Witt in 1926, was destined never to be read before a party convention.

Legatee of a variety of political and administrative headaches bequeathed by the defunct CPPA, Johnston's committee deserves commendation not only for its efforts to preserve the spark of progressivism, but also for the manner in which it manfully shouldered the unmet obligations of the CPPA. By raising several hundreds of dollars itself and through a generous contribution from the railroad unions, National Progressive Headquarters, under Dr. Mercer Johnston, paid off the greater part of the ten thousand dollar debt inherited from the CPPA.[41]

Several issues of *The Progressive Bulletin,* official organ of the new political group, were issued from headquarters in Baltimore in 1926. Various efforts were made to effect a union with the Farmer-Labor Party of Minnesota, one of the few vital progressive units functioning in the late 'Twenties. But it was not enough. Labor had returned to the protective folds of the old parties; the Socialists, unconvinced by the sincerity of their 1924 associates, had moved back to their position of uncompromising Marxism. The vigorous voices of protest fell on ears deafened by the comfortable blandishments of Coolidge prosperity. The legendary figure in the White House, with his magic formula for accomplishing much by doing nothing, was gaining the blind devotion of an ever greater multitude of Americans. It was not yet 1929.

In such an atmosphere, with Coolidge's world too much with them, National Progressive Headquarters sadly gave up the ghost on November 3, 1927. On that day, with only three members present, the motion to adjourn *sine die* was

40 *Ibid.*

41 *Minutes,* Meeting of Exec. Comm., Nat. Prog. Hdqtrs., Baltimore, Md., Feb. 20, 1926, (M. G. Johnston papers).

carried.[42] The motion had been preceded by a long consideration of correspondence from progressive leaders throughout
the country, most of which indicated that no worthwhile
purpose could be served by continuance of the national Progressive organization.

In a letter sent to all members of the Executive Committee on
January 3, 1928, Dr. Johnston pointedly explained the reason
for the decision to dissolve the Progressive organization: [43]

> . . . First, as to the decision reached at this meeting to ad-
> journ *sine die*. At no time since I became a member of the
> Committee appointed at the Chicago Convention with Wm.
> H. Johnson as its chairman has it seemed possible to carry out
> the duty imposed upon the Committee. Both before and after
> the chairmanship devolved upon me, I was wholly ready to go
> as far as the hard facts our Committee had to face warranted.
> We sought in vain to find facts more favorable than those
> that hemmed us in. Only by ignoring the facts could our Com-
> mittee have gone ahead and called a National Convention.
> If there remained in any mind a last lingering doubt of the
> truth of this, it was dispelled by reports and letters presented
> at the meeting of November 3. . .

In an expression of deep faith and prophetic perception, Dr.
Johnston concluded his final report with a poignantly sincere
command for progressives to stand fast.

> . . . .The adjournment of the Executive Committee of Na-
> tional Progressive Headquarters does not mean the end of the
> Progressive Movement—by no means. It still possesses ele-
> ments of great strength. The power exercised by the Progres-
> sives in Congress was never greater than it is at this time.
> Sooner or later the principles for which the Progressives
> fought in 1924 will assume definite militant form.

42 *Minutes*, Meeting of Exec. Comm., Nat. Prog. Hdqtrs., Washington,
D. C., Nov. 3, 1927, (M. G. Johnston papers).

43 *Report* of M. G. Johnston, Chairman, to members of Executive Committee, National Progressive Headquarters, Jan. 3, 1928, (M. G. Johnston
papers).

Little could Dr. Johnston, or anyone else, on that morning when the obituary of the 1924 progressive movement was prepared, know how soon the cautious conservatism of a Republican Administration would be rejected by a weary and hungry electorate. Little could anyone, in 1928, appreciate how quickly and how completely militant ideas of political and social change would catch hold in an America overwhelmed by the greatest economic distress in its history. The seeds of progressivism had not been destroyed; they lay scattered, to grow and to be nourished in the tragic soil of depression.

CHAPTER XII
AFTER LAFOLLETTE

SENATOR LaFollette, who had been for the greater part of his career the embodiment of progressive ideals: dynamic, indefatigable and implacable, was coming to the end of the road. His days beyond the last CPPA conference were numbered. The strain of the campaign, added to his seventy years and coupled with a recent period of frail health, proved too much.

LaFollette lived long enough to give the Republicans the satisfaction of punishing him for his political heresy. As reprisal, the party regulars ousted him from Republican caucus, consequently depriving him—and the score of other Republican congressmen who had supported him in the election—of committee rank. LaFollette's 1924 bolt had provided the party leaders with a splendid opportunity to replace him with a dependable, conservative regular, James Watson of Indiana, on the important Interstate Commerce committee in the Senate.

The final personal blow to the CPPA came on June 18, 1925, when, exhausted and weary, unable any longer to resist the maladies afflicting him, Senator LaFollette passed away at his home in Washington. The hopes for a third party in 1928 died with Senator LaFollette. He would have been too aged to lead another political revolt himself, but the devotion of his admirers might have endowed the progressive movement with the cohesive quality without which, after 1925, the whole conglomeration of agrarians, Socialists, liberals and labor men fell apart and disappeared.

It was fitting that Senator LaFollette should pass away at the moment when America had chosen to accept the materialistic creed of the 'Twenties. LaFollette's faith in the common man seemed out-of-date in a nation spellbound by the exploits of wealth and bigness. His capacity for vigilance and criticism seemed unwanted by a people which had condoned corruption in high places. His Jeffersonian distrust of the powerful few, the oligarchy of rank and riches, struck a discordant note in the market-place, the market-place where all Americans, of course, could become millionaires by buying the right stock, the same market-place which assured a chicken in every pot and two cars in every garage.

LaFollette had left his mark upon the American political scene. His contribution might be better assayed, not in 1925, but in 1940 or 1950. It was going to take the American people a long time to evaluate the man properly. LaFollette's life had been long filled to overflowing, with both the fury of combat and the remorse and sorrow of defeat. " His role was that of an awakener of thought, a stimulator of action, a purifier of the public life. There was sacrifice in it, and suffering. There was also satisfaction. It is the only role a Robert LaFollette could have played." [1]

The collapse and disappearance of the progressive movement after the 1924 election cannot be fully explained in terms of the particular conditions and circumstances which blighted the La-Follette campaign. To establish—let alone win elections—a third party is a Herculean assignment; a task multiplied many times when the new organisation is liberal or radical, as was the case in 1924. The two-party system is so strongly ingrained in the structure of American politics that efforts to coalesce the opposition elements are likely to accomplish little beyond re-affirming the strength of the old parties. If the principles and policies espoused by the third party are unpopular, the leaders of the major parties can safely denounce or ignore them. If the new party has a live issue, capable of attracting votes, the old party leaders will probably steal it. In either case, a new party's lot is not a happy one. Unless it chooses, like the Socialist and Prohibition parties, to continue tasting the bitter dregs of defeat in election after election, a new party is almost certainly

---

1 Ogg, F. A., "LaFollette in Retrospect," *Current History Magazine,* 33:5, Feb. 1931, p. 691. See also Sayre, W., *Robert M. LaFollette, A Study in Political Methods,* Unpublished Doctor's Thesis, N.Y.U., 1930, for a brilliant appraisal of Senator LaFollette.

doomed to an early death. In dying it may often be comforted by the thought that its policies, having been kidnapped, are in safe and strong hands.

To be permanent, a party must be organised from its roots *advice* upward. The hasty collapse of the Bull Moose movement, a decline quite as metoric as its rise, is eloquent testimony to the temporary nature of parties which appear fullgrown from the brow of some great political hero. The pathetic lack of organisation of the Progressives in 1924 is further evidence that, in a nation with the geographical scope and magnitude of the United States, the groundwork for the construction of a new political party is a gigantic undertaking. Considerations of local office-seeking are of such vital importance in determining the success of an entire party ticket that it becomes futile for a national candidate to expect success without diligent preparation in county and precinct spadework.

To the dismay of the Progressives, the 1924 experience demonstrated the effectiveness with which the various state election laws hamper—intentionally or not—the efforts of a third party movement. Running for office is not merely a matter of placing one's name in a space provided on the ballot. Long, wearisome days of legal study and consultation, precious—and expensive —weeks collecting signatures and perhaps even funds for election fees are prerequisites for getting one's party on the ballot. The election machinery, in the hands of members of the old parties, is manipulated so as to discourage, if not to prevent, the appearance of a new party column on the election ballot.

And the plans, ambitious as they must be, of a third party take money and willing hands. In a country where campaigns last for several months and millions of dollars are spent on traveling expenses, rentals, campaign literature, radio time and all the incidental expenses, success at the polls must be predicated upon ample and sufficient financial support. Those affluent enough to finance a new party, even if not frightened off by the purposes of the rebel group, will hesitate to contribute to a party which can hold out little promise of success. The *quid pro quo* arrangement, which so often is a determining factor in campaign donations, is hardly applicable when the chance of rewarding the party angels is so remote. Thus a kind of vicious circle restricts the new party from achieving results. Because it has no money, it is unable to organise. Because it is unorganised—and likely to lose, it attracts little financial support. The " cohesive power of public plunder " cannot be generated for any prospect so lean as the political dividends of a protest vote.

What has been said of money applies equally to political workers. With his characteristically pragmatic approach, the politician is unwilling to associate himself with a losing cause. After all, he is primarily interested in winning his own—or his own candidate's—election. If supporting a new party jeopardises his prospect of winning, then, naturally, it will have to wait to secure his endorsement; wait until it has demonstrated its ability to win elections. The bandwagon did not go out of date with the horse and buggy. In 1924, neither Senator Borah nor Senator Norris, notwithstanding their personal admiration and friendship for LaFollette, campaigned for him. In fact, while Norris remained silent, Borah endorsed Coolidge and the Republican ticket. There is evidence that both these great Western leaders, while probably unmoved by selfish considerations, were convinced of the futility of a third party. Among politicians less powerful and less independent than men like Borah and Norris there was the fear of reprisals after Election Day when the old parties would still be around, working at the same old stand.

It seems a practical impossibility for a new party to erect a national organization, penetrating into the smallest towns and counties and supported by experienced local politicians or leaders capable of getting out the vote. To do so takes time, patience, volunteers and money far in excess of the amount produced by the progressive crusade of 1924. The Bull Moosers of 1912, with Munsey and Perkins funds behind them, were at least in possession of one of these much needed ingredients for success. The LaFollette Progressives, of course, were in dire financial stress all the time. In fact, if we may judge from 1924, the only effect, from a financial viewpoint, of the emergence of a liberal third party like LaFollette's is to facilitate the task of the revenue collectors of the old parties. Just when the major parties were in need of some extra cash, LaFollette or Wheeler would considerately blast again at the Supreme Court or " big business " and the flow of checks and money orders into Republican and Democratic headquarters would resume.

Moreover, for many persons, voting the old ticket has become an environmental or cultural characteristic. Such persons would no more think of deserting their party than their families. Their political behavior is as predictable as the salivary response of a conditioned dog in Prof. Pavlov's laboratory. " To many good Americans, there is something peculiarly sacred about the two party system. It is like the decalogue, or the practice of monogamy, or the right of the Supreme Court to declare a law of Congress unconstitutional." [2] In striking contrast to social politics abroad, the United States has never witnessed any permanent, effective alliance of farmers and laborers. Perhaps the singularly dynamic development of the nation, with its abundance of cheap land and pioneer opportunities, has been chiefly responsible for this. Occasionally—when their immediate interests coincide, as in 1932—farmers and workers vote together, but more frequtently they are opposed.

> The farmers want lower freight rates, while railroad employees demand higher wages. Daylight saving meets the need of city workers, but is objectionable to the farmers. Higher prices for farm products do not seem reasonable to workingmen in cities. The farmer is individualistic and capitalistic in

2 Hicks, J. D., " The Third Party Tradition in American Politics," *Mississippi Valley Historical Review*, 20:1, June 1933, p. 3.

his views. He is group-conscious, but not class-conscious. Only when some emergency arises does he turn to the state for help.[3]

Whether the cause is to be found in some such tangible conflict of interest or as a result of the farmer's preoccupation with his property interests, the net effect is an almost complete lack of the class feeling noticeable in Europe. Farm-labor political alliances have been temporary expediencies here, with the two groups finding common cause in opposing conservative forces but falling apart as soon as more definite and positive policies take shape. " What it takes to arouse resentment and revolt they have; what it takes to go forward on a line of action they have not." [4]

American farmers, clinging to a political habit which contradicts Marxist concepts of group solidarity, have persistently declined to identify their own welfare with that of the industrial proletariat. American farmers " disbelieve in industrial evolution." They prefer to adhere to their faith in a Jeffersonian Utopia, where each man has his plot of land and the right to buy more land. Their panacea for the social and economic ills of the nation lies not so much in extensions of government controls as in limitations and safeguards upon the freedom of the industrialists to convert the nation into a bustling urban community of factories, technological skills and hired workers. Their reluctance to co-operate politically with the proletarian victims of the industrial process has been a consequence of their refusal to accept, in their thinking and political attitudes, this condition of change. Mid-West farmers may have voted for La-Follette because his principles reminded them of Populism, or

3 Haynes, F. E., " The Significance of the Latest Third Party Movement," *Mississippi Valley Historical Review*, 12:2, Sept. 1924, p. 182.

4 Tugwell, R. G., " Is a Farmer-Labor Alliance Possible," *Harper's Magazine*, 174:1044, p. 651.

5 Macmahon, A., " Political Parties—The United States," *Encyclopedia of the Social Sciences*, Vol. II, p. 599.

because his swing around the circuit was Bryanesque, or because, like Mary Lease, they just felt like raising less corn and more hell. To them, LaFollette was in the tradition of those great champions of the soil of that West whose economic conditions and grievances had cradled so many rebel party movements. To them, LaFollette's party was another party of agrarian dissent, a latter-day collection of Free-Soilers, Greenbackers and Populists. They voted for LaFollette because he seemed to express so abundantly their wrath and their loathing for the malefactors of great wealth who had tinkered with the order of things.

The Progressives did not receive a full measure of support from organised labor. Labor's original reluctance to endorse LaFollette and Wheeler before alternative courses were exhaustively explored, its wavering, inadequate support during the campaign, its early retreat in the face of defeat, its indecent haste to abandon the progressive movement and humbly solicit the old parties for a share of the political swag once more, all of this demonstrated that organized labor—at least, large and controlling sections of it, particularly in the American Federation of Labor and the Railroad Brotherhoods, were not prepared to face the logical consequences of a real break with the entrenched political machines.

Looking back on 1924 now, we can discern certain difficulties of this particular third party—features which, in all probability, would also hamper other progressive movements. First of all, there was not time enough. From July 4 to November 4 was inadequate for the construction of a new political organization. Painstaking time and energy must precede the actual launching of a national party.

Then, too, prosperity—the Coolidge variety—beckoned with too many material comforts. Attuned to the low emotional vibrations of Coolidge's negative policies, the nation was in no mood to hear the Progressive plea. Indeed, theirs were voices crying in a wilderness, a wilderness crowded with popular-

priced automobiles, golf courses and service club outings. La-
Follette and the Progressives raised their voices when the business interests were apparently more thoroughly entrenched,
in both political power and public esteem, than at any time since
the days of Harrison and McKinley. Despite the wishful
dreams of intellectuals, the nation was not ready for a counterpart of the British Labour Party in 1924. Neither the intellectuals, who had failed to prepare the way as the Fabians had
done in England, nor the labor unions, which were still frankly opportunistic, were adequately equipped to launch the new
party. Major political movements are the products of their
times, with economic and social factors strong enough to compel changes in voting behaviour and to remold party lines.
There was no such compulsion about 1924.

There were too many dissensions within the CPPA. La-
Follette's mixed army went in too many directions, all at once.
The heterogeneous nature of the movement undermined confidence. Not only was there the obvious difficulty of conciliating
trade-union ideas with Western agrarian principles and Non-
Partisan League practical politics with the idealism of Eastern
intellectuals, but there was always the fear on the part of each
group that it might be swallowed up by the others. This feeling implanted in all of them a sense of inferiority, a need for
being on guard. The Socialists distrusted the labor unions; the
unions feared Socialism. The farmers were hostile to the Socialists and in economic disagreement with the labor unions.
Jockeying for position in the new organization, the different
parts of the CPPA found difficulty in watching the common
enemy. One effect of the internecine dissensions was to make the
movement more and more dependent upon LaFollette. The temporary basis for agreement among agrarians, labor unions, intellectuals, Single Taxers, the Committee of Forty Eight and all
the rest had been the endorsement of LaFollette and Wheeler.
It was both a strength and weakness of the movement. The extent to which the CPPA was dependent upon LaFollette and
submissive to his desires was shown when it permitted him, as

its candidate, to dictate the platform. As the campaign progressed, it became increasingly the "LaFollette movement" and the terms "Progressive" and "CPPA" were much less in evidence. While a tribute to his personal magnetism and the force of his character and personality, such a development heightened the impression that the progressive effort was a one-man show, which, instead of laying the foundation for a new party, would culminate in victory or defeat for LaFollette on Election Day. The 1924 progressive movement, under these circumstances, became as vulnerable and as mortal as La-Follette.

In spite of LaFollette's attempts to make monopoly the major issue, there was no paramount issue in the campaign.[6] This coincided with Republican strategy to divert attention from the Harding scandals. LaFollette often lashed out against the "interests"; Wheeler generally denounced "the Ohio Gang." Frequently, the Progressive leaders would condemn imperialism or high tariff policies. Often they called for agricultural relief. But none of these appeals had political glamour in 1924. The apathetic electorate seemed bored by the charges of Republican scandal and corruption. Monopoly was not the torch word LaFollette expected it to be. At best, it was an issue which lacked constructive character, largely negative by nature. LaFollette seemed to be thinking still in terms of 1905 or 1910, little aware that the problems of the 'Twenties called for remedies more complex than the dissolution of trusts and the elimination of the private monopoly system. In the campaign, as he denounced monopoly, LaFollette was constantly reiterating the battle cries and suggesting the panaceas of an earlier day. Trustbusting days were over, but the Senator did not realize it. "In final judgment the veteran warrior turned again to the veteran issues—and decided to march his legions out to familiar shell-torn battlefields."[7]

6 See Sullivan, M., "Looking Back on LaFollette," *World's Work*, 49:3, Jan. 1925, p. 326.

7 Richberg, D., *Tents of the Mighty*, p. 135.

Issues which LaFollette did not intend to emphasize were cleverly accentuated by the old-line politicians. In particular, three issues stand out as distinct liabilities to LaFollette. They were the Court issue, LaFollette's alleged pro-German sympathies, and the threat of an election deadlock. The first of these, as we have already seen, alienated countless sincere voters concerned about the dignity of the Court or the preservation of civil liberties. In the minds of many substantial God-fearing citizens, the members of the Supreme Court were close to demigods. Any attack, even indirect, upon them approximated blasphemy. Mark Sullivan has described how some voters made up their minds. After describing the venerable, dignified justices in their solemn robes he says:

> The voter looked on the photograph of the Supreme Court and saw all that. Then the same voter turned to the campaign photographs of LaFollette, some of which were not of La-Follette at his best, he saw in LaFollette something of that unusualness, that aberration from the conventional, which is frequently a deterrent from confidence in the average man's mind, the pompadour hair that suggests emotional excitability—the voter turned from one photograph to the other and decided to stand by what seemed to be the picture of greater stability.[8]

It may be amusing to think of anyone to whom campaign issues and choices can all be simplified into a comparison of two photographs. Nevertheless this psychology must have been effective in swelling the Coolidge total on Election Day.

Allusions to LaFollette's war record, as already indicated, were frequent and effective. LaFollette's poor showing in Missouri may be evidence that his lack of ardor for the Allies lost him more votes among patriots whose enthusiasm had not yet abated than it gained for his ticket in German sections.

The apprehensions over the possibility of a deadlocked election served the Republicans well. The fearful picture drawn

8 Sullivan, M., *op. cit.*, p. 331.

by the nimble imagination of many a Republican editor of the disastrous confusion sure to follow in the event of an indecisive electoral count seemed to provide tangible evidence of the dangers foreseen by George Harvey when he cried out that the paramount issue was " Coolidge or Chaos." [9] By " Chaos," as he was careful to point out, Harvey meant the paralysing consequences of a deadlocked electoral college. That George Harvey's exuberant desire for Republican success in the election temporarily exceeded his faith in the American constitutional system was obscure to many alarmed voters.

Although its leader had passed away and its official organization was stillborn, the ideas and the men of the progressive movement marched on. From 1925 until the coming of the New Deal, it was the undercurrent of reform and rebellion, an undercurrent dramatically re-emerging in the places of the mighty in 1933. Intermittent efforts to organise a third party of Progressives on a national scale continued. Progressive leaders concentrated, in the late 'Twenties, on maintaining and enlarging the liberal bloc in Congress, a group sufficiently large and influential enough to embarass the Coolidge and Hoover Administrations. As a Congressional group it reflected in large part the agrarian policies of Northwesterners like Shipstead and Frazier. Perhaps its greatest victory was the passage of the McNary-Haugen farm relief bill, although President Coolidge killed the bill by veto.

The 1928 national election provided no opportunity for progressives to offer their program to the country. Confused by irrelevant issues and misled by whispered canards, the American voter found himself on a holiday from thinking, his choice at the polls often determined by Al Smith's pronunciation of *radio* or the latest rumor about the Free Masons or the Knights of Columbus.[10] Repeating again and again the pragmatic idiom,

9 Harvey, G., " The Paramount Issue—Coolidge or Chaos," *North American Review*, 220:824, Sept. 1924, pp. 1-9.

10 See Peel, R. V., and Donnelly, T. C., *The 1928 Campaign*, pp. 112-128, for an analysis of the factors in this election.

Mr. Hoover sought and secured election as the guardian of material comforts, of prosperity, and the American way of life. These major issues of 1928—prosperity, religion and Prohibition—cut directly across ordinary political affiliations. Kansas farmers suspected Al Smith's Tammany connections; Herbert Hoover lost the votes of thirsty Republicans in the great cities of the East.

On Mar. 11, 1931, a conference of progressives was called in Washington by five liberal Senators—G. W. Norris of Nebraska, Edward Costigan of Colorado, Bronson M. Cutting of New Mexico, Robert M. LaFollette, Jr. of Wisconsin, and Burton K. Wheeler of Montana. By 1931, the depression, which had begun early in the Hoover Administration, had deepened. Liberal and reform groups, despairing of any assistance from the White House, were calling upon Congress to assert itself in taking positive steps for the alleviation of the nation's economic ills. In such a political climate, so different from that of 1924, these liberals met. The purpose of the meeting was " to outline a program of constructive legislation dealing with economic and political conditions for presentation to the first session of the 72nd Congress." [11] Unlike the CPPA, this group explicitly announced that the meeting would not consider a basis for a new party. Rather it was to be devoted to an exchange of ideas looking solely to the formulation of a sound legislative program for liberals. Many names familiar to the 1924 Progressive campaign reappear at this conference. From Congress came men like Brookhart, Cutting, Norris and LaGuardia. From the ranks of labor came William Green, Sidney Hillman and D. B. Robertson. LaFollette men of 1924 like Donald Richberg and Joseph Bristow joined with farm representatives like Milo Reno and George Huddleston. Present were such intellectuals as Charles Beard, Bruce Bliven and E. A. Ross. While accomplishing little more than afforded by the opportunity to meet each other and exchange ideas, the

11 *Proceedings*, Conference of Progressives, Washington, D. C., Mar. 11-12, 1931, title page.

progressives of 1931 found common ground in their uncompromising and unreserved disapproval of the Hoover Administration. The 1931 conference was a suggestion of the shape of things to come, when farm and labor voters would join to oust the Republicans from control of the national government.

Spasmodically between 1928 and 1932, liberal groups had sought to prepare the way for another progressive electoral campaign. Even before the great depression had underlined the need for social and economic reform, Paul Douglas and others, in 1928, had organized the League for Independent Political Action, devoted to the principles of increased social control and fundamental realignment of the American party system.[12] John Dewey became its Chairman and Howard Y. Williams its national organiser. The League was intended to act as a co-ordinating agency, rather than to become a new party itself. The response to the formation of the League was disappointing. Prominent liberals, like Norris and Cutting, preferred to remain within the old parties and to work as regulars for a more liberal program. As the 1932 presidential election approached, the League for Independent Political Action presented a program of progressive policies—called a " Four Year Presidential Plan"—which was largely an anticipation of the program which Franklin D. Roosevelt was later to unfold.[13] During the 1932 campaign, the League endorsed the Socialist candidacies of Norman Thomas and James Maurer.[14]

How much did the 1924 Progressives contribute to Franklin D. Roosevelt's victory in 1932? To what extent did the LaFollette Progressives move into the Democratic party as the Populists had entered the Democratic ranks in 1896?

As the Democratic national convention of 1932 approached, it became increasingly apparent that the delegates would divide

12 See Douglas, P. H., *The Coming of a New Party*.

13 *Nation*, " The Four Year Presidential Plan," complete text of the L.I.P.A. platform, 134:3476, Feb. 17, 1932, special section.

14 *New York Times*, July 11, 1932.

into two opposing factions: those supporting Governor Roosevelt's presidential candidacy, and those opposed to it, the latter drawn together by their common desire to "stop Roosevelt." In this group were the loyal followers of Al Smith, Governor Ritchie of Maryland, Newton D. Baker of Ohio, James Reed of Missouri and a host of others. Although the issues were blurred, as they usually are at a national political convention, by maneuvering and hotel-room deals, it is probably correct to say that the opposition to Roosevelt came chiefly from conservatives already alarmed by some of Roosevelt's measures of social reform in the State of New York, and city bosses anxiour to deadlock the convention in order to nominate a candidate more directly obligated to them than the ambitious Franklin D. Roosevelt. Thus, Democrats like John W. Davis and Boss Hague joined to stop Roosevelt. Jim Farley, Roosevelt's energetic campaign manager, had been busy collecting votes before the delegates assembled. Roosevelt's success in the state conventions and preference primaries brought him into the convention with a majority, but not the requisite two-thirds.[15]

The convention itself provides no clear-cut lines to the behaviour of progressives in 1932. Occasionally there was an indication that progressive sympathies lay mostly with Roosevelt. The Roosevelt forces supported Tom Walsh of Montana for permanent chairman, action which precipitated one of the early tests of strength of the respective Roosevelt and anti-Roosevelt forces. The balloting for the presidential nomination disclosed the liberal-conservative division in the 1932 convention. The opposition to Roosevelt—expressed as votes for Smith, Reed, Ritchie, Baker or some other of the Stop-Roosevelt group—came largely from boss-dominated states like New York, New Jersey and Illinois. The states like Wisconsin, the Dakotas and Minnesota, where LaFollette had been strong in 1924, voted for Roosevelt.[16] A rather dramatic portent of the

15 Farley, J., *Behind the Ballots*, pp. 112-122.

16 *New York Times*, July 2, 1932.

position many progressives would take in the forthcoming election was provided when the assembled delegates, awaiting Roosevelt's arrival to accept the nomination, were informed that the party's candidate had received the unqualified support of George Norris of Nebraska, grand old man of the Progressive bloc in the Senate.[17]

Partly, perhaps, as the result of a natural desire to get on the bandwagon, and partly because of general—though unexicited —approval of Roosevelt's program as it was slowly revealed through campaign speeches, the progressive element lent support to the Democratic ticket during the campaign. In Wisconsin, the LaFollettes came out in complete endorsement of the Democratic candidates.[18] As the campaign progressed, such outstanding liberals as Norris of Nebraska, Cutting of New Mexico, Richberg and Manly of Illinois, and Frank Walsh of New York were actively campaigning for Roosevelt. Paul Anderson, one of the most acute political observers of the 'Thirties, had been extremely skeptical about the Democratic candidate. But, by early October, he was writing that one of the " most heartening aspects of the 1932 campaign is (Franklin D. Roosevelt's) demonstrated eagerness to associate himself openly with progressives of . . . .unquestionable sincerity." [19] The Norman Thomas Socialist vote, which had appeared so substantial in numerous straw ballots, was inconsequential on Election Day. There is a strong likelihood, as one magazine supporting Thomas suggested, that many Thomas supporters, alarmed by Republican claims of a " ground swell " for Hoover as the election approached, voted for Roosevelt. Needless to say, the reports of a " ground swell " for Hoover were, like the news of Mark Twain's death, greatly exaggerated!

17 *Ibid.*, July 3, 1932.

18 Evjue, W. T., " Wisconsin Turns to Roosevelt," *Nation,* 135 :3513, Nov. 2, 1932, p. 425.

19 Anderson, P. Y., " Roosevelt Woos the Progressives," *Nation,* 135 : 3510, Oct. 12, 1932, pp. 331-332.

How much did the 1924 Progressives contribute to the New Deal in power? Most certainly, whatever the contribution has been, the New Deal and its leaders have never acknowledged it. A comparative study of the Progressive platform of 1924 and the policies enacted into law by Franklin Roosevelt and his New Deal would indicate that, perhaps unintentionally, much of the latter was plagiarised. The Progressives get no credit line for the TVA, the " rapidly progressive " income (and inheritance) tax schedules, the Wagner Labor Relations Act, the various New Deal aids to agriculture, the Securities Exchange Commission and the abolition of child labor. Yet all these demands, and others later incorporated as part of the body of New Deal legislation, are to be found in the Progressive platform of 1924.[20] What prophets those distressful and dismal days in March 1933 made of the LaFollette insurgents who, in the midst of prosperity and complacency, foresaw the inevitable consequences of reckless financial manipulation and shameless exploitation! Undismayed by threats of coercion and unreceptive to seductive promises of lush materialism, the Progressives of 1924 saw their apprehensions confirmed by the disastrous events of the depression years.

In their hour of economic and social peril, the American people, reacting in accordance with the prescribed practice of American political behaviour, had decided to " turn the rascals out" and to elect a Democrat as President. Perhaps H. L. Mencken's hardy Chinaman could have been elected in 1932 provided he had been running as a Democrat. But the choice of the Democrats was Franklin D. Roosevelt, Governor of New York, generally regarded as sympathetic to those people, farmers, laborers, small business men, who had felt the full brunt of the depression. His plan of action, reluctantly and only partially disclosed during the campaign, was " an indistinctly liberal program, patterned generally after the progressivism of his late cousin and of the late Robert LaFollette." [21] But, for the large

20 See Appendix 4.
21 Allen, F. L., The Lords of Creation, pp. 420-421.

part, Roosevelt was elected not because his program incorporated progressive policies. The American people were chiefly motivated, as they voted for him by the millions, by their resentment at Hoover and the Republican Party and a feeling, born of pathetic desperation, that any change would be a change for the better. Preoccupied by their powerful urge to change administrations, they had little time to make a reasoned choice. Hence the kind of providential luck which had assisted Calvin Coolidge on so many occasions thrust Mr. Roosevelt and his advisors into positions of great responsibility. That these advisers were often Progressives, of the 1924 variety, was not the result of an expression of preference on the part of the American electorate so much as it was the deliberate choice of advisers made by the new President, choosing men like David K. Niles to serve as an Executive Secretary, Harold L. Ickes as Secretary of the Interior, and Basil Manly as a member of the Federal Power Commission. A veteran of many sessions of Congress noticed the connection.

> If one will take the trouble to examine the platform of 1924 on which Robert M. LaFollette ran for Senator (*sic*) he will find very many of the identical propositions embodied that are now being put into execution by the administration of Franklin D. Roosevelt and, furthermore, a closer examination will reveal the fact that many of the very men who are now engaged in aiding President Roosevelt were in Wisconsin at that time helping LaFollette.[22]

Support, sometimes even before the party had nominated him, from such respected liberals as George Norris, Burton K. Wheeler and young Bob LaFollette was sufficient evidence to many a progressive voter that Roosevelt had challenged the power of the vested interests.

But progressivism had changed in shape—though perhaps not in substance—by 1932. Progressivism as an independent

22 Watson, J. E., *As I Knew Them*, p. 297. Copyright 1936. Used by special permission of the publishers, Bobbs-Merrill Company.

movement of farmers and workers had disappeared, only to reappear as a powerful and influential wing of the resurgent Democratic party, carrying weight among the leaders close to the ear of the Chief Executive. That the term " Progressive " was drowned out in the torrent of political discussion and debate over the " New Deal " should not obscure the thread of continuity which connects 1924 with 1932 and 1936. The overwhelming support which Roosevelt received from farmers and workers, in 1932 and 1936, proves that these groups will unite when a coherent program appealing to both of them is presented and when the leadership is adequate.[23] " The LaFollette movement has never died." [24] Roosevelt, with some less liberal program would have won in 1932—the tide against Hoover was so strong—but not with such an overwhelming endorsement from farmer and worker. Perhaps that endosement strengthened the hand of those progressives around the President who guided and charted a course for the new Administration.[25]

The overwhelming Roosevelt landslide in 1932 and the subsequent preoccupation of the New Deal with matters of social and economic reform retarded the development of Paul Douglas' idea of a new party of progressives in the 'Thirties. Many liberals, as we have noted, were playing an active role within the Administration. Even those who were not identified with the New Deal hesitated to divide the forces of reform by joining a party whose votes would be drawn from supporters of President Roosevelt. In 1933, a futile attempt had been made to coalesce the elements left of Roosevelt at a conference held in Chicago.[26] Despite the able and energetic support of Alfred

23 Tugwell, R. G., *op. cit.*, p. 655.

24 *Ibid.*

25 Oswald G. Villard vigorously dissents from this opinion that the New Deal has been influenced by progressive ideals. Correspondence, O. G. Villard to author, 1944.

26 Bingham, A. M., " The Farmer Labor Political Federation," *Common Sense*, 2:4, Oct. 1933, pp. 18-20. *Common Sense* (1932-1944) is a rich source of material on the progressive movements of the 1930's.

Bingham's *Common Sense,* which had, to all intents and purposes, become the official organ of Douglas' League for Political Action, the conference did little except hear an excellent speech delivered by Thomas Amlie of Wisconsin. In 1935, another attempt was made, again in Chicago.[27] With some of the old timers of 1924 like Ray McKaig and Nathan Fine in attendance, a much more serious effort to launch a new party came to the same end. Lured by William Lemke's presidential candidacy, some Non-Partisan League supporters sought temporary sanctuary in Father Coughlin's ill-starred potpourri of dissidents called the Social Justice Party in 1936. That same year, liberals within New York State organised the American Labor Party.[28] In 1938, a new effort on the part of progressives led by the LaFollettes, quickly produced both a name—the National Progressive Party and an emblem—a red, white and blue design.[29] But the November elections—so satisfactory to the Republicans throughout the nation—swept Phil LaFollette from the Governor's chair in Madison and put an early end to the national aspirations of the progressives.[30] Undeterred by what they considered to be temporary setbacks, the Wisconsin progressives—with little encouragement from the rest of the nation—continued to dwell upon ways and means of expanding their state organization into a national political structure.

The fate of third parties in American history—to expire after their contributions have been adopted (or stolen) by one of the major parties—has blinded many students to their real

27 See Amlie, T. R., "The American Commonwealth Federation," *Common Sense,* 4:8, Aug. 1935, pp. 6-7. This issue of *Common Sense* also includes the complete platform of the "American Commonwealth Federation" organised at Chicago by the progressives.

28 *New York Times,* July 17, 1936.

29 *New York Times,* Apr. 29, 1938. The Wisconsin Progressive Party had been founded in 1934.

30 See LaFollette, P., "They Wanted Something New," *Nation,* 147:43, Dec. 3, 1938, pp. 586-587.

significance. "Looked at from the social point of view, the chief function of third parties has been to bring new issues before the people; they force new policies upon the older parties, and after accomplishing their work, they pass away." [31]   The major parties, dominated by the prime consideration of effecting a majority on Election Day out of countless sectional and economic blocs, cannot afford to be so definite or articulate in facing the issues of the day.   As a rule, only a minor party can afford the luxury of expecting defeat at the polls; it can afford to be recklessly courageous.   Our weakest parties are our most unequivocal parties.   In contributing new issues, the third parties become the trial horses of the American party system.   When a good race is run, the horse may find himself suddenly transferred to one of the elegant stables of the old parties.   Hence the value of a third party must be accepted in terms of its effects upon the other parties rather than by an exclusive history of its own efforts and achievements.   There is no way of evaluating the influence of the 1924 Progressives upon the New Deal beyond recognising the familiar faces and comparing the LaFollette program with the Roosevelt record. But, basically, the same social and economic forces which were responsible for nearly five million votes of protest in 1924, manifested themselves in the formulation of that program of recovery and reform which we have come to refer to familiarly as the New Deal. Without that base, how firm a foundation would the New Deal have had at the beginning of Franklin Roosevelt's administration?

The real political alignments in America are local, consisting of innumerable parochial factions whose interests are are often in sharp conflict.   The American party system has evolved as an ingenious device for creating national majorities out of conglomerate local interests and particularist groups. The American political party is a kind of huge circus tent beneath whose broad canopy a startling variety of characters per-

31 Hayes, F. E., *Social Politics in the United States*, p. 154.

form, some of them acrobats, others skilled actors and a great many well-paid clowns. The only practical substitute—and would it be so practical?—is a multiple-party system under which the United States would be exposed to the irresolute and vacillating fruits of bloc government. The two-party system in America represents not a consolidation of the various local factions, but rather a working union in which the common objective of victory is more of a cohesive factor than the various group interests.

> That the two-party system does not under these conditions produce a direct conflict of principle is understandable. The victorious faction has not only to conciliate the defeated faction in its own party but it must bid for the movable vote in the other party. Therefore, the progress of an election campaign tends to show a steady closing up of issues that would divide men, a steady approach to the same apparently popular cries, a constantly increasing neutralization of the conflict. I have often thought during a national election that if it ran another six months the candidates would be using each other's speeches.[32]

Viscount Bryce was noticing the same feature of the American party system when he commented that the parties in the United States are pure home growths, developed by the circumstances of the nation. [33] Woodrow Wilson recognised the role of our parties in holding together disconnected and dispersed elements and in lending coherence to the action of political forces which might otherwise have a disruptive effect.[34] The anxiety of the average politician to conciliate the groups which might turn against him reminds one of the remark in *The Biglow Papers*—

32 Lippman, W., " Birds of a Feather," *Harper's Magazine*, 150:898, Mar. 1925, p. 409.

33 Bryce, J., *The American Commonwealth*, Vol. II (1927 edition), p. 5.

34 Wilson, W., *Constitutional Government in the United States*, p. 206.

Every fool knows that a man represents
Not the fellers that sent him but them on the fence.

What, then, becomes the role of a third party like LaFollette's in 1924? If the major party organizations in America are sufficiently flexible and embracing to absorb movements of protest and revolt, how can a group like the Progressives hope to make any contribution, beyond swelling the vote for one of the old parties? The answer lies in the concessions and alignments which go to make up the substance of a political party. In 1932 Governor Roosevelt aligned himself, first, to secure the Democratic nomination, and later, to win the election, with progressive elements from industrial centers and the agrarian West. In doing so, the nominee of the Democratic party added progressive spice to the Democratic pie. It is no curious coincidence that it was those states of the Middle Border, where long the banners of progressivism had been displayed, which supported Mr. Roosevelt most loyally at the 1932 Convention. In one of those marriages of convenience so characteristic of American political behavior, progressives were joining city boss-dominated machines, like Kelly's and Hague's, the overlords of the South, Democratic state organizations and a horde of discontented resentful voters in a determined, united effort to get rid of Hoover. Thus, in 1933, on a memorable day when a new President was inaugurated, the remnants of the progressive movement of 1924 provided one of the mosaics in the baffling, sometimes inharmonious, but unvariably vivid pattern of that New Deal which was to contribute such a lengthy chapter to American history.

APPENDIX No. 1

THE RAILROAD BROTHERHOODS, 1924
(The names of the executive officers of each union are also listed)

Brotherhood of Locomotive Engineers
    (W. S. Stone)
Brotherhood of Locomotive Firemen and Enginemen
    (D. B. Robertson)
Brotherhood of Railway Carmen of America
    (Martin F. Ryan)
Brotherhood of Railroad Signalmen
    (D. W. Helt)
Brotherhood of Railway Steamship Clerks, Freight Handlers, Express and Station Handlers
    (E. H. Fitzgerald)
Brotherhood of Stationary Firemen and Oilers
    (Timothy Healy)
Amalgamated Sheet Metal Workers' International Alliance
    (J. J. Hynes)
International Association of Machinists
    (W. H. Johnson)
International Brotherhood of Blacksmiths and Helpers of America
    (J. W. Kline)
International Brotherhood of Boilermakers, Iron Shipbuilders and Helpers of America
    (J. A. Franklin)
International Brotherhood of Electrical Workers
    (James P. Noonan)
Order of Railway Conductors of America
    (L. E. Sheppard)
Order of Railroad Telegraphers of America
    (E. J. Manion)
Switchmen's Union of North America
    (T. C. Cashen)
Railway Employes' Department, American Federation of Labor
    (B. M. Jewett)
United Brotherhood of Maintenance of Way Employes and Railway Shop Laborers
    (F. H. Fljozdal)

                —from the files of *Labor*

APPENDIX No. 2

THE NATIONAL COMMITTEE OF FIFTEEN

(Chosen by the Conference for Progressive Political Action
at St. Louis, Mo., February 22, 1922)

J. G. Brown
> Farmer-Labor Party

Mrs. Edward P. Costigan
> National League of Women Voters

Joseph A. Franklin
> President, Brotherhood of Boilermakers and Iron Ship-
> builders

George H. Griffin
> Non-Partisan League

Sidney Hillman
> President, Amalgamated Clothing Workers

Frederic C. Howe

Morris Hillquit
> Socialist Party

William H. Johnson
> President, International Association of Machinists

Edward Keating
> Editor, *Labor*

E. J. Manion
> President, Order of Railroad Telegraphers

Basil M. Manly
> Director, People's Legislative Service

Benjamin C. Marsh
> Director, Farmers' National Council

Agnes Nestor
> Women's Trade Union League

William Green
> Secretary, United Mine Workers of America

Warren S. Stone
> G. E. C., Brotherhood of Locomotive Engineers.

APPENDIX No. 3

TO THE PEOPLE OF THE UNITED STATES:

After mature deliberation, and with a full sense of our responsibility, this conference of American citizens, assembled without regard to party, section, class or creed, to take counsel in this hour of national crisis, reassert, upon this 190th anniversary of the birth of Washington, the fundamental principles upon which this nation was founded.

"We hold these truths to be self-evident, that all men are created equal, that they are endowed by their Creator with certain inalienable Rights, that among these are Life, Liberty and the pursuit of Happiness. That to secure these rights, Governments are instituted among Men, deriving their just powers from the consent of the governed.

"That Government is instituted for the common good, for the protection, safety, prosperity and happiness of the people and not for the honor or profit of any man, family or class of men.

"That no man, corporation or group of men shall have any other title to receive compensation from the public than that which is measured by the value of the services they render to the public."

Reasserting these fundamental doctrines as the corner stones of liberty, we proclaim that we do earnestly seek to restore the Government of the United States to the noble ends and high purposes for which it was conceived.

We hold that the splendid structure of the visible American Government is sound and well adapted to the genius of our people. But through the apathy of the people and their division upon false issues, the control of this visible government has been usurped by the "invisible government" of plutocracy and privilege and, administered in every branch by their creatures and servitors, has become destructive of those sacred rights to secure which it was established.

The history of recent years is a history of repeated injuries and usurpation by the servants of this oligarchy in both the dom-

267

inant parties; all having in direct object the establishment of an absolute Tyranny and Plutocratic Dictatorship within these states. Life, Liberty and Happiness all have been sacrificed upon the altar of greed. To prove this, let Facts be submitted to a candid world.

They have stifled free speech, throttled free press and denied the sacred right of assembly.

They have sanctioned wholesale corruption of the electorate by seating in the Senate of the United States, Newberry, its most notorious beneficiary.

They have used the Federal Reserve System, controlling the life blood of the nation's credit, as an instrument to deflate and crush farmers and independent business men and cause nation-wide unemployment.

They have obstructed every honest effort to relieve the distress of Agriculture thus caused, and have used every influence to secure betrayal of the farmers' interests.

They have conscripted four million men and boys while they permitted corporations and individuals to extort unconsionable war profits and have sacrificed the soldiers' just demands for equitable compensation to the dictates of Mellonism and the selfish interests of tax-dodging capitalists and war profiteers.

They have abolished the taxes upon excess profits of corporations and have reduced the taxes upon the incomes of millionaires.

They have squandered the resources of the nation in wasteful and fraudulent contracts and subsidies.

They have permitted the railroads, the arteries of the nation, to be operated not for service but for speculative gain and, after subsidizing them heavily and guaranteeing their income, have allowed them to be looted by financial manipulation and by contracts to corporations controlled by favored railroad directors.

They have engaged in a campaign of ruthless imperialism in Haiti and San Domingo and have permitted the arms and resources of the United States to be used to crush nations and peoples struggling for freedom and self-government.

They have through the Courts nullified righteous laws of state and nation for the protection of human rights and exalted judge-made law above the statutes.

They have permitted organized crimes and conspiracies of Trusts to go unhampered and have turned the sword of the Anti-Trust Law only against organizations of farmers and industrial workers.

They have held in prison men convicted of no crimes and have pardoned without warrant notorious profiteers and monopolists.

They have used the Army and the troops and police forces of states and cities to crush labor in its struggles to secure rights guaranteed by the Constitution.

They have prostituted the highest offices of government as channels of pernicious propaganda.

They have surrendered Americanism to Garyism, creating now privileges and immunities for capital and trampling under foot the rights of man.

In every stage of these Oppressions, We have Petitioned for Redress in the most humble terms: Our repeated Petitions have been answered only by repeated injury. Any administration, whose character is thus marked by every act which may define a Tyrant, is unfit to be the ruler of a free people.

WE, THEREFORE, CITIZENS OF THE UNITED STATES OF AMERICA, in Conference Assembled, do solemnly publish and declare that our Government of right ought to be administered for the common good and for the protection, prosperity and happiness of the people; that its present usurpation by the invisible government of plutocracy and privilege must be broken; that this can be best accomplished by united political action suited to the peculiar conditions and needs of each section and state; and that to this end, we do hereby pledge ourselves to organize for the coming campaign in every state and congressional district so that this may become once more in very truth a GOVERNMENT OF THE PEOPLE, FOR THE PEOPLE, AND BY THE PEOPLE.

APPENDIX No. 4

For one hundred and forty-eight years the American people have been seeking to establish a government for the service of all and to prevent the establishment of a government for the mastery of the few. Free men of every generation must combat renewed efforts of organized force and greed to destroy liberty. Every generation must wage a new war for freedom against new forces that seek through new devices to enslave mankind.

Under our representative democracy the people protect their liberties through their public agents.

The test of public officials and public alike must be: Will they serve, or will they exploit, the common need?

The reactionary continues to put his faith in mastery for the solution of all problems. He seeks to have what he calls the " strong men and best minds " rule and impose their decisions upon the masses of their weaker brethren.

The progressive, on the contrary, contends for less autocracy and more democracy in government and for less power of privilege and greater obligations of service.

Under the progressive principle of co-operation, that government is deemed best which offers to the many the highest level of average happiness and well-being.

It is our faith that we all go up or down together—that class gains are temporary delusions and that eternal laws of compensation make every man his brother's keeper.

In that faith we present our program of public service:

(1) The use of the power of the federal government to crush private monopoly, not to foster it.

(2) Unqualified enforcement of the constitutional guarantees of freedom of speech, press and assemblage.

(3) Public ownership of the nation's water power and creation of a public superpower system. Strict public control and permanent conservation of all natural resources, including coal, iron and other ores, oil and timber lands, in the interest of the people. Promotion of public works in times of business depression.

(4) Retention of surtaxes on swollen incomes, restoration of the tax on excess profits, taxation of stock dividends, profits undistributed to evade taxes, rapidly progressive taxes on large estates and inheritances, and repeal of excessive tariff duties, especially on trust-controlled necessities of life and of nuisance taxes on consumption, to relieve the people of the present unjust burden of taxation and compel those who profited by the war to pay their share of the war's costs, and to provide the funds for adjusted compensation solemnly pledged to the veterans of the World War.

(5) Reconstruction of the Federal Reserve and Federal Farm Loan System to provide for direct public control of the nation's money and credit to make it available on fair terms to all, and national and state legislation to permit and promote co-operative banking.

(6) Adequate laws to guarantee to farmers and industrial workers the right to organize and bargain collectively through representatives of their own choosing for the maintenance or improvement of their standards of life.

(7) Creation of a government marketing corporation to provide a direct route between farm producer and city consumer and to assure farmers fair prices for their products, and protect consumers from the profiteers in foodstuffs and other necessaries of life. Legislation to control the meat-packing industry.

(8) Protection and aid of co-operative enterprises by national and state legislation.

(9) Common international action to effect the economic recovery of the world from the effects of the World War.

(10) Repeal of the Cummins-Esch law. Public ownership of railroads, with democratic operation, with definite safeguards against bureaucratic control.

(11) Abolition of the tyranny and usurpation of the courts, including the practice of nullifying legislation in conflict with the political, social or economic theories of the judges. Abolition of injunctions in labor disputes and of the power to punish for contempt without trial by jury. Election of all federal judges without party designation for limited terms.

(12) Prompt ratification of the child labor amendment and subsequent enactment of a federal law to protect children in industry. Removal of legal discriminations against women by measures not prejudicial to legislation necessary for the protection of women and for the advancement of social welfare.

(13) A deep waterway from the Great Lakes to the sea.

(14) We denounce the mercenary system of degraded foreign policy under recent administrations in the interests of financial imperialists, oil monopolists, and international bankers, which has at times degraded our State Department from its high service as a strong and kindly intermediary of defenceless governments to a trading outpost for those interest and concession seekers engaged in the exploitations of weaker nations, as contrary to the will of the American people, destructive of domestic development and provocative of war. We favor an active foreign policy to bring about a revision of the Versailles treaty in accordance with the terms of the armistice, and to promote firm treaty agreements with all nations to outlaw wars, abolish conscription, drastically reduce land, air and naval armaments, and guarantee public referendums on peace and war.

In supporting this program we are applying to the needs of today the fundamental principles of American democracy, opposing equally the dictatorship of plutocracy and the dictatorship of the proletariat.

We appeal to all Americans without regard to partisan affiliation and we raise the standards of our faith so that all of like purpose may rally and march in this campaign under the banners of progressive union.

The nation may grow rich in the vision of greed. The nation will grow great in the vision of service.

SEPARATE RESOLUTIONS

(1) Resolved, that we favor the enactment of the postal salary adjustment measure for the employes of the postal service passed by the first session of the 68th Congress and vetoed by President Coolidge.

(2) Resolved, that we favor enforcement and extension of the merit system in the federal civil service to all its branches

and transfer of the functions of the Personnel Classification Board to the United States Civil Service Commission.

(3) Resolved, that we favor the immediate and complete independence of the Philippine Islands, in accordance with the pledges of the official representatives of the American people.

(4) Resolved, that appropriate legislation be enacted which will provide for the people of the Virgin Islands a more permanent form of civil government such as will enable them to attain their economic, industrial and political betterment.

(5) Resolved, that we deeply sympathize with the aspirations of the Irish people for freedom and independence.

(6) Resolved, that in the prevailing starvation in Germany, which, according to authoritative evidence, is beyond the scope of private charity, and in the event of like destitution in any other country, we consider it humane and just, and in conformity with our traditions and former practices, that the aid of our government should be extended in the form of the delivery of surplus food supplies to a reasonable amount, and upon such conditions as the emergency may justify.

(7) Resolved, that we denounce every such use of the armed forces of the United States to aid in the exploitation of weaker nations, as has occurred all too frequently in our relations with Haiti, San Domingo, Nicaragua and other nations of Central and South America.

APPENDIX No. 5

PRESIDENTIAL ELECTION RESULTS, 1924

(Represented as state percentiles in order of Progressive strength.)

	PROG.	DEM.	REP.
Wisconsin	.540	.081	.371
North Dakota	.453	.070	.477
Minnesota	.413	.068	.511
Montana	.378	.194	.425
South Dakota	.370	.133	.497
Idaho	.365	.164	.471
Nevada	.362	.219	.418
Washington	.358	.102	.522
California	.332	.082	.572
Wyoming	.315	.161	.524
Iowa	.281	.166	.551
Oregon	.245	.242	.511
Arizona	.233	.355	.413
Nebraska	.229	.296	.471
Utah	.208	.299	.493
Colorado	.204	.220	.573
Ohio	.176	.237	.586
Illinois	.175	.234	.588
Kansas	.149	.236	.615
New York	.144	.292	.559
Pennsylvania	.143	.191	.653
Maryland	.132	.414	.453
Massachusetts	.125	.249	.622
Connecticutt	.106	.275	.615
Michigan	.105	.131	.754
New Jersey	.100	.265	.621
Arkansas	.095	.612	.293
New Mexico	.085	.430	.485
Florida	.079	.568	.286
Oklahoma	.078	.484	.428
Georgia	.076	.739	.181
Texas	.065	.737	.198

	PROG.	DEM.	REP.
Missouri	.064	.439	.497
West Virginia	.062	.441	.495
Maine	.059	.213	.720
Vermont	.059	.157	.782
Indiana	.056	.387	.553
Delaware	.054	.368	.577
New Hampshire	.054	.347	.598
Kentucky	.050	.460	.489
Alabama	.049	.678	.270
Virginia	.046	.624	.328
Tennessee	.035	.528	.436
Louisiana	.033	.764	.202
Rhode Island	.032	.365	.596
Mississippi	.031	.893	.076
North Carolina	.014	.588	.397
South Carolina	.010	.966	.022

APPENDIX No. 6

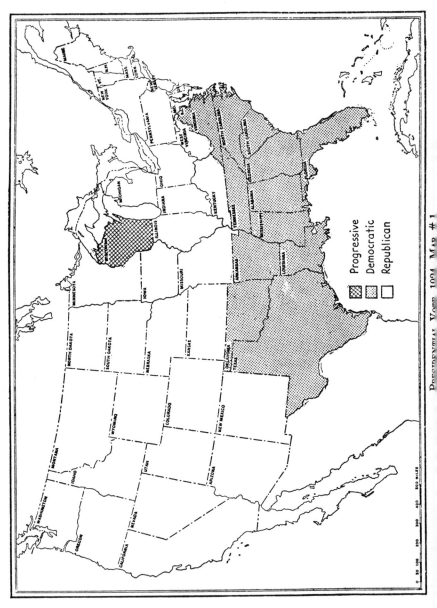

Presidential Vote 1904 Map #1

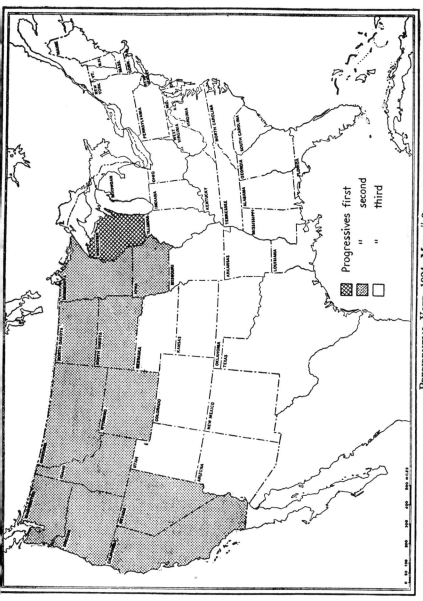

PRESIDENTIAL VOTE, 1924, MAP #2

BIBLIOGRAPHY

LETTERS AND MANUSCRIPTS

A—*Confidential Manuscript Sources.* Some of the material which has gone into the shaping of this work was examined under the pledge that the identity and location of the contents be kept confidential for the present. When these sources become available to the public, more specific citations will be possible.

B—*Private Collections of Letters and Manuscripts.* While the author is indebted to many of the persons interviewed for the privilege of perusing and utilising private files, he is especially grateful for permission to draw upon the rich collections listed below, several of which were examined for the first time by a research student.

1—*Morris Hillquit Papers,* Custodian, Miss Nina E. Hillquit, New York, N. Y.

An invaluable collection carefully preserved and filed, providing a running account of the whole left-wing movement in the 'Twenties.

2—*Mercer Green Johnston Papers,* Dr. M. G. Johnston, Washington.

The last Chairman of the 1924 Progressives has preserved the irreplaceable journals and minutes of the CPPA Convention, 1924, and conferences, 1924-1927, and plans to contribute them to the Library of Congress.

3—*Oswald Garrison Villard Papers,* Mr. O. G. Villard, New York, N. Y.

These papers are of especial value in throwing light upon campaign organization, financing, strategy, etc.

4—*Frank P. Walsh Papers,* Custodian, Mr. Robert W. Hill, New York Public Library, New York, N. Y.

This collection, now available to the research student, offers perhaps the best single source of material relating to the illimitable problems which beset a third party movement. The late Frank P. Walsh acted as Senator LaFollette's counsel during the 1924 campaign.

5—*American Civil Liberties Union Cases, 1924-1925,* on deposit, New York Public Library, New York, N. Y.

Complete files of correspondence dealing with alleged violations of basic rights and liberties during the campaign are included.

PERSONAL INTERVIEWS

The following list of names does not purport to be a complete roster of those men and women who, through their generous recollections and interpretations, have furnished this work some small measure of that vitality which comes with first-hand information. Each of the following was, however, through his intimate knowledge of or association with some phase of the 1924 campaign, able to make singular and significant contributions of enduring worth.

Mr. John M. Baer of North Dakota, first candidate of the Non-Partisan League to be elected to the United States Congress.

Mr. Roger Baldwin, Director of the American Civil Liberties Union and an active supporter of LaFollette and Wheeler in Connecticut.

Dr. William E. Bohn, Editor of the *New Leader,* New York, N. Y.

Mr. Hartwell L. Brunson, member of the National Progressive Executive Committee and close associate of the late William H. Johnston, CPPA National Chairman.

Hon. John W. Davis, Democratic candidate for the Presidency, 1924.

Mr. Herman Ekern, Senator LaFollette's campaign manager in Wisconsin and former Attorney-General of that state.

Dr. Nathan Fine, writer and historian, active in the Socialist Party in 1924.

Mr. J. A. H. Hopkins, Founder and National Chairman, The Committee of Forty Eight.

Dr. Mercer G. Johnston, Committee of Forty Eight, Chairman, National Progressive Headquarters, 1925-1928.

Mr. Edward Keating, Editor, *Labor,* official publication of the Railroad Brotherhoods, and former Congressman from Colorado.

Mr. Judson King, Director, National Popular Government League, and close associate of the late George Norris, Senator from Nebraska.

Miss Fola LaFollette, daughter of the late Robert M. LaFollette, Senator from Wisconsin.

Hon. Robert M. LaFollette, Jr., Senator from Wisconsin.

Mr. Basil Manly, Campaign Manager, LaFollette-Wheeler Headquarters, Washington, D. C., 1924.

Mr. Benjamin Marsh, Director of The People's Lobby and member of the CPPA National Executive Committee.

Mr. James E. Pope, LaFollette organiser in New Jersey and close associate of George Record, New Jersey reformer.

Mrs. Gilbert Roe, widow of the late Gilbert Roe, Senator LaFollette's law partner, who managed New York campaign headquarters in 1924.

Mr. Norman Thomas, Socialist candidate for Governor of New York in 1924 and member of the CPPA National Executive Committee.

Mr. Oswald Garrison Villard, Editor of the *Nation* in 1924 and Treasurer of the LaFollette-Wheeler Eastern Campaign Headquarters.

Hon. Burton K. Wheeler, Senator from Montana and Progressive candidate for the Vice Presidency, 1924.

Mrs. Bertha Hale White, Executive Secretary of the Socialist Party in 1924.

MINUTES, PROCEEDINGS, AND REPORTS

American Federation of Labor, *Proceedings,* 43rd and 44th Annual Conventions, 1923 and 1924.

Conference for Progressive Political Action

Report, Committee on Organization, CPPA, Chicago, Ill., Feb. 20-21, 1922.

Report of the Chairman, W. H. Johnston, Chairman, to the Executive Committee, CPPA, Washington, Mar. 15, 1922.

Report of the Proceedings, Second Conference for Progressive Political Action, held at Cleveland, Ohio, Dec. 11-12, 1922.

Proceedings, Third Conference for Progressive Political Action, held at St. Louis, Mo., Feb. 11-12, 1924.

Proceedings, Conference for Progressive Political Action Convention, held at Cleveland, Ohio, July 4-5, 1924, 2 vols. (M. G. Johnston Papers).

Minutes, Meeting of the Joint Executive Committee, LaFollette-Wheeler Campaign Headquarters, Chicago, Ill., Sept. 26, 1924.

Proceedings, National Progressive Convention, sometimes referred to as the 4th CPPA, held at Chicago, Ill., Feb. 21-22, 1925, (M. G. Johnston Papers).

Report to Progressives, W. H. Johnston, Chairman, National Progressive Headquarters, Washington, Mar. 1, 1925, (Benjamin Marsh Papers).

Minutes, Meetings of the Executive Committee, National Progressive Headquarters, held variously at Washington and Baltimore, Md., 1925-1927, (Johnston Papers).

Report, M. G. Johnston, Chairman, to Members of the Executive Committee, National Progressive Headquarters, Jan. 3, 1928, (Johnston Papers).

Conference of Progressives, *Proceedings,* Conference of Progressives to Outline a Program of Constructive Legislation, Washington, Mar. 11-12, 1931.

Democratic National Convention, *Proceedings,* Democratic National Convention, held at New York, N. Y., June 24-July 9, 1924.

Republican National Convention, *Proceedings,* 18th Republican National Convention, held at Cleveland, Ohio, June 10-12, 1924.

State Conference for Progressive Political Action, *Proceedings,* State CPPA, held at Albany, N. Y., July 29-30, 1932 (Hillquit Papers).

UNPUBLISHED MANUSCRIPTS

Crews, Cecil Robert, *Farm Labor Parties in the United States, 1918-1925,* Master's essay, University of Wisconsin, Madison, Wis., 1935.

Guttmann, Harry H., *Labor and the Election of 1924,* Master's essay, Columbia University, New York, 1938.

Parzen, Herbert, *A Comparative Study of the Progressive Presidential Campaigns of 1912 and 1924,* Master's essay, Columbia University, New York, 1926.

Sayre, Wallace S., *Robert M. LaFollette: A Study in Political Methods,* Doctor's thesis, New York University, New York, 1930.

Ullman, Albert C., *The Third Party As an American Political Instrument,* Master's essay, Columbia University, New York, 1939.

UNITED STATES GOVERNMENT DOCUMENTS

Sixty-eighth Congress, second session:
  Senate Report No. 1100, *Investigation of Campaign Expenditures,* 1924.
Sixty-ninth Congress, first session:
  Senate Document No. 15, *Memorial Services, Robert M. LaFollette,* 1925.
Supreme Court Cases cited:
  Duplex Printing Press Corporation v. Deering, 254 US 443 (1921).
  Newberry v. United States, 256 US 312 (1921).
  Truax v. Corrigan, 257 US 312 (1921).
  United Mine Workers v. Coronado Coal Co., 259 US 344 (1922).
  Wolff Packing Co. v. Court of Industrial Relations, 262 US 522 (1923).

CAMPAIGN LITERATURE

Campaign Handbook of the Eastern District, "The Facts about LaFollette and Wheeler," LaFollette-Wheeler Campaign Committee, New York, 1924.
Campaign Textbook, "The Facts," LaFollette-Wheeler Campaign Headquarters, Chicago, 1924.
Democratic Campaign Book, Democratic National Committee, Washington, 1924.
Lovestone, Jay, *The LaFollette Illusion,* Workers' Party Headquarters, Chicago, 1924.
Republican Campaign Book, Republican National Committee, Chicago, 1924.
Various pamphlets, etc. (especially complete collections of 1924 campaign literature are to be found in the Library of Congress and in the New York Public Library's *Scrapbook of the 1924 Presidential Campaign.*)
Private collections of papers examined were often rich in campaign literature, some being more extensive than the available public collections. Many of these memorabilia, it is to be hoped, will find their way into public collections.

GENERAL REFERENCES

American Labor Year Book, New York, Rand School, 1919-1928.
American Year Book, (A. B. Hart, ed.), New York, Macmillan, 1925.
Atlas of Historical Geography, (C. O. Paullin, ed.), Washington, Carnegie, 1932.
The World Almanac and Book of Facts, New York, World Pub. Co., 1918-1928.
Yearbook of Agriculture, U. S. Department of Agriculture, Washington, Government Printing Office, 1918-1928.

BOOKS AND MONOGRAPHS

Adams, Samuel H., *Incredible Era, The Life and Times of Warren Gamaliel Harding*, Boston, Houghton Mifflin, 1939.

Agar, Herbert, *The Pursuit of Happiness, the Story of American Democracy*, Boston, Houghton Mifflin, 1938.

Allen, Frederick Lewis, *Only Yesterday*, New York, Harper, 1931.

Anonymous, *Behind the Mirrors*, New York, Putnam, 1922.

Bean, Louis H., *Ballot Behavior*, Washington, American Council on Public Affairs, 1940.

Beard, Charles A., *The American Party Battle*, New York, Macmillan, 1928.

Bimba, A., *History of the American Working Class*, New York International, 1927.

Binkley, Wilfred E., *American Political Parties*, New York, Knopf, 1943.

Bizzell, William Bennett, *The Green Rising, An Historical Survey of Agrarianism*, New York, Macmillan, 1926.

Brooks, Robert Clarkson, *Political Parties and Electoral Problems*, New York, Harper, 1933.

Bruce, A. A., *The Non-Partisan League*, New York, Macmillan, 1921.

Bryce, James, *The American Commonwealth*, 2 Vols., Macmillan, 1916.

Buck, Solon Justice, *The Agrarian Crusade*, (*The Chronicles of America* series, Alvin Johnson, ed.), New Haven, Yale, 1920.

Capper, Arthur, *The Agricultural Bloc*, New York, Harcourt, Brace, 1922.

Chamberlain, John, *Farewell to Reform; The Rise, Life and Decay of the Progressive Mind in America*, New York, Liveright, 1932.

Cochran, Negley D., *E. W. Scripps*, New York, Harcourt Brace, 1933.

Committee on Recent Economic Changes, *Recent Economic Changes in the United States*, 2 Vols., New York, McGraw-Hill, 1929.

Commons, J. R., et al., *History of Labour in the United States*, 4 Vols., New York, Macmillan, 1918-1935.

Coolidge, Calvin, *The Autobiography of Calvin Coolidge*, New York, Cosmopolitan Book, 1929.

Cousens, Theodore W., *Politics and Political Organizations in America*, New York, Macmillan, 1940.

Croly, Herbert, *The Promise of American Life*, New York, Macmillan, 1914.

Curti, Merle, *The Growth of American Thought*, New York, Harper, 1943.

Dawes, Charles G., *Notes as Vice-President*, Boston, Little, Brown, 1935.

DeWitt, Benjamin Parke, *The Progressive Movement*, New York, Macmillan, 1915.

Douglas, Paul H., *The Coming of a New Party*, New York, McGraw-Hill, 1932.

Durand, D. L., *From Roosevelt to Roosevelt*, New York, Henry Holt, 1937.

Ewing, Cortez, *Presidential Elections*, Norman, Okla., Univ. of Oklahoma, 1940.

Filler, Louis, *Crusaders for American Liberalism*, New York, Harcourt, Brace, 1939.

Fine, Nathan, *Labor and Farmer Parties in the United States, 1828-1928,* New York, Rand School, 1928.

Fite, Emerson D., *The Presidential Campaign of 1860,* New York, Macmillan, 1911.

Flint, Winston Allen, *The Progressive Movement in Vermont,* Washington, American Council on Public Affairs, 1941.

Frankfurter, F., and Greene, N. V., *The Labor Injunction,* New York, Macmillan, 1931.

Fuess, Claude M., *Calvin Coolidge, The Man from Vermont,* Boston, Little Brown, 1940.

Gardner, Gilson, *Lusty Scripps; The Life of E. W. Scripps,* New York, Vanguard, 1932.

Gaston, Herbert E., *The Nonpartisan League,* New York, Harcourt, Brace, 1920.

Gilbert, Clinton, *You Takes Your Choice,* New York, Putnam, 1924.

Gitlow, Benjamin, *I Confess,* New York, Dutton, 1939.

Gompers, Samuel, *Seventy Years of Life and Labor,* 2 Vols. New York, Dutton, 1925.

Gosnell, Harold F., *Getting Out the Vote,* Chicago, Univ. of Chicago, 1927.

Harris, Frank, *Contemporary Portraits,* New York, Brentano, 1923.

Harris, Herbert, *American Labor,* New Haven, Yale, 1939.

Harris, Joseph P., *Registration of Voters in the United States,* Washington, Brookings, 1929.

Haynes, Fred Emory, *Social Politics in the United States,* Boston, Houghton Mifflin, 1924.

———, *Third Party Movements since the Civil War,* Iowa City, Ia., State Historical Society, 1916.

Hays, Arthur Garfield, *City Lawyer,* New York, Simon and Schuster, 1942.

Hechler, Kenneth William, *Insurgency: Personalities and Politics of the Taft Era,* New York, Columbia, 1940.

Hicks, John D., *The Populist Revolt,* Minneapolis, Univ. of Minnesota, 1931.

Hillquit, Morris, *History of Socialism in the United States,* New York, Funk and Wagnalls, 1906.

———, *Loose Leaves from a Busy Life,* New York, Macmillan, 1934.

Hines, W. D., *War History of American Railroads,* New Haven, Yale, 1928.

Holcomb, Arthur N., *The New Party Politics,* New York, Harper, 1923.

———, *The Political Parties of Today,* New York, Harper, 1924.

Howe, Frederic C., *The Confessions of a Reformer,* New York, Scribner, 1925.

———, *Wisconsin: An Experiment in Democracy,* New York, Scribner, 1912.

Ickes, Harold L., *Autobiography of a Curmudgeon,* New York, Reynal and Hitchcock, 1943.

Jenks, Leland Hamilton (ed.), *The Future of Party Government,* Winter Park, Fla., Rollins, 1929.

Johnson, Claudius O., *Borah of Idaho,* New York, Longmans, Green, 1936.

Kent, Frank R., *The Democratic Party*, New York, Century, 1928.

Kirkland, Edward Chase, *A History of American Economic Life*, New York, 1939 (Rev. Ed.)

Knoles, George Harmon, *The Presidential Campaign and Election of 1892*, Stanford University, Cal., Stanford Univ., 1942.

LaFollette, Robert Marion, *LaFollette's Autobiography*, Madison, Wis., LaFollette Publishing Co., 1913.

Lief, Alfred, *Democracy's Norris*, New York, Stackpole, 1939.

Lorwin, Lewis L., *The American Federation of Labor*, Washington, Brookings, 1933.

Malin, James Claude, *The United States After the World War*, Boston, Ginn, 1930.

McAdoo, William Gibbs, *Crowded Years*, Boston, Houghton Mifflin, 1931.

McCarthy, Charles, *The Wisconsin Idea*, New York, Macmillan, 1912.

MacVeagh, Rogers, *The Transportation Act of 1920*, New York, Holt, 1923.

Merriam, C. E., and Gosnell, H. F., *The American Party System*, New York, Macmillan, 1929.

Morison, S., and Commager, H. S., *The Growth of the American Republic*, 3rd Ed., 2 Vols., London and New York, Oxford, 1942.

Mullen, Arthur F., *Western Democrat*, New York, Wilfred Funk, 1940.

Myers, William Starr, *The Republican Party; A History*, New York, Century, 1928.

Neuberger, R. and Kahn, S. B., *Integrity, The Life of George Norris*, New York, Vanguard, 1937.

Nourse, Edwin G., *American Agriculture and the European Market*, New York, McGraw-Hill, 1924.

O'Connor, Harvey, *Mellon's Millions*, New York, John Day, 1933.

Odegard, P., and Helms, E. A., *American Politics*, New York, Harper, 1938.

Oneal, James, *American Communism*, New York, Rand School, 1927.

Overacker, Louise, *Money in Elections*, New York, Macmillan, 1932.

———, *The Presidential Primary*, New York, Macmillan, 1926.

Ostrogorski, M., *Democracy and the Organization of Political Parties*, 2 Vols., New York, Macmillan, 1902.

———, *Democracy and the Party System in the United States*, New York, Macmillan, 1910.

Parkes, H. B., *Recent America*, New York, Crowell, 1941.

Paxson, Frederic L., *Recent History of the United States*, Boston, Houghton Mifflin 1937.

Peel, R. V., and Donnelly, T. C., *The 1932 Campaign*, New York, Farrar and Rinehart, 1935.

———, *The 1928 Campaign*, New York, R. R. Smith, 1931.

Perlman, Selig, *A History of Trade Unionism in America*, New York, Macmillan, 1922.

Perlman, S., and Taft, P., *History of Labor in the United States*, 1896-1932, (Vols. III and IV of Commons, J. R. et al., *History of Labor in the United States*), New York, Macmillan, 1935.

Platt, Chester C., *What LaFollette's State is Doing,* Batavia, N. Y., Batavia Press, 1923.

Porter, Kirk H., *National Party Platforms,* New York, Macmillan, 1924.

President's Research Committee on Social Trends, *Recent Social Trends in the United States,* 2 Vols., New York, McGraw-Hill, 1933.

Pringle, Henry F., *Alfred E. Smith,* New York, Macy-Masins, 1927.

——, *Theodore Roosevelt,* New York, Harcourt, Brace, 1931.

Quick, Herbert, *The Real Trouble with the Farmers,* Indianapolis, Bobbs-Merrill, 1924.

Raney, William F., *Wisconsin, A Story of Progress,* New York, Prentice-Hall, 1940.

Rice, Stuart, *Farmers and Workers in American Politics,* New York, Columbia, 1924.

Richberg, Donald, *Tents of the Mighty,* New York, Willet, Clark and Colby, 1930.

Robinson, Edgar E., *The Evolution of American Political Parties,* New York, Harcourt, Brace, 1924.

——, *The Presidential Vote, 1896-1932,* Stanford University, Cal., Stanford, 1934.

Robinson, Henry Morton, *Fantastic Interim,* New York, Harcourt, Brace, 1943.

Russell, Charles E., *The Story of the Nonpartisan League,* New York, Harper, 1920.

Sait, Edward M., *American Parties and Elections,* New York, Appleton-Century, 1927.

Slosson, Preston William, *The Great Crusade and After, 1914-1928,* (*History of American Life* Series, ed. by D. R. Fox and A. M. Schlesinger), New York, Macmillan, 1931.

Steffens, Lincoln, *Autobiography of Lincoln Steffens,* 2 Vols., New York, Harcourt, Brace, 1931.

——, *Struggle for Self-Government,* New York, McClure, Philips, 1906.

Stirn, Ernest W., *An Annotated Bibliography of Robert M. LaFollette,* Chicago, Univ. of Chicago, 1937.

Stoddard, Henry L., *As I Knew Them,* New York, Harper, 1927.

Stone, Irving, *They also Ran,* Garden City, Doubleday, Doran, 1943.

Sturmthal, Adolf F., *The Tradegy of European Labor,* New York, Columbia, 1943.

Sullivan, Mark, *Our Times; The United States, 1900-1925,* 7 Vols., New York, Scribner, 1926-1935.

Torelle, Ellen (Comp.), *The Political Philosophy of Robert M. LaFollette,* Madison, Wis., LaFollette Publishing Co., 1920.

Tucker, R., and Barkley, F. R., *Sons of the Wild Jackass,* Boston, L. C. Page, 1932.

Villard, Oswald Garrison, *Fighting Years,* New York, Harcourt, Brace, 1939.

——, *Prophets True and False,* New York, Knopf, 1928.

Walling, William English, *American Labor and American Democracy*, New York, Harper, 1926.

Watson, James E., *As I Knew Them*, Indianapolis, Bobbs-Merrill, 1936.

Webb, Walter Preston, *Divided We Stand*, New York, Farrar and Rinehart, 1937.

White, William Allen, *Masks in a Pageant*, New York, Macmillan, 1928.

———, *Politics: The Citizen's Business*, New York, Macmillan, 1924.

———, *A Puritan in Babylon: The Story of Calvin Coolidge.*

Wiest, Edward, *Agricultural Organizations in the United States*, Lexington, Ky., Univ. of Kentucky, 1923.

Wilson, Woodrow, *Constitutional Government in the United States*, New York, Columbia, 1921.

Wittke, Carl, *A History of Canada*, 3rd Ed., New York, Crofts, 1941.

Wood, Louis A., *A Union-Management Cooperation on the Railroads*, New Haven, Yale, 1931.

MAGAZINE AND PERIODICAL ARTICLES AND PAMPHLETS
OF SPECIAL INTEREST

Abbott, Lyman, "Mr. LaFollette As Seen from the Gallery," *Outlook*, 100:5, Feb. 3, 1912.

Alderfer, Harold F., "Presidential Elections by Pennsylvania Counties, 1920-1940," *Pennsylvania State College Bulletin* (State College, Pa.), 35:34, June 9, 1941.

Amblie, Thomas R., "The American Commonwealth Federation," *Common Sense*, 4:8, Aug. 1935.

Anderson, Paul Y., "Roosevelt Woos the Progressive," *Nation*, 135:3510, Oct. 12, 1932.

Anonymous, "John Davis, Democrat," *World's Work*, 48:5, 48:6, Sept. and Oct. 1924.

Bean, L., and Stine, O. C., "Income from Agricultural Production," *Annals, American Academy of Political and Social Science*, 126:206, Jan. 1925.

Bendiner, R., "Burton K. Wheeler," *Nation*, 150:17, Apr. 27, 1940.

Benedict, Bertram, "The Socialist Movement in Great Britain and the United States," *American Political Science Review*, 18, May 1924.

Bingham, Alfred M., "The Farmer Labor Political Federation," *Common Sense*, 2:4, Oct. 1933.

Bittleman, Alexander, "Parties and Issues," *Workers' Party Pamphlet*, Workers Party, Chicago, 1924.

Bliven, Bruce, "LaFollette's Place in Our History," *Current History*, 12:2, Aug. 1925.

Bryan, William J., "My Brother Charles," *World's Work*, 48:5, Sept. 1924.

Evjue, W. T., "Wisconsin Turns to Roosevelt," *Nation*, 135:3513, Nov. 2, 1932.

Gannett, Lewis, "A Party Struggles to be Born," *Nation*, 120:3113, Mar. 4, 1925.

Gardner, Gilson, "Our Next President: LaFollette or Wheeler," *Nation*, 119:3089, Sept. 17, 1924.

Genung, A. B., "The Purchasing Power of the Farmer's Dollar from 1913 to Date," *Annals, American Academy of Political and Social Sciences*, 126:206, Jan. 1925.

Gompers, Samuel, "Should a Labor Party Be Formed?", *AFL Pamphlet*, Amer. Fed. of Labor, Washington, D. C., 1918.

Harvey, George, "The Paramount Issue,—Coolidge or Chaos," *North American Review*, 220:824, Sept. 1924.

Haynes, Fred Emory, "The Significance of the Latest Third Party Movement," *Mississippi Valley Historical Review*, 12:2, Sept. 1925.

Hicks, John D., "The Third Party Tradition in American Politics," *Mississippi Valley Historical Review*, 20:1, June 1933.

Ickes, Harold L., "Who Killed the Progressive Party?," *American Historical Review*, 46:2, Jan. 1941.

Johnson, Claudius O., "Third Parties," *Quarterly Journal of the University of North Dakota*, 15:1, Nov. 1924.

Keenleyside, Hugh L., "The American Political Revolution of 1924," *Current History*, 21:6, Mar. 1926.

LaFollette, Philip, "They Wanted Something New," *Nation*, 147:43, Dec. 3, 1938.

League for Independent Political Action, "The Four Year Presidential Plan," (Platform of the L.I.P.A.), *Nation*, 134:3476, Feb. 17, 1932 special section.

Lippmann, Walter, "Birds of a Feather," *Harper's Magazine*, 150:898, Mar. 1925.

Lovett, Robert M., "The Farmer Labor Communist Party," *New Republic*, 39:500, July 2, 1924.

———, "The Farmer Labor Fiasco at Chicago," *New Republic*, 35:450, July 18, 1923.

———, "A Party in Embryo," *New Republic*, 83:3, July 24, 1935.

Lowry, Edward G., "LaFollette's Own Platform," *World's Work*, 48:5, Sept., 1924.

Macmahon, Arthur E., "Political Parties and Elections," *Political Science Quarterly*, Special Supplement to Vol. XL, Mar. 1925.

———, "Political Parties—The United States," *Encyclopedia of the Social Studies*, Vol. XI.

McCurdy, Allen, "The Forty-Eighters' Position," *Nation*, 111:2874, July 31, 1920.

McKaig, Ray, "The Nonpartisan League and Its Independent Press," *The Public* 22:1083, Jan. 4, 1919.

Ogg, Frederic A., "Robert M. LaFollette in Retrospect," *Current History*, 33:4, Feb. 1931.

Oneal, James, " Changing Fortunes of American Socialism," *Current History*, 20:1, April, 1924.

Orton, William, " American vs. British Progressivism," *New Republic*, 42:536, Mar. 11, 1925.

Paxson, Frederic, " Robert M. LaFollette," *American Dictionary of Biography*, Vol. X.

Plumb, Glenn E., " Labor's Plan for Government Ownership and Democracy in the Operation of the Railroads," *Pamphlet*, Plumb Plan League, Washington, 1919.

' Potomacus ', " Wheeler of Montana," *New Republic*, 108:13, Sept. 20, 1943.

Richberg, Donald R., " Future Prospects of the Progressive Movement ", *Locomotive Engineers' Journal*, 59:1, Jan. 1925.

Ring, Elizabeth, " The Progressive Movement of 1912 and the Third Party Movement of 1924 in Maine," (University of Maine Studies Series II, No. 26), *Maine Bulletin*, 35:5, Jan. 1933.

Rowell, Chester H., " The Political Cyclone in North Dakota," *World's Work*, 46:1, July, 1923.

Steuben Society of America, " The Republican Victory Analyzed," *Pamphlet*, New York, Nov. 1924.

Stolberg, Benjamin, " LaFollette Crosses the Rubicon," *Independent*, 113:-3873, July 19, 1924.

———, " The Peter Pans of Communism," *Century*, 110:3, July 1925.

Sullivan, Mark, " Looking Back on LaFollette," *World's Work*, 49:3, Jan. 1925.

Thomas, Norman, "Progressivism at St. Louis," *Nation*, 118:3060, Feb. 27, 1924.

Tugwell, Rexford G., " Is A Farmer-Labor Alliance Possible? ", *Harper's Magazine*, 174:1044, May 1937.

Walling, William A., " Labor's Attitude toward a New Party," *Current History*, 21:1, Oct. 1924.

Warren, Louis A., " The Lincoln and LaFollette Families in Pioneer Drama," *Wisconsin Magazine of History*, 12:4, June 1929.

Wheeler, B., Gale, Z., and Pezet, W., " LaFollette and His Platform (Three Points of View)," *Forum*, 72:5, Nov. 1924.

FARM PERIODICALS

American Agriculturist (Ithaca N. Y.)
Breeders' Gazette (Spencer, Ind.)
Capper's Farmer (Topeka, Kan.)
Country Gentlemen (Philadelphia, Pa.)
Cow Country (Cheyenne, Wyo.)
Dakota Farmer (Aberdeen, N. D.)
Farm Journal (Philadelphia, Pa.)
The Farmer (St. Paul, Minn.)
Kansas Farmer (Topeka, Kan.)
Michigan Farmer (Detroit, Mich.)

National Farm News (Washington, D. C.)
National Livestock Producer (Chicago, Ill.)
Ohio Farmer (Cleveland, O.)
Pacific Rural Press (San Francisco, Cal.)
Pennsylvania Farmer (Pittsburgh, Pa.)
Progressive Farmer and Southern Ruralist (Birmingham, Ala.)
Rural New Yorker (New York, N. Y.)
Wallace's Farmer (Des Moines, Ia.)
Wisconsin Agriculturist (Racine, Wis.)
Wisconsin Farmer (Madison, Wis.)

LABOR AND GROUP INTEREST PERIODICALS
(affiliation indicated in right-hand column)

Advance (Long Island City, N. Y.)	Amalgamated Clothing Workers of America
Afro-American (Baltimore, Md.)	
American Labor Monthly (New York, N. Y.)	
Daily Worker (New York, N. Y. and Chicago, Ill.)	Workers' Party
Irish World (New York, N. Y.)	
Justice (New York, N. Y.)	International Ladies' Garment Workers
Labor (Washington, D. C.)	Railroad Brotherhoods
Labor Age (New York, N. Y.)	
Labor Herald (New York, N. Y.)	Trade Union Educational League
Locomotive Engineers' Journal (Cleveland, O.)	
Locomotive Firemen's Magazine (Cleveland, O.)	
Machinists' Monthly (Washington, D. C.)	
Minnesota Leader (Minneapolis, Minn.)	Non-Partisan League of Minnesota
New Leader (New York, N. Y.)	Socialist Party
New Majority (Chicago, Ill.)	Farm-Labor Party of Illinois
New York Call (New York, N. Y.)	Socialist Party
Non-Partisan Leader, later Non-Partisan National Leader (Minneapolis, Minn.)	Non-Partisan League
People (New York, N. Y.)	Socialist Labor Party
The Public (New York, N. Y.)	Single Taxers
Railroad Trainman (Mt. Morris, Ill.)	
Railway Carmen's Journal (Kansas City, Mo.)	
Railway Maintenance of Way Enployes' Journal (Detroit, Mich.)	
Railroad Telegrapher (St. Louis, Mo.)	
United Mine Workers' Journal (Indianapolis, Ind.)	

GENERAL PERIODICALS AND MAGAZINES

American Historical Review
American Political Science Review
Century
Common Sense
Current History Magazine
Everybody's Magazine
Forum
Harper's Magazine
Independent
LaFollette's Magazine
Literary Digest

Nation
New Republic
North American Review
North Dakota Quarterly Journal
Outlook
Review of Reviews
Saturday Evening Post
Scribner's Magazine
Wisconsin Magazine of History
World's Work

NEWSPAPERS

Baltimore (Morning and Evening)
    Sun
Boston Globe
Chicago Herald
Chicago Tribune
Christian Science Monitor (Boston)
Cincinnati Enquirer
Cleveland Plain Dealer
Cleveland Press
Indianapolis Star
Los Angeles Times
Madison (Wisconsin) Capital-Times
Milwaukee Journal
Newark Evening News

New York American
New York Evening Post
New York Sun
New York Times
New York Tribune, Herald-Tribune
New York World
Omaha Bee
St. Paul Pioneer-Press
St. Louis Post-Dispatch
San Francisco Chronicle
Washington Post
Washington Times
Wisconsin State Journal (Madison
    Wis.)

INDEX